AF446775

Autonomy and Control of State Agencies

Public Sector Organizations

Editors: **B. Guy Peters**, Maurice Falk Professor of Government, Pittsburgh University, USA, and **Geert Bouckaert**, Professor at the Public Management Institute, Katholieke Universiteit Leuven, Belgium

Organizations are the building blocks of governments. The role of organizations, formal and informal, is most readily apparent in public bureaucracy, but all the institutions of the public sector are composed of organizations, or have some organizational characteristics that affect their performance. Therefore, if scholars want to understand how governments work, a very good place to start is at the level of the organizations involved in delivering services. Likewise, if practitioners want to understand how to be effective in the public sector, they would be well-advised to consider examining the role of organizations and how to make the organizations more effective.

This series will publish research-based books concerned with organizations in the public sector and will cover such issues as: the autonomy of public sector organizations, networks and network analysis, bureaucratic politics; organizational change and leadership and methodology for studying organizations.

Titles include:

Koen Verhoest, Paul G. Roness, Bram Verschuere, Kristin Rubecksen and Muiris Mac-Carthaigh
AUTONOMY AND CONTROL OF STATE AGENCIES
Comparing States and Agencies

Forthcoming titles:

Geert Bouckaert; B. Guy Peters; Koen Verhoest
THE COORDINATION OF PUBLIC SECTOR ORGANIZATIONS
Shifting Patterns of Public Management

Amanda Smullen
TRANSLATING AGENCY REFORM
Rhetoric and Culture in Comparative Perspective

Public Sector Organizations Series
Series Standing Order ISBN 978–0–230–22034–8 (Hardback)
978–0–230–22035–5 (Paperback)
(*outside North America only*)

You can receive future titles in this series as they are published by placing a standing order. Please contact your bookseller or, in case of difficulty, write to us at the address below with your name and address, the title of the series and the ISBNs quoted above.

Customer Services Department, Macmillan Distribution Ltd, Houndmills, Basingstoke, Hampshire RG21 6XS, England

Autonomy and Control of State Agencies

Comparing States and Agencies

Koen Verhoest

Assistant Professor and Research Manager, Public Management Institute, Catholic University of Leuven, Belgium

Paul G. Roness

Professor, Department of Administration and Organization Theory, University of Bergen, Norway

Bram Verschuere

Lecturer in Public Management, University College Ghent, Belgium

Kristin Rubecksen

Research Fellow, Department of Administration and Organization Theory, University of Bergen, Norway

Muiris MacCarthaigh

Research Officer, Institute of Public Administration, Ireland

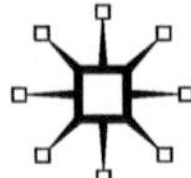

Contents

List of Tables and Figures

Tables

Figures

Acknowledgements

The process of writing a book is never a solitary one. We extend our gratitude to several individuals who have provided us with inspiration and help in the development of this volume.

First, we thank Amy Lankester-Owen, Allison Howson and Gemma d'Arcy Hughes from Palgrave Macmillan for the trust they placed in us and for providing us with fulsome support during the editorial process.

Second, we would like to thank the many colleagues who commented on previous papers on which this book has drawn. In particular we recognise the contribution of the members of the 'Comparative Public Organization Data Base for Research and Analysis (COBRA) network' (http://www.publicmanagement-cobra.org/), which is an academic research collaboration in the field of public management. The COBRA network gathers and analyses similar survey data on agency autonomy and control in a large number of participating countries, allowing the comparison of agency types and features operating in different politico-administrative cultures. This book draws on three such surveys which were conducted at the initiation of the network. In a similar vein we would like to thank our colleagues of the COST Action IS0601 'Comparative Research into Current Trends in Public Sector Organization' (www.soc.kuleuven.be/io/cost). Within this network, high-quality European public management research teams from 22 countries are joining their forces in a common research strategy on public sector organisation. A central research focus in this work is the changing autonomy, control and coordination of public agencies, as well as the explanations and consequences of this trend.

Among this excellent group of scholars we especially would like to thank Geert Bouckaert (Catholic University of Leuven), B. Guy Peters (University of Pittsburgh), Per Lægreid (University of Bergen), Peter C. Humphreys (Institute of Public Administration), Sandra van Thiel (Erasmus University), Tom Christensen (University of Oslo), and Kutsal Yesilkagit (University of Utrecht).

As this book is based on survey data of originally more than 300 public organizations in Norway, Ireland and Flanders, we want to express our enormous respect and gratitude to all the senior managers who have taken the time to fill in the survey and to give us supplementary information where required. Without their efforts, this comparative study would not have been possible. We hope that when reading this book, these officials will affirm the value of comparative studies on autonomy and control of public sector organizations, both from a scientific and practical point of view.

We all want to thank our home institutions and respective colleagues for granting us the time and support to do this study. Moreover, we want to thank our partners and families for their patience and encouragement when writing this book.

This publication is supported by COST. Therefore, we gratefully acknowledge the European Science Foundation and COST for allowing the COST Action ISO601 to fund the involved network activities, which has further enabled this comparative research.

COST – the acronym for European Cooperation in Science and Technology – is the oldest and widest European intergovernmental network for cooperation in research. Established by the Ministerial Conference in November 1971, COST is presently used by the scientific communities of 35 European countries to cooperate in common research projects supported by national funds. The funds provided by COST – less than one per cent of the total value of the projects – support the COST cooperation networks (COST Actions) through which, with EUR 30 million per year, more than 30,000 European scientists are involved in research having a total value which exceeds EUR two billion per year. This is the financial worth of the European added value which COST achieves. A 'bottom up approach' (the initiative of launching a COST Action comes from the European scientists themselves), 'à la carte participation' (only countries interested in the Action participate), 'equality of access' (participation is open also to the scientific communities of countries not belonging to the European Union) and 'flexible structure' (easy implementation and light management of the research initiatives) are the main characteristics of COST.

As precursor of advanced multidisciplinary research COST has a very important role for the realisation of the European Research Area (ERA) anticipating and complementing the activities of the Framework Programmes, constituting a 'bridge' towards the scientific communities of emerging countries, increasing the mobility of researchers across Europe and fostering the establishment of 'Networks of Excellence' in many key scientific domains such as: Biomedicine and Molecular Biosciences; Food and Agriculture; Forests, their Products and Services; Materials, Physical and Nanosciences; Chemistry and Molecular Sciences and Technologies; Earth System Science and Environmental Management; Information and Communication Technologies; Transport and Urban Development; Individuals, Societies, Cultures and Health. It covers basic and more applied research and also addresses issues of pre-normative nature or of societal importance.

Web: http://www.cost.esf.org.

List of Abbreviations

NPM	New Public Management
GDP	Gross Domestic Product
MBOR	Management by Objectives and Results
SMI	Strategic Management Initiative
DBG	Delivering Better Government
BBB	Beter Bestuurlijk Beleid (Better Administrative Policy)
FTE	Full Time Employee
OECD	Organisation for Economic Co-operation and Development
IMF	International Monetary Fund
HRM	Human Resource Management
FM	Financial Management
EU	European Union
EEA	European Economic Area
CEO	Chief Executive Officer
CAF	Common Assessment Framework

Notes on the Authors

Muiris MacCarthaigh (Dr) is a research officer with the Institute of Public Administration, Dublin. His research interests include public sector organization and reform, governance and accountability regimes and legislative studies. He has published a number of articles and books on these topics, as well as several studies about state agencies and commercial state-owned enterprises.

Paul G. Roness (dr.philos) is a professor at the Department of Administration and Organization Theory, University of Bergen. He has published widely on organization theory and public administration reform. Among his recent books are *Organization Theory and the Public Sector* (with Tom Christensen, Per Lægreid and Kjell Arne Røvik, 2007) and *Change and Continuity in Public Sector Organizations* (edited with Harald Sætren, 2009).

Kristin Rubecksen is a research fellow and doctoral candidate at the Department of Administration and Organization Theory, University of Bergen. Her research interests are in public sector organizations. She has published articles on this topic in *Financial Accountability and Management, International Public Management Journal, Scandinavian Political Studies* and *Public Organization Review*.

Koen Verhoest (Dr) is Assistant Professor and Research Manager at the Public Management Institute (Catholic University of Leuven, Belgium) where he studies organization, control and marketization of public tasks. He has published articles in *Governance, Public Administration and Development, International Review of Administrative Sciences* and *Public Organization Review*.

Bram Verschuere (Dr) is a lecturer in public management at University College Ghent (Belgium). Previously he worked at the Public Management Institute (Catholic University of Leuven, Belgium). His research interests are in public sector organization and state third-sector relationships. Part of his work has been published in *Public Management Review, Governance* and *Public Administration and Development*.

Part I
Introduction

1
Central Research Questions and Argument

1.1 General aim and scope of the book

Since the 1980s, the structuring and functioning of the Organisation for Economic Co-operation and Development (OECD) public sector has undergone major shifts (cf. OECD 2002a; Pollitt and Bouckaert 2004). One of the most observed trends in public sector organization in OECD states is the shift from a centralized and consolidated public sector to a decentralized, structurally devolved and 'autonomizing' public sector, including the disconnection of policy design, implementation and evaluation (Christensen and Lægreid 2001a, 2006). Systems of public administration have been disaggregated into a multitude of different kinds of (semi-)autonomous organizations, denoted as 'agencies' or 'quangos' (cf. Flinders and Smith 1999; Pollitt and Talbot 2004). This disaggregation through 'agencification' is the result of a process of vertical and horizontal specialization, based on geography as well as on different types of purposes, tasks, customer groups or processes (Christensen et al. 2007; Roness 2007). In this process of agencification and autonomization, the responsibilities and autonomy of public organizations are redefined (structural aspect). Moreover, the way that they are controlled by government, including the mechanisms of accountability, are redesigned, mostly from *ex ante* to *ex post*, and from input to results based rationals (functional aspect).

The New Public Management (NPM) doctrine, propagated by several international bodies (like the OECD, the IMF, the World Bank and, to some extent, the EU), takes a normative stance about the conditions under which (semi-)autonomous agencies should be created, as well as on the kind of control arrangements and autonomy levels for such agencies. Although one should expect a substantial degree of convergence between states, in practice, agencies in different states still exhibit significant differences in their prevalence, in their legal-structural form, their control arrangements and autonomy (see, for example, Pollitt et al. 2004). But the question remains as to whether or not we see convergence across states for agencies with similar features, such as the same size, task or governance structure.

Moreover, according to the NPM doctrine, the creation of agencies with greater management autonomy, combined with performance-based pressures to perform, will induce public sector organizations to modernize their management and optimize their functioning, which will ultimately improve their performance. However, while these effects are often promised or assumed they are seldom well documented (Christensen and Lægreid 2001a, 2006; Pollitt 2004; Verhoest et al. 2004a, 2007).

This phenomenon of agencification poses major conceptual, empirical, methodological and theoretical challenges to public organization research with regard to different basic questions: What are 'agencies', what are their features and how can we map them? How can we measure their autonomy and control? To what extent do agencies in different states and sectors differ and how can we explain these differences and similarities? What characteristics influence the autonomy and control of agencies? To what extent does the level of autonomy and control of agencies affect their internal management and their performance?

Despite a considerable body of scientific research into the world of 'agencies', several aspects of the above questions remain unanswered, or else the results are inconclusive (see for example Bouckaert and Peters 2004; Pollitt 2004; Verhoest et al. 2004a). In part, this is because these questions call for clear conceptualizations, broad data gathering strategies and international comparative research designs as well as multi-faceted theoretical frameworks. Although there are some exceptions (for example, Pollitt et al. 2004; Christensen and Yesilkagit 2006), this is mostly lacking in contemporary agency research.

In this book, we deal with most of these questions by describing, comparing and explaining the features of a large number of agencies in three states: Norway, Ireland and Flanders as a member state of the federal kingdom of Belgium. This comparison is particularly interesting because, on the one hand, they are European states of similar size and with comparable political systems (parliamentary democracies). Moreover, all three states are generally considered to be quite impervious to administrative reforms along NPM lines. On the other hand, they represent three different politico-administrative regimes and traditions (Nordic, Anglo-Saxon and Latin-European) with different cultures and views on the role of the state. The relevance of such regimes, traditions and cultures are most important in explaining differences in the way internationally diffused reform trends are implemented in different 'implementation habitats' (Lijphart 1999; Christensen and Lægreid 2001b; Lalenis et al. 2002; Pollitt and Bouckaert 2004; Wollmann 2004).

Drawing on data from recent and standardized surveys covering a large set of comparable public sector agencies in Norway, Ireland and Flanders, we compare the autonomy, control and internal management of these orga-nizations in the three states. The focus is on the autonomy of an agency vis-à-vis the responsible minister and department and their control by minister/department. Moreover, we explain the similarities and differences in the autonomy, control and internal management of agencies by referring to characteristics at the level of states (such as politico-administrative regime and history) and at the level of agencies (such as size, task and age). In addi-tion, we analyse the effect of characteristics of agencies and their autonomy and control on the internal management of agencies.

Based on ideas from organization theory and different strands of institu-tional theory (rational choice, sociological and historical institutionalism), and by using statistical techniques, we elaborate four different sets of empirical and theoretical research questions:

Describing agencies:

RQ 1: Background: To what extent are agencies created by the governments of the three states, in what form, with what legal-structural status, and in which policy domains? What tasks are they performing? How is the creation of agencies evolving over time?

Comparing states:

RQ 2: Do agencies in general, or with similar features, in the three states show similar or dissimilar levels and patterns of autonomy, control and internal management? Do these patterns match the features of the NPM ideal type?

RQ 3: How can similar/dissimilar levels and patterns of autonomy, control and internal management between the three states be explained by referring to aspects of their politico-administrative regime (state-level characteristics)?

Comparing agencies:

RQ 4: Which agency-level characteristics (such as size or task) influence the level and pattern of autonomy and control of agencies in general?

RQ 5: Which agency-level characteristics influence the internal manage-ment of agencies in general? To what extent does the level of autonomy and control affect the internal management (the use of management techniques)?

Explaining autonomy, control and internal management:

RQ 6: How do agency-level characteristics interact with state-level character-istics in explaining agency autonomy, control and internal management?

RQ 7: Which theoretical perspective has the strongest explanatory power with respect to the level and pattern of autonomy, control and internal management of agencies in the three states?

The research design is cross-sectional and compares states as well as agencies. For the empirical part of this book we use two main kinds of data sources. For answering the first research question on describing agencies we rely on state-specific databases on public sector organizations, which were constructed from information in various official documents in each state. For answering the comparative and explanatory research questions we rely on survey data, which were collected in quite similar ways in the three states during the period from late 2002 until early 2005 (cf. Chapter 4, p. 74 – ending in February 2005 in Norway). We include survey data from 226 organizations.

1.2   The NPM ideal-type agency model as basis for comparison

We ask what agencies' autonomy, control and management looks like in the three states, and how these specific features can be explained, taking, as a starting point, the pressure for conformity that comes from international NPM doctrines. We assume all three states to be influenced by this international-level pressure for convergence. Indeed, agencification is to be observed in almost all developing countries (OECD 2002a) to such an extent that scholars refer to the emergence of a contagious agency fever (Pollitt et al. 2001).

This international pressure to agencify is expected to lead to isomorphic administrative reforms, whereby, in the three states studied here, organizational structures are adjusted towards the internationally propagated 'ideal-type agency' image. As such, we would expect agencies in the three states to be quite similar in terms of autonomy, control and internal management, and in line with the NPM ideal-type agency. As this ideal-type is our point of departure, we must first identify the basic elements of such agencies in terms of autonomy, control and internal management.

NPM is a set of ideas that has gained ascendancy in political circles and that includes several intellectual and ideological dimensions (Aucoin 1990). It combines public choice-based ideas about re-establishing the primacy of government over bureaucracy, and ideas from managerialism concerned with re-establishing the primacy of managerial practices over bureaucracy (for example fighting 'red tape'). Inspired and spread by an NPM-rhetoric (Trosa 1994; Massey 1995; Laking 2002) an ideal-type agency form emerged along with some key dimensions such as structural disaggregation, managerial freedom, results control and the 'policy-operations' split. According to its advocates, this ideal-type agency is the best way to have public services delivered in a transparent, customer-oriented and effective and efficient way.

The first feature is *structural disaggregation*. The large monolithic departments that characterized the earlier governmental bureaucracies should be disaggregated into single-purpose and client-oriented organizations that have a service delivery focus. Agencies are assumed to be closer to the citizens, and hence more 'customer-oriented'. Also, increased transparency is assumed, since agencies can be subjected to contract-like regimes (Pollitt et al. 2001). All agencies studied in this book are structurally disaggregated from their parent department.

Structural disaggregation cannot be equated with autonomy (Pollitt et al. 2004). Autonomy revolves around the level of choices that the organization can make about internal arrangements, or the extent to which these are externally imposed. In the NPM ideal-type model, agencies are given a great deal of managerial autonomy in order to be able to act more or less independently of their core governmental departments. The goal is to improve and allow modern management, which should provide for increasing efficiency and decrease 'waste' (Hood 1991). Rational choice theories, such as property rights theory, state that by receiving managerial responsibilities the managers of agencies may be more inclined to behave efficiently since they are made responsible for 'their' resources. Next to that, letting managers 'manage' will encourage professionalism in public agencies.

Moreover, NPM emphasizes the need to shift the control of agencies from *ex ante* to *results-based control*, based on contractual instruments. By relaxing controls on inputs and procedures, agencies are freed from cumbersome regulations, which hamper the efficient use of resources and effective organization of processes. Instead, agencies are set clear organizational goals, targets and indicators of organizational success, which are monitored, evaluated and eventually sanctioned by political and administrative principals (Hood 1991).

Managerial autonomy and results control point to two inherently linked conditions for the efficient and effective behaviour of public managers (Aucoin 1990; Christensen and Lægreid 2001b; Norman 2003). First, '*Let* public managers manage'. Managerial autonomy enables and facilitates efficient behaviour, but does not in itself induce public managers to behave efficiently. Therefore, pressure is needed. Thus, the second condition is to '*Make* public managers manage' by putting managerial and market-like pressures on them (OECD 1997; Kettl 2000). Results control is crucial to increasing pressures on agency managers. Hence, according to NPM doctrines, high levels of autonomy must be counterbalanced by high levels of results control. Theoretically, this pattern of autonomy and control is firmly grounded in principal-agent theory. This theory proposes that agents will perform most efficiently if they have autonomy that allows them to specialize, on the one hand, and they are controlled strongly by the principal through results monitoring, bonding and risk-turnover, on the other. This control is needed to minimize agency problems, like opportunistic behaviour (moral hazard and adverse selection) stemming from goal incongruence and information asymmetry (Pratt and Zeckhauser 1991). This refers to the so-called paradox of autonomization in which the autonomization of public agencies may imply stricter central regulation (Kickert 1998; Smullen et al. 2001). This paradox is essentially about a reduction of extensive input and process control, combined with a stricter control on performance (Bouckaert and Verhoest 1999).

The fourth feature of the NPM ideal-type agency refers to the *'policy-operations' split* (Boston et al. 1996; Schick 2002). The idea is to divide public sector tasks into policy preparation and policy operations. The former, which is a 'political' task, is to be performed by those who are directly democratically legitimated and their direct subordinate core departments. The latter, which is an 'administrative' task, is to be performed by 'arm's length' agencies, which are more or less free of ministerial interference. Again, this element is founded in principal-agent theory, in which minister–agency relations can be framed as a purchaser–provider relationship based on contractual terms. In order to avoid agencies setting their own contractual terms, policy design and decisions should be conducted by ministers and departments. Moreover, this policy-operations split allows agencies to specialize in efficient policy implementation (Hood and Jackson 1991). The NPM doctrines consider agencies to be mainly implementers of policy, set from above, with either no role, or only a small one, in policy design or decision making. This implies that such agencies would have low levels of policy autonomy.

In sum, if public sector reformers follow this NPM ideal-type agency model, we would expect to find agencies which *have considerable degrees of managerial autonomy, rather low levels of policy autonomy, and which are controlled by results.* Such agencies are considered by advocates of the model as being effective and efficient vehicles, as they will behave in a more businesslike manner, and modernize their internal management and adopt management techniques that are prominently used by private sector firms. Therefore, such agencies are expected to perform better in terms of efficiency, effectiveness, quality of service delivery and accountability towards stakeholders (OECD 1994). Indeed, there is a growing literature on 'management matters', which assumes that modern management practices seem to influence the performance of public organizations (for example, Ingraham et al. 2003; O'Toole and Meier 2003; Boyne 2004).

To what extent is this ideal-type NPM agency to be found in the real world? This question is related to the 'convergence–divergence' debate (Pollitt and Bouckaert 2004). According to adherents of the convergence thesis, the ideal-type agency would be observed very often and in different contexts. Adherents of the divergence thesis are more likely to see a lot of empirical variation within the ideal-type agency form. Empirical evidence collected in recent years suggests that the normative ideal-type agency is only rarely observed. Moreover, a closer examination of individual countries' reform projects reveals variation in reform practices across states and sectors (Premfors 1998; OECD 2002a; Fedele et al. 2007). Pollitt et al. (2001: 278) found that 'empirical research has suggested that in practice the choice of organizational form by ministers and civil servants tends to be fairly ad hoc and that the [normative model of agencification] features more from text-books and lectures than from the reality of politico-administrative decision making', referring to research by Gains (1999), Van Thiel (2001) and Boston et al. (1996). The *variation in individual agency forms* has been studied in case studies, with scholars searching for interpretative explanations (Smullen 2004) or historical explanations (Gains 2004), or explanations based on agency-specific characteristics such as, for example, the political salience of the task that counts for different steering and control practices (Pollitt 2004). Most studies focus either on agency-specific characteristics or on more institutional environments as explanations for these variations. Studies combining both sets of explanatory characteristics are very rare, except for the multiple-case study research done by Pollitt et al. (2004).

Recent research has shown that agencies actually differ quite substantially across, and within, states with respect to their main features – that is, autonomy, control and internal management. In this book we study this issue of similarity and dissimilarity, allowing theoretically not only for international pressures, but also for state-level and agency-level characteristics that may explain these phenomena. In this model, the international pressure for agencification is transformed when it meets state-specific polity and cultural features, which may lead to different responses and reform programmes (that is, state-level pressures for divergence and dissimilarity). But these potentially different reform programmes may be reformulated and adapted again when they are applied to agencies with different tasks, sizes or governance structures. As will be shown, in more depth, later in this book, one can expect agencies with similar tasks, for example, to have somewhat similar levels of autonomy and control (that is, agency-level pressures for convergence or similarity). This could be due to the demands of agencies with these tasks, to judgements and to the views of the political principals, or to internationally proclaimed doctrines (for example, about the desirability of independent regulatory agencies). Both the drivers for convergence/similarity and divergence/dissimilarity at the different levels (international, state and agency level) will ultimately determine the extent to which agencies with similar features in states with different polity and cultures will show similar agency features. Moreover, these characteristics help us to explain the observed levels of agency autonomy and control.

1.3   **Relevance of the book**

A major part of public sector organization research is focused on specialization and agencies. This research could be sub-categorized around three basic questions:

1. What are the facts and figures about the phenomenon of agencies and other autonomous bodies (descriptive; for example OECD 2002a; Talbot and Caulfield 2002; Pollitt and Talbot 2004; Verhoest et al. 2004a, Jann and Döhler 2005; Christensen and Yesilkagit 2006; Ongaro 2006)?
2. Why do agencies emerge and with such variety (explanatory; for example James 2003; Van Thiel 2004; McGauran et al. 2005)?
3. Are these types of organizations more effective than others (predictive; for example Pollitt et al. 1998; Flinders and Smith 1999; Ingraham and Moynihan 2001)?

Other studies are more normative in nature or formulate practitioners' models (Trosa 1994; Massey 1995). These questions are also embedded in a broader set of research on governance and coordination (based on hierarchies, markets and networks) in OECD states (for example Painter and Pierre 2005; Bouckaert et al. forthcoming).

However, despite the vast literature on agencification, many questions remain unanswered or have led only to inconclusive results. In their overviews of the agency literature, Pollitt (2004) and Bouckaert and Peters (2004) identify what is missing in the agency literature:

- Theoretically: There is a need for more studies in which two or more rival or complementary theoretical approaches are brought to bear on the same issue or question.
- Explanatory: We need a clearer articulation of middle-range theories, which will help us to classify and interrelate the kinds of variables that explain variations between superficially similar organizational forms within a single jurisdiction or even within a single programme.
- Empirical – methodologically: 'this is a field which is crying out for real comparative research. [...] a research project which deliberately and systematically compared an (apparently) similar development in different countries, and then attempted to explain perceived variations between those countries' (Pollitt 2004: 339–40). Up to now, the research conducted comprises predominantly single-country or single-sector studies, except for a few (albeit high-quality) cross-comparative multiple case studies (see mainly Pollitt et al. 2004). Bouckaert and Peters (2004) point at the usefulness of surveys, besides case studies, but until recently no such survey-based international comparisons have been undertaken.

- Conceptually: There is a need for a clear definition of what agencies are, but also clear conceptualizations of core concepts such as autonomy and control (Verhoest et al. 2004a). Whereas recent front-line research (Pollitt et al. 2004) delineates the field of agencies in a clear way, large-scale empirical comparative research based on strict conceptualizations of autonomy and control is harder to find.

The comparative research of agencies in Norway, Ireland and Flanders presented in this book explicitly takes these lacunae of previous research as a starting point. The research is clearly internationally comparative, based on very clear common multi-dimensional conceptualizations, operationalizations and measurements, using survey data from 226 organizations with all kinds of tasks and covering all kinds of policy sectors.

The research is based on similar survey questionnaires, leading to identical variables and indexes. Moreover, the interpretation of the survey data is to some extent facilitated by making reference to case studies and previous research by the research teams involved. Through the use of simple and advanced statistical techniques, we compare agencies from different states, policy areas, size and age as well as governance structure. Moreover, through a careful delineation of the state samples, we are comparing agencies with broadly similar legal–formal status (excluding core-ministerial units and private law agencies). The research presented is based on a theoretical framework with explanatory factors at international, state and agency level. Each set of factors leads to competing explanatory models and hypotheses. These relationships can be considered as middle-range theories, linking autonomy, control and the use of management techniques with explanatory factors at different levels.

How does this relate to the recent authoritative study by Pollitt et al. (2004) of agencies in four countries and four sectors? This is perhaps the most comprehensive study so far of, as the subtitle says, 'how governments do things through semi-autonomous organizations'. They concentrate on three questions that are seen as among the more general and basic questions about the recent international wave of 'agencification': 1) Why has the agency form seemed to become so popular over the past 15 years or so? (Why is it chosen, Why has it spread?); 2) How can agencies best be 'steered' by their parent departments?; 3) What are the conditions under which agencies perform well (or badly?). They try to answer these questions through a research design comparing four countries and four comparable sets of public sector tasks which were delivered through agencies. They also develop a theory on autonomy and control of agencies that combines a perspective on path-dependency (among others, based on politico-administrative culture) and a perspective linked to the task of that agency.

Their aim was to see how these agencies were organized and how they fit into national patterns of politico-administrative structure and agencification, as well as task-specific patterns. They were particularly interested in how autonomous and performance-managed they were. Quite similar to us, they compare agencies in different countries in one part of the book and tasks in another. The findings are interpreted in a concluding chapter, in which they construct their task-specific path dependency model and contrast it to the bureau-shaping model and the practitioner model. Where the path-dependency points more to dissimilarities, the task-specificity refers to similarities in autonomy and control of agencies. Relevant task features, which have an impact on the way agencies are controlled by their parent departments and political principals, are features such as political salience (as evoked by size or budgetary weight), measurability of tasks and the level of expertise needed for tasks.

Our study aims to complement this recent research in different ways: First, the research design allows for checking the external validity of the task-specific path dependency perspective in a large number of cases (226 agencies in total) and for three different small European states. Second, we explicitly study the impact of state-level characteristics (pointing at potential path dependency) and the impact of agency-level characteristics (of which some are related to task) on the autonomy and control of agencies. But our set of explanatory factors is broader, using a wide range of competing theoretical models. We also study how state-level characteristics and agency-level characteristics interact in explaining agencies' autonomy, control and internal management. Moreover, we do not only seek explanations for autonomy and control of agencies, but also study the impact of autonomy and control on the internal management of agencies, which is operationalized as the use of specific management techniques. This part of the research brings greater insight into the issue of the extent to which agencification affects the management and, consequently, performance of public organizations. Lastly, instead of focusing on typical high-profile states, which figure in most comparative public management studies (like the United Kingdom, Sweden, the Netherlands), we focus on states that are generally neglected, because they are small and not considered to be radical reformers. This focus gives a more nuanced view of public management reform in European countries.

Finally, this study will contribute to the explanatory research perspective that has focused on the effects of agencification for agency performance. In this quite large field of research, the influence of agencies' autonomy and the (results) control practices that agencies face on their performance has been studied (Dunsire et al. 1991; Wolf 1993; Pollitt et al. 1998; van Thiel 2001; Christensen and Lægreid 2001a; Verhoest 2002; see for an overview Verhoest et al. 2004a). Overall, the findings of this research tradition are inconclusive. This has to do first with conceptualization problems (Verhoest et al. 2004a), and with problems of performance measurement, such as the lack of data and the problem of attribution, as reported by several studies (for example, Pollitt et al. 1998). Second, the inconclusiveness also relates to the need to study variables which intervene in this relationship between autonomy, control and performance. Potential intervening variables are suggested by other research, such as organizational routines and norms, actor preferences, organizational dependence on technology (Pollitt et al. 1998), organizational culture, tangibility of organizational objectives (Ter Bogt 1998), age, political support, leadership features (Wolf 1993), corporatism, agency size and the extent to which the agency faces competition (van Thiel 2001). In this study we avoid the problem of conceptualizing and measuring performance by taking modern internal management as a proxy. In fact, we assume that this (measured by the use of internal management techniques) will enhance organizational performance (Ingraham et al. 2003; O'Toole and Meier 2003). When studying the effect of autonomy and control arrangements on the internal management of agencies we check for the direct influence of some of the intervening variables suggested, including size, age and measurability of task outputs.

1.4   Structure of the book

In the following chapter, we outline the major concepts, including agencies, autonomy, control and internal management. In Chapter 3, we present the main aspects of the theoretical lenses used in this book, and explain our selection in relation to alternative theories adopted in other agency research. Drawing on ideas and concepts from organization theory and rational, sociological and historical institutional schools, four theoretical perspectives are elaborated: 1) a structural-instrumental perspective (emphasizing formal organization structure and instrumental action), 2) a cultural-institutional perspective (emphasizing organizational culture and organizational path dependency), 3) a task-specific perspective (emphasizing the characteristics of organizational tasks) and 4) an environmental perspective (emphasizing institutional environments, isomorphism and myths). In order to integrate these perspectives, we develop a theoretical framework for comparing and explaining features of agencies in the three states. Based primarily on a transformative perspective (cf. Christensen and Lægreid 2001b, 2001c, 2007a), this theoretical framework points to explanatory factors at three levels of analysis: the international level, the state level and the agency level (for example, policy areas, tasks and size).

In the final chapter of Part I (Chapter 4) we discuss methodological aspects of the research, including the operationalization and measurement of concepts, the strategies for data gathering and analysis, the delineation of similar samples of agencies within the joint database as well as the selection of the states.

In Part II, we set the scene and describe the prevalence, types, features and history of agencies (Chapter 6) within the broader politico-administrative context of the three states (Chapter 5), by dealing with the following descriptive research questions:

RQ 1:   *Background: To what extent are agencies created by the*
           governments of the three states, in what form, with what
           legal-structural status, and in which policy domains? What
           tasks are they performing? How is the creation of agencies
           evolving over time?

In Part III, in which we compare states, we come to one of the core issues of this book and ask to what extent the autonomy, control and internal management of agencies in the three states may be influenced by *state-level pressures for divergence*. Based on a literature review and two competing frameworks, Chapter 7 first identifies the main characteristics at state level and clusters them in four main sets: environmental aspects, dimensions of politico-administrative culture, actor constellations and deliberate actions taken by these actors. Theoretically, these characteristics are embedded in the environmental perspective.

Chapter 8 compares the patterns of autonomy, control and use of management techniques across the three states for all agencies. Additionally, these patterns are compared across states for subgroups of agencies with similar governance structure, tasks, size and age. Hence, the second research question will be dealt with in this chapter:

RQ 2:   *Do agencies in general or with similar characteristics in the*
           three states show similar or dissimilar levels and patterns of
           autonomy, control and internal management? Are
           similarities between agencies in the three states in line
           with the NPM ideal-type agency model?

In Chapter 9 we discuss the relevance of each of the state-level characteristics in explaining systematic similarities and differences between agencies in the three states. As such, we tackle the related explanatory question:

RQ 3:   *How can similar or dissimilar levels and patterns of autonomy,*
           control and internal management between the three states be
           explained by referring to aspects of their politico-administrative
           regime (state-level characteristics)?

In Part IV we look for agency-level characteristics that explain the levels of autonomy and control of agencies across the three states for the total sample of agencies. Moreover, we analyse the extent to which the internal management of agencies is influenced by their autonomy and control, as well as by agency-level characteristics. In Chapter 10 we outline the relevant theoretical landscape, and argue for expectations and hypotheses based on the structural-instrumental perspective, the cultural-institutional perspective, as well as the task-specific perspective. Chapters 11 and 12 present the findings of bivariate and multivariate regression analyses. These chapters deal with the following research questions:

RQ 4: *What agency-level characteristics (such as size, task) influence the level and pattern of autonomy and control of agencies in general?*

RQ 5: *What agency-level characteristics influence the internal management of agencies in general? To what extent does the level of autonomy and control affect their internal management?*

In Chapter 13 we bring the analysis to its final stage. Having analysed the influence of state-level characteristics and of agency-level characteristics separately in earlier chapters, we now focus on the interaction effects of state-level with agency-level characteristics. More specifically, we examine which agency-level characteristics affect agency autonomy, control and internal management in a direct way, and independently from the influence of state-level characteristics. Integrating the findings on state-level characteristics outlined in Chapter 9, we can then outline which characteristics, both at state level and at agency level, affect agency autonomy, control and internal management directly and independent from one another. Chapter 13 thus deals with the final explanatory questions:

RQ 6: *How do agency-level characteristics interact with state-level characteristics in explaining agency autonomy, control and internal management?*

RQ 7: *Which of the four theoretical perspectives has the strongest explanatory power with respect to the level and pattern of autonomy, control and internal management of agencies in the three states? Or do all four theoretical perspectives add explanations to the empirical data?*

For each of the theoretical perspectives and hypotheses, we discuss the relevance of the corresponding state-level and agency-level characteristics in explaining systematic similarities and differences between agencies in each of the three states. We conclude by linking back to the four theoretical perspectives on which we have built our expectations. We also discuss the relevance of our findings in the light of previous agency research and important theoretical frameworks. Methodological lessons are drawn about the relevance and limitations of survey research and the need for methodological triangulation. Finally, some directions for future research are outlined.

2
Central Concepts

In order to compare the autonomy, control and internal management of state agencies we must clarify what we are studying. This requires us to define the central concepts: agencies, autonomy, control and management techniques. In doing so we draw on relevant literature from academics as well as practitioners in public administration.

2.1 Agencies

The focus of this book is on specific types of public sector organizations, which we refer to as *agencies*. These are variously described internationally as non-departmental public bodies, hybrids, quangos, fringe bodies, non-majoritarian institutions, quasi-autonomous public organizations, and distributed public governance (see, for example, Wettenhall 2005; Christensen and Lægreid 2006; Roness 2007). How an agency is defined, and what it does, varies considerably across national and organizational cultures, legal systems and political systems (Smullen 2004). Drawing on some elements of Pollitt et al. (2004) and Talbot (2004), we focus on those public sector organizations which have the following features:

- *They are public law bodies*, meaning they are set up by a public law instrument (such as a statute, law, constitution, ministerial order or a formal decision of cabinet or minister) and their main features are predominantly described by this instrument. This criterion excludes private law bodies, which are created with their own constitution or deed of trust under a private law instrument (for example, under a Companies Act or an act regulating the establishment of trusts, cooperatives and societies) and whose basic features are predominantly described by this instrument.
- *They have some capacity for autonomous decision making either with respect to management or policy.* This autonomous decision-making capacity is granted by statute (law or ministerial order) or is generally accepted by consensus.

- *They are structurally disaggregated* from other organizations or from units within core departments. This excludes government departments and ministries that have direct ministerial-level representation in cabinet, and also regional and local offices of departments.
- *They are formally under at least some control of ministers (and departments),* which encompasses more than just control as shareholder or market regulator. Moreover, there is formally a reporting and accountability relationship to departments or the minister. This excludes agencies directly and solely accountable to Parliament.
- *They have some expectation of continuity over time.* This excludes purely temporary (advisory) committees, interdepartmental teams, task forces and tribunals of inquiry.
- *They have some resources (financial and personnel) of their own.*

This means that the following sets of public sector organizations are excluded from our understanding of agencies:

- Companies and corporations with a commercial focus, which have to closely observe the laws regulating private companies, or which are registered under a Companies Act as a company: Since 'commercial functions' are, of themselves, hard to define and subject to changes over time, we deal with this pragmatically by excluding the following large groups in each state: state-owned companies (including limited companies with the state as majority owner) in Norway; private companies in Ireland; private law bodies in the form of companies in Flanders.
- Governmental foundations, trusts, cooperative societies and voluntary organizations: In order to deal with this pragmatically, we exclude from the analysis: governmental foundations in Norway; trusts and charities in Ireland; and private law bodies in Flanders.

What this actually implies, in terms of which public sector organizations are included in this study, is more fully discussed in Chapter 6.

2.2 Autonomy

One of the defining characteristics of agencies is that they have some form, and degree, of autonomy from superior bodies. The concept of *autonomy* is also used in different ways in the study of agencies. The focus is mostly on structural and formal autonomy and on agency design (for example Moe 1990; Christensen 2001; Yesilkagit 2004a). Other studies are more interested in de facto autonomy, taking autonomy as the level of decision-making competencies of agencies as the point of departure. Thus, autonomy is about discretion, or the extent to which an agency can decide itself about matters that it considers important (Verhoest et al. 2004a; Verschuere 2007; Roness et al. 2008).

This study focuses on the latter way of defining agency autonomy. Autonomy as decision-making power can be split into two kinds, based on two different scopes of discretion. When agencies have some decision-making competencies delegated from superior bodies with regard to the choice and use of inputs, they have some degree of *managerial autonomy*. This implies that agencies are exempted from certain rules and regulations concerning input management, which traditionally enhance the legality and economy of governmental transactions and constrain managerial discretion. An agency can have managerial autonomy with regard to human resource management, financial management or the management of other production factors such as logistics, organization and housing. But the scope of autonomous decision-making capacity may also vary because of the structuring of the primary production processes of the agency and the policies themselves. In contrast with managerial autonomy, the level of *policy autonomy* of an agency indicates the extent to which the agency itself can take decisions about: the (sub)processes and procedures it has to conduct to produce the externally prescribed goods or services; the policy instruments used to implement the externally set policy and the quantity and quality of the goods or services to be produced; and the target groups and societal objectives and outcomes to be reached by the policy. Policy autonomy indicates, for example, that agencies may take decisions on individual cases within externally set regulations and laws.

In this study we examine only certain forms of agency autonomy. For managerial autonomy this includes some forms of human resource management (HRM) autonomy and financial management autonomy, while for policy autonomy we focus on autonomy in the choice of policy instruments. Moreover, we focus on the level of de facto autonomy, as perceived by the senior management of the agency. This is dealt with in Chapter 4.

2.2.1 Human resource management autonomy

Human resource management autonomy is measured on both a *strategic* level (as in whether or not agency managers can set general rules with respect to that element of HRM) and an *operational* level (as in whether or not agency managers can take decisions on individual cases with respect to that element of HRM). In our study, three elements of HRM autonomy are included: autonomy with respect to salaries, promotion and evaluation of personnel.

Modern HRM policies in public sector organizations encompass decisions concerning personnel planning (including staff number controls), selection and appointment, personnel evaluation, career management, promotion, and mobility, pay and rewards, and dismissal (see for example Armstrong 1988). Optimally, these decisions are interrelated and connected to one another, based on an integrated vision of the efficient use of human resources. Since human resources are usually by far the most important production factors for agencies, the allocation of decision-making power concerning these issues has been a hotly debated issue since the 1980s in most OECD states. Centralizing such decision-making power in the hands of the government may secure uniformity of personnel-related decisions throughout state administration, enhancing mobility and economies of scale and protecting the employees from nepotism and arbitrariness by line managers.

The power of labour unions within the civil service may be an additional factor in motivating the government to adopt centralized decision making with regard to human resource policies. Furthermore, by deciding criteria for selection, evaluation and promotion, the government may, to a large extent, influence the kind of employees that come into, and rise through, the state administration. Moreover, HRM decisions, in particular those related to staff numbers, appointment and pay and rewards have long-term financial implications, which may endanger the sustainability of the state budget to a large extent (Heyman 1988). For example, several OECD states face the challenge of controlling state pensions over the longer term. Therefore, staff numbers may principally be decided on from above, and pay schemes may be strictly regulated. For all of these reasons, governments, and particularly the ministers responsible for state administration and finances, may prefer to control human resource policies in the different agencies quite strictly and uniformly. This may apply either at the level of actual decision making on individual employees (that is, at the operational level), or at least at the level of general regulations and procedures on HRM issues (that is, at the strategic level) (Verhoest 2002).

However, managers of individual agencies may prefer rather high levels of autonomy in relation to these issues. Operational autonomy on individual decisions within regulations set by the government may be appreciated, since it allows the managers to speed up the procedures for personnel selection and movements, and gives some discretion to put 'the right man on the right job' (at least, if central regulations allow such personnel allocations). Moreover, most agency managers may also prefer strategic autonomy, giving them leeway in regulating criteria and procedures for personnel selection, promotion and evaluation. Such strategic autonomy may enable the manager involved to tailor the HRM policy to the specific agency. Managers may generally prefer some degree of flexibility in staff numbers in the form of a budgetary limit on personnel costs, rather than a strict *ex ante* regulation in terms of quantity and quality. Similarly, as personnel evaluation may be the best way for a manager to form a view on the functioning, performance and career possibilities of the personnel, and because the criteria for evaluation are guiding principles for the behaviour of personnel, it may be advantageous for the manager to be able to set evaluation criteria and procedures. In order to fully utilize their employees, managers may strive for autonomy with regard to career patterns and promotion criteria. Discretion on pay schemes and rewards may also help to increase the attractiveness of employment and personnel motivation.

2.2.2 Financial management autonomy

Flexibility in the way an agency receives its financial resources and uses them for its activities is often highly valued by agency managers. Discretion on financial management can be related to several decisions, such as the design and approval of the agency budget, the execution of the budget (including budget shifts during and over years), the format and rules for accounting systems, the management of incomes and savings, the acquisition and selling of assets, the management of cash resources and long-term loans, as well as the creation of subsidiaries and financial participation in other organizations (Coe 1989; McKinney 1995).

On all of these dimensions governments have traditionally issued strict regulations, sought uniform and detailed formats, and strictly controlled compliance. Line-item budgets specified *ex ante* in detail what budget was to be used for what kind of expenses, without a link to objectives or performance. Highly detailed accounting plans and rules, mainly based on cash accounting principles, allowed an intensive and thorough financial and budgetary accounting regime. The acquisition of resources or selling of assets was subjected to prior regulation or approval, and capital spending was usually appropriated and controlled separately from current expenditure (Heyman 1988). Line managers were allocated an annual budget and were usually not free to borrow or lend against that budget (Heyman 1988). The strict position of the government, and in particular the minister of finance, is related to the sustainability of the state budget in the short and long run, the economy of resources used at the macro level, the need for an annual equilibrated budget as well as the prevention of misuse or fraud. A central objective of such financial and budgetary input controls is to 'maintain the integrity of an aggregate expenditure constraint', as Horn (1995: 89) explains: 'A simple annual expenditure limit [as one of the most important forms of control by the legislature on the public organizations] would not be effective if officials were left with an unrestricted ability to make intertemporal transfers.'

However, agency managers may generally prefer flexibility in acquisition and use of financial resources for reasons of organizational efficiency, tailored financial practices and more speedy financial procedures (Coe 1989). Moreover, financial management autonomy may allow them to more easily align their financial management practices to the strategic objectives of their organization. Following the logic of public choice and principal-agent theorists, flexibility in terms of financial management would be valued by agency managers because greater financial resources might influence their prestige and organizational power, enabling them to expand capacity or increase the opportunities to create organizational slack (Niskanen 1971; Migué et al. 1974).

An agency has essentially three ways of financing investments: using cash resources, saving cash resources for future investments or taking loans in the capital market (McKinney 1995). As such, the ability to take loans may be important for agencies with capital-intensive activities. Traditionally, governments have been reluctant to give subordinate bodies full autonomy to take out loans, because most of these transactions entail a government guarantee in case the bodies fail to repay the loan. If that happens, the debt ratio and rating of the government may deteriorate, endangering the sustainability of the state budget and precipitating a rise in the interest rate for loans for the government. Moreover, loans place a burden on the agency budget for several years, which must be funded either by government or by users. Governments must carefully choose which agencies to grant this kind of autonomy, set restrictions with regard to the kind of loans and the maximum amount of capital to be lent, or make the actual loan-taking dependent on a government authorization for each individual transaction.

The ability of agencies to set tariffs for their services and products is another important autonomy dimension. Agencies generate income through the performance of their activities and tasks. This could include different types of fees, taxes or tariffs related to different types of service delivery, such as provision of health services, selling products, informational services or case management. The extent to which agencies are able to keep or actually use self-generated income varies. Traditionally, the ability of agencies to generate their own income and to set tariffs themselves has been strictly regulated by government. Allowing them to generate their own income is only useful from a macro point of view if this managerial freedom enables governmental funding to be reduced. Agencies may only use such self-generated sources of income for activities that fit within their statutory tasks and objectives. Moreover, tariff setting may be tightly regulated in order to ensure the equal treatment of all citizens and to avoid abuses.

For agencies, the freedom to set their own tariffs may be important as it allows them to adjust the tariffs in line with their cost structure. Moreover, it may allow the top management of the agency to maximize the budget in order to increase their service delivery output, to perform new and additional tasks or to increase organizational slack. Public choice theorists like Niskanen (1971) build their models of bureaucratic behaviour on the assumption that bureaucrats aim for budget maximization, or the maximization of 'managerial discretionary profit' or 'organizational slack' that allows them to realize personal objectives (for example, lower workload by taking on additional personnel).

Being able to shift budgets between years or budget terms represents an important tool for financial flexibility in agencies. Traditional line-item budgets restrict the agency in that it cannot shift budget between budget posts during the year or shift budgets over years. The principle of budget annuality obliges agencies to return the non-consumed budgetary resources to the government at the end of the year. Often, the following year's budget of the agency will then be reduced by the non-consumed amount. For the government, this may allow for maximization of the economy at a macro level. It also helps to prevent agencies from accumulating non-used financial resources to the detriment of the financial health of the whole state administration. Moreover, the principle of budget annuality is based on the democratic right of Parliament to approve the state budget in its totality every year. However, within agencies, this annuality may create perverse effects, forcing them to consume the full budget by the end of the year, even if these resources could be more effectively used the following year. Moreover, as agencies may work on multi-year projects and on an accrual basis, they may prefer to allocate resources to activities and increase their efficiency. The ability to shift budgets between years allows agencies to save or to lend on their own budget, enabling multi-year financial flexibility and efficiency.

2.2.3 Policy autonomy

As shown above, the level of policy autonomy refers to the type of issues an agency can take decisions about. This ranges from more strategic issues to more operational ones, including the objectives the agency pursues and the effects it wishes to deliver, the policy instruments it employs, the target groups it focuses its actions on, the output quantity and quality it aims for, and the way it structures its primary production processes internally. Traditionally, legislators and ministers have taken such policy decisions themselves, at least, with regard to those strategic level decisions (for example, objectives, target groups and policy instruments). But even operational decisions on the way primary processes are structured can be enshrined in laws voted by Parliament, or in orders issued by the cabinet or individual ministers. In such cases, politicians micro-manage agencies in order to avoid 'bureaucratic drift' or deviation from the policy content intended by the legislators or ministers (Huber and Shipan 2002; Verhoest et al. 2004a). Politicians may want to achieve some policy goals in order to satisfy their constituencies and get re-elected. This may imply that allowing agencies to define policy goals, instruments and target groups themselves happens only in exceptional cases, and based on very specific grounds such as enhancing the credible commitment of government regulation in economically liberalized sectors.

However, agencies may advocate more autonomy on these issues, certainly when it comes to the way the primary processes are structured internally. Autonomy in designing processes and procedures may enable the agency managers to fulfil their tasks in a more efficient way. However, they may also strive for more extended levels of policy autonomy by influencing the delineation of target groups or the exact use of policy instruments. The argument is that such agencies are much closer to their service users, and that they may therefore have much more information about circumstances which may demand changes in aspects of policy. Hence, policies may be easier to implement and more realistic if such issues are left for agencies to define.

Public choice and principal-agent theorists would argue that extended levels of policy autonomy allow agency managers to maximize their benefits or to shirk. Leeway for agencies to influence and define aspects of policy-making seems counter-intuitive. Following these rational choice theorists, the NPM-inspired idea of ideal-type agencies calls for the strict separation of policy and operations, with policy design and policy making being allocated to parent departments and politicians, and agencies being involved as mere implementers of clearly defined policy (OECD 1994, 1999; Pollitt et al. 2004: 41–2). However, many reports of agencies in OECD states point to the existence of such influence and autonomy because of the lack of counter-expertise in their parent department or with the legislators. Rather abstract government legislation can be another cause for such influence (OECD 2002a).

2.3 Control

In general, control refers to the mechanisms and instruments that are used by a controlling actor in order to influence the decisions and the behaviour of the controlled actor with the aim of fulfilling the objectives of the controlling actor. In our case, the minister/departments and other superior bodies will be the controlling actors, while agencies are the controlled actors. Control relationships can be unilateral or mutually-reciprocal, or vertical, horizontal or diagonal (Verschuere et al. 2006). As a concept, control has a particular relationship with the concept of autonomy (Verhoest et al. 2004a). In this study, control focuses upon the constraints which the ministers/departments and other superior bodies can develop to influence the actual use of the decision-making competencies of agencies in order to influence how those decisions are subsequently made.

More generally, in cybernetics, the control system contains three sub-systems: an *ex ante* sub-system of planning and target setting, an *ex nunc* measurement and monitoring sub-system, and an *ex post* sub-system of evaluation, rewards and sanctions and feedback (Kaufmann et al. 1986). These three sub-systems assume another focus and content in the case of the three fundamental forms of control, referring to the basic mechanisms of social interaction (hierarchy, market and networks), which are discerned in the literature on (management) control, policy analysis and governance (cf. Lindblom 1977; Dunsire 1978; Ouchi 1979; Kaufmann et al.

1986; Thompson et al. 1991; Peters 1998; Verhoest 2005). Firstly, an actor can control another actor through authority by orders, rules, procedures or standards, in other words, by hierarchically based means. One specific form is structural control, by which the superior bodies may influence the agencies' decisions through hierarchical and accountability lines towards the chief executive officer (CEO) of the agency or through a governing board. Market-like forms of control emphasize exchange (based on demand), offer and price. Here, financial control is included, influencing the agencies' decisions by changing the level of budget granted to the agency, the composition of its incomes and changing the level of risk-turnover, as well as control by putting the agency into competition with other organizations. Network-based forms of control refer to social mechanisms based on cooperation and solidarity. Control is achieved by persuasion, reputation, informal contacts and by establishing common values, common problem definitions and objectives. In this context, it can be done by, for example, enhancing the creation of cooperation networks of which the agency is a part.

Accountability is also an ambiguous concept, but in the context of governance it is closely related to steering and control (cf. Flinders 2001; Mulgan 2003). One actor is accountable to another for achieving objectives, fulfilling tasks or respecting norms, which are set and/or controlled by the second actor. In this study we are interested in upwards or vertical accountability of (the CEO of) agencies towards ministers and departments (cf. Verschuere et al. 2006).

Forms of agency control may differ in the emphasis placed on a certain phase in the control cycle (inputs and processes versus results and performance). But these features mostly come in pairs. Therefore, two forms of control are discernible. In the case of *ex ante* control of input and processes, the emphasis is on the 'before-the-fact' formulation of detailed rules, standard operating procedures and approval requirements (or nullification rights) that give direction to the agency in order that the desired objective (from the viewpoint of the ministers/departments) will be achieved. The intention is 'to minimize risks and to increase certainty of performance processes before they begin' (Wirth 1986). Input control (Heyman 1988) can range from extensive control, such as centralization of financial transactions, through moderate control, such as centrally prescribed procedures for financial transactions, to low control by, for example, regulating the general principles to which the financial procedures and transactions of the agency must comply. The criteria on which an agency is controlled and on the basis of which it has to be held accountable for its actions when regulated *ex ante* on inputs and processes, are *legality*, defined here as compliance to rules and standards, fairness, integrity and procedural correctness (Verhoest 2005; Verschuere et al. 2006).

In contrast, by using control of results (outputs and effects, or quality), the superior body can check whether or not the intended set of organizational goals and result targets have been achieved by the agency, and whether there is a need for corrective future actions by means of 'after-the-fact' controls (Thompson 1993), such as *ex post* monitoring and evaluation. Accountability here is focused on achieved results and performance, which can be formulated as efficiency, effectiveness, quality, value for money and responsiveness.

Both forms optimally include the application of rewards and sanctions as part of the control cycle. These can take several forms, for example, wage increases or decreases for personnel, increased or decreased resource alloca-tion, and greater or reduced discretion. The last tool is an example of how control of agencies may be connected to autonomy, if autonomy is seen as the exemption from constraints on the actual use of decision-making competencies (cf. Verhoest et al. 2004a; Verschuere 2007).

More specifically, we distinguish in our analysis between three elements of control and steering in public agencies. First of all we look at the account-ability of the top manager (CEO) in terms of accountability towards results or towards legality. Next, we focus on control of agencies through the use of rewards or sanctions, partly of a financial kind related to individuals (wages/bonuses) or to the organization as a whole (increased budget alloca-tion), and partly in terms of increased or decreased autonomy levels for the organization vis-à-vis superior bodies. Moreover, we analyse the extent of result control to which an agency is subjected. The extent of result control is measured by the extent to which an agency CEO is accountable for results, and whether or not this result accountability goes hand in hand with the promise (or threat) of potential performance-based rewards and sanctions.

2.4 Internal management of agencies: The use of management techniques

The final concept of importance to this study is *management techniques*. The way we employ it here refers to the tools that agency managers can use in order to improve the internal management of their organization. Several techniques that were previously only applied in private sector orga-nizations are now often observed in the public sector. Thus, concepts such as customer-orientation, quality control and cost-calculation have gained increased influence in the public sector. To a large extent, the adoption of private sector management techniques by the public sector is the result of the '*management matters*' thesis that has been inspired by the doctrines of 'managerialism' and NPM. These doctrines advocate the adoption of pri-vate sector management techniques within public sector organizations in order to increase efficiency, effectiveness and quality (Osborne and Gaebler 1992; Osborne 2002). From an academic point of view, the topic of mod-ern management tools has gained growing attention in the past few years. Using management techniques is assumed by some authors to be a crucial step towards enhancing the performance of organizations (Naschold 1996; Ingraham et al. 2003). This literature can be linked to the growing body of empirical evidence about the influence of management on performance of public organizations, showing that 'management does indeed matter' (Ingraham et al. 2003; O'Toole and Meier 2003; Boyne 2004). For example, some research has already been conducted about the effects of specific management techniques on the performance of organizations (Kravchuk and Leighton 1993; Berman and West 1995).

The concept of management techniques is, however, very heterogeneous in itself. There exist a large variety of techniques or tools that can be included under this umbrella. Our point of departure is the distinction between four organizational management sub-systems, as identified in the literature (Lawton and Rose 1994; Pollitt 1995; Flynn 2002; Ingraham et al. 2003): financial management, performance management, human resources management and quality management. For each management sub-system, we can identify a number of important and frequently mentioned techniques. Innovations in the financial management of public organizations include cost-calculation systems and the transfer of financial management autonomy to lower units in the organizational hierarchy. In relation to performance management, public organizations tend to apply more and more tools or techniques such as steering on organizational objectives and results, and multi-year planning. Human resources management in many public organizations has been modernized by management techniques such as results-driven HRM (for example, pay for performance) and fixed-term mandates for leading civil servants (instead of career-long positions in the same office). Finally, innovations in the quality management of public organizations may include the increased use of customer surveys and the use of quality management systems such as Balanced Score Card (BSC), Common Assessment Framework (CAF) and ISO standards. In our analysis we focus on techniques related to systems of performance management, financial management and quality management.

More specifically, six specific management techniques or tools are selected for empirical inquiry. These techiques were selected because of their relevance and use in the three states being examined, as well as in the OECD states in general. Next to that, these six techniques are to some extent representative of three out of four organizational management sub-systems discussed above:

- the use of planning over years, or multi-year planning (performance management)
- the reporting on organizational performance and results to the general public, called public reporting (performance management)
- the internal allocation of resources to organisational units on the basis of performance (financial management)

- the development of cost-calculation systems (financial management)
- the use of quality management systems, such as CAF (quality management)
- the use of customer surveys, such as service quality surveys (quality management).

We will regard the use of management techniques partly from above as an expression of regulation inside government, and partly from below as a wilful choice from agencies (cf. Lægreid et al. 2007).

2.5 Conclusion

The central concepts in our study are all somewhat ambiguous and are being defined and used in different ways in the academic literature. With regard to the concept of *agency* we apply it in a wider (or softer) sense than that restricted to the new types of state organizations that have become popular in some OECD states (for example, executive agencies in the United Kingdom), but not as wide as to include state-owned companies (cf. the discussion of 'soft' versus 'hard' definitions by Wettenhall 2005). Moreover, with regard to the concept of *autonomy*, we focus on de facto autonomy and discretion in deciding on issues of importance for the agencies, and not on formal-legal autonomy through agency design.

With regard to *control* we also examine the importance of other constraints, which superior bodies can develop to influence the actual use of the decision-making competencies of agencies, like rewards and sanctions and result control. Finally, for management techniques, we focus on some modern tools that are related to various management sub-systems.

3
Theoretical Lenses

3.1 Introduction

In this book we compare and contrast the autonomy, control and internal management of agencies across states and agencies, and attempt to explain these similarities and differences. We examine whether, and how, specific factors affect their autonomy, control and use of management techniques. These explanatory factors and their importance are linked to certain theories, that is, ideas concerning the relationships between independent and dependent variables and why the independent variables matter.

In this chapter we present the principal aspects of the theoretical lenses used in this book, and determine our selection in relation to alternative theories used in other agency research. Our research is primarily based on ideas from organization theory and three different institutional schools (cf. Hall and Taylor 1996; Scott 2001; Peters 2005): rational choice institutionalism with the emphasis on rational behaviour by politicians and administrators, sociological institutionalism with the central concepts of isomorphism, myths and decoupling (Meyer and Rowan 1977; DiMaggio and Powell 1983), and historical institutionalism with path-dependency and punctuated equilibrium (Krasner 1988; Pierson 2004; Thelen 2004).

We argue that explanations as to why agencies have specific levels and patterns of autonomy and control, and why they have specific forms of internal management, are based on two major logics of action (cf. March and Olsen 1989). The first is that they are chosen by actors following a 'logic of consequentiality', in order to meet certain goals. This logic refers to instrumental perspectives, in which organizations and forms of autonomy, control and internal management are used as instruments in the hands of leaders, pursuing specific goals (Christensen et al. 2007). Alternatively, these forms are chosen by actors because they regard it as being in accordance with what has worked well for the organization in the past, or because they regard it as being acceptable in the environment of the organization at the present time. The second logic is the 'logic of appropriateness', which is prominent in institutional perspectives. Keeping these two logics of action in mind, we distinguish between four different theoretical lenses, or perspectives. These perspectives emphasize different types of independent variables and/or different ideas as to why they are important:

(1) a structural-instrumental perspective, emphasizing formal organizational structure and rational choice of actors;
(2) a cultural-institutional perspective, emphasizing organizational culture and organizational path dependency;
(3) a task-specific perspective, emphasizing the characteristics of organizational tasks;
(4) an environmental perspective, emphasizing institutional environments and other elements of politico-administrative environment.

We begin by presenting the core ideas of each of the four perspectives. We elaborate on how the perspective links with major strands in organization theory and institutional theory, including whether it is based on a logic of consequentiality or a logic of appropriateness. We then discuss briefly what the potential relevance of the perspective is for our discussion on autonomy, control and the internal management of agencies. In Chapters 7 and 10 we draw on the existing literature on organizations and public administration in general, and on the literature on agencies in particular, to formulate expectations and hypotheses on similarities and dissimilarities across states and agencies with regard to autonomy, control and internal management.

Following a more general discussion of the four theoretical perspectives, we build a layered explanatory model for comparing and explaining autonomy, control and internal management of agencies within, and across, the three states. In this model we combine theoretical elements that predict and explain similarities and dissimilarities among states and agencies. This theoretical framework points at explanatory factors at three levels of analysis: the international level, the state level and the agency level (for example, policy area, task and size). The importance of the relevant factors at both state level and agency level are developed further in Chapters 7 and 10. Though we draw on a broad set of ideas from organization theory and institutional theory, we do not use, to any significant extent, other theoretical perspectives that may be potentially relevant to the study of public sector organizations, like game theory (Scharpf 1997), grid/group cultural theory (Hood 1998), population ecology, network theory (Kickert et al. 1997) and postmodern theories (Miller and Fox 2007). Although these theories could provide interesting insights, the kind of data we have collected does not allow the testing of such theories in this book.

3.2 A structural-instrumental perspective on public sector organizations: Structure matters

The importance of organizational structure for organizational behaviour has been among the central topics in the study of organizations and of public administration throughout the history of these academic fields. Questions such as how a given structure may constrain and enable instrumental rational action in, and by, organizations, and how it is possible to affect actual organizational behaviour indirectly by structural design, have been discussed for a long time, and remain highly relevant. According to this perspective, organizations are seen as tools or instruments for achieving certain goals that are viewed as important in society. This can be expressed partly as public sector organizations and their members acting with instrumental rationality according to a logic of consequentiality in fulfilling tasks and achieving the desired results. They assess the available alternatives or tools according to their consequences and in relation to the chosen goals, make wilful choices among alternatives and thereby achieve the desired effects. Yet instrumentality can also be expressed in the structural design of an organization in accordance with means-ends assessments, which, in turn, determine how its members behave while carrying out tasks. Instrumental rationality can thus involve both the effects of organizational structure and the process whereby that structure is determined and formed (Christensen et al. 2007).

The formal structure of an organization consists of positions and rules deciding who shall, or can, perform a particular task, and defines how various tasks should be executed (cf. Christensen et al. 2007). Organizations are composed of a set of positions and subordinated units and can themselves fall under other larger units. In addition, organizational units can be divided up and coordinated in different ways. For agencies, *vertical specialization* concerns whether and how they consist of subordinate bodies, as well as how they relate to superior bodies. In this study, the formal relationship between agencies and their parent departments are particularly relevant. *Horizontal specialization* expresses how different tasks are thought to be allocated on a certain level by means of organizational structure. Thus, agencies may be structured on certain principles of specialization, like purpose (sector), process, clientele or geography (cf. Gulick 1937). Through the superior–subordinate relationship between different levels in a hierarchy, there will be a great degree of *vertical coordination* within and between organizations. In central governments of most representative democracies, vertical coordination is expressed in the principle of ministerial responsibility, in other words, the cabinet minister is responsible to the Parliament for activities in his or her own department and subordinate agencies. At the same time, the minister, through participation in the cabinet, is responsible for shaping the cabinet's general policy, and this entails elements of horizontal coordination at this level. Hierarchy can also involve vertical specialization, in that different types of tasks are assigned to different levels in the organization, or to organizations at different levels. *Routines* can constitute a form of coordination both vertically and horizontally. Procedural rules can be used as tools within an organization, but can also be used to coordinate activities in a way that cuts across organizations. For agencies, this can apply, for example, to general rules for financial management and human resource management, which restrict the managerial autonomy of public sector organizations.

The importance of the formal organizational structure is related to its impact on rational calculation and social control (cf. Dahl and Lindblom 1953). Like other organizations, agencies often operate under bounded rationality (cf. March and Simon 1958). This means that they have a limited amount of time, attention and analytical capacity for the tasks and problems they face, and their attitudes and actions are constrained by the organizational structure in which they are placed. Even if they try to act instrumentally, they have neither the possibility nor the capacity to review all the goals, all the alternatives or all the potential consequences of the various alternatives. Hence, they face problems of capacity and understanding. This necessitates a process of selection. Through the formal structure, some aspects grab their attention and focus, while other aspects are ignored or neglected.

Like other organizations, agencies may serve as instruments for the agency leaders as well as for superior bodies. The formal structure determines whether, and how, agencies may be controlled internally and externally, and the structure may be designed in order to obtain desired results. Even though the formal organizational structure poses clear limitations on an individual organizational member's choice of actions, it simultaneously creates the possibility for the organization to realize specific goals. Put differently, rationality at the organizational level can be strengthened through structural features, which both constrain and enable the organization's instrumental rational actions.

While some parts of the literature based on a structural-instrumental perspective emphasize how formal organizational structures are designed, other parts emphasize how existing organizational structures and changes in these structures affect organizational behaviour (cf. Egeberg 2003; Christensen et al. 2007). In this study, we draw on contributions from both types of literature. As with other theories, they take some relationships as given and explore others.

Many strands of economic organization theory (like transaction cost theory, property rights theory, agency theory and public choice theory) and rational choice theory in political science may be of relevance for explaining autonomy and control of public sector organizations (cf. Bouckaert and Verhoest 1999). For example, Moe (1990) discusses the structural design of agencies (and the formal level of autonomy that stems from this design) as resulting from processes of political and technical uncertainty, and of political compromise. Thus, autonomy is related to the formal, legal design of agencies. Elaborating on Moe, Yesilkagit (2004a) sees the structural design of agencies (and formal level of autonomy) as a result of the prevalence of certain logics (commitment and agency). Applied to public administration, the focus is often on delegation (of formal authority) *from the principal(s) to the agent(s)*. For example, Müller et al. (2003: 20) outline a parliamentary chain of delegation with four discrete steps:

(1) delegation from voters to their elected representatives;
(2) delegation from legislators to the executive branch, specifically to the head of government (the prime minister);
(3) delegation from the head of government (prime minister) to the heads of different executive departments;
(4) delegation from the heads of different executive departments to civil servants.

They add that this chain of delegation is mirrored by a corresponding chain of accountability that runs in the reverse direction, including mechanisms for controlling representatives (and other agents). Thus, delegation and accountability is related to what we call (formal) autonomy and control.

In the comparative study coordinated by Strøm et al. (2003a), it is somewhat unclear whether the last step comprises only civil servants in the ministries, or also includes those in the agencies. However, Braun and Gilardi (2006: 4) explicitly add a fifth step, which often seems to be neglected in this literature: delegation to independent agencies, or what Thatcher and Sweet (2002) call non-majoritarian institutions, that is, organizations that enjoy considerable independence from elected officials.

This structural-instrumental perspective focuses on how formal structure is designed in an instrumental rational way, as well as on how the existing formal structure affects rational behaviour within the organization. Thus, this perspective is potentially highly relevant in order to answer our basic explanatory research questions: How do aspects of formal organizational structure influence the (perceived) autonomy and control of agencies? How does the structure (including the degree of autonomy and control) of the agency affect its internal management (the use of management techniques)? In Chapter 10 we develop this perspective further and formulate specific hypotheses on the autonomy, control and internal management of agencies.

3.3 A cultural-institutional perspective on public sector organizations: Culture matters

The second theoretical perspective focuses on organizational culture and organizations as institutions. Although organizational culture has been used as a major concept in the study of organizations and of public administration for less than three decades, some of the general ideas on the importance of institutionalization are older. Like structure, culture may constrain and enable what an organization and its members are doing. In this respect, however, action is regarded as being based on prevalent norms and values rather than goals, and in accordance with a logic of appropriateness rather than with a logic of consequentiality. Normally, it is also seen as more difficult to affect behaviour indirectly through changing culture than through changing structure.

Organizational culture is concerned with the informal norms and values that are important for the activities of organizations (cf. Scott 2001; Christensen et al. 2007). Like other public sector organizations, agencies can have distinct organizational cultures. The emphasis is not on goals, but on informal norms, values and identities that develop gradually. The classic distinction made by Selznick (1957: 17) is between the organization as an instrument for obtaining goals, and the *institution*, where an organization, through a process of institutionalization, is 'infused with value beyond the technical requirements of the task at hand'. Thus, in addition to solving tasks in an instrumental sense, an organization like an agency has then become a value-bearing institution with its own distinct identities and opinions about what the relevant problems and solutions are. This makes for a more complex organization that is less flexible or adaptable to new demands, but also one equipped with the new and essential qualities that can, potentially, help the organization to solve tasks more expediently and function well as a socially integrated unit.

The importance of organizational culture is related to its impact on what is seen as *appropriate behaviour* in, and by, organizations (cf. March and Olsen 1989). Like other institutionalized organizations, agencies develop distinctive identities. Faced with a new situation, they have to recognize the nature of that situation and find a rule for action that is consistent with their identity. Organizational culture entails a relatively consistent set of rules and identities, so that such links are simple to make. What makes an action appropriate in a particular organization is a normative and institutional foundation that may differ greatly from that found in other organizations, depending on how the organizational culture has evolved and what its dominant informal norms and values are. Thus, an agency's culture demarcates organizations from one another, and through mechanisms of socialization strengthens cohesion and commitment among its members. Culture provides members of the organization with a sense of belonging to a community with a shared goal and mission (Wilson 1989; Yesilkagit 2004b).

A central concept in the political science literature on institutionalization and organizational culture is *path dependency*. In the context of what since the early 1990s has been called *historical institutionalism*, path-dependency refers to the tendency of actors to make choices (for example, on organizational design) that are consistent with formerly taken 'paths' (Thelen 1999; Pierson 2004; Peters 2005). These 'paths' or legacies are quite resistant to change. In general, historical institutionalism includes ideas of rational calculation as well as of organizational culture (cf. Hall and Taylor 1996). Based on ideas of rational calculation, the 'increasing returns' over time of previously created institutions and the huge cost of such change will imply a large degree of stability (Pierson 2000, 2004). Based on ideas of organizational culture, the socialization of organizational members over time will also result in a considerable level of stability (Pollitt 2008). In both instances, major changes are only possible or probable at *critical junctures*, for example, when an organization is created or when it is exposed to a crucial external shock. This means that the norms and values that make their mark on an organization in its early and formative years will have considerable influence on the path of development it follows (cf. Stinchcombe 1965). A public sector organization is established at a specific time, and is therefore shaped by particular cultural contexts or norms and values that leave a permanent impression on it.

Norms and values within agencies are also important for agency autonomy and control. Organizational path dependencies constrain what is regarded as appropriate and possible to move to agency status and determines the way those agencies will operate. What happens in one agency is not, however, a blueprint for developments in other agencies. Organization-specific traditions represent 'filters' producing different outcomes in different agencies. Internal forces contributing to the organization's robustness and stability will be more important than shifting political signals, and the links between general doctrines of reform and any actual changes will be rather loose. Reforms that are incompatible with the established organizational culture will not be followed through. Thus, from a cultural-institutional perspective, we expect the fate of reform initiatives from superior bodies to depend on the degree to which there is normative correspondence between them and the organization as it already exists. Reform initiatives that are incompatible with established norms and values in organizations will be rejected and controversial parts will be adapted so as to be made acceptable, while parts that are compatible will be implemented (cf. Christensen et al. 2007).

The main types of explanatory factors emerging from a cultural-institutional perspective are connected to the constraints inherent in established traditions and cultures within organizations, as developed over time. In Chapter 10 we expand on this perspective and formulate specific hypotheses on the autonomy, control and internal management of agencies.

3.4   A task-specific perspective on public sector organizations: Task matters

While the previous perspectives have focused on the structural and cultural aspects of organizations, in this perspective, and the one that follows, we focus more on the effect of organizations' environments. This perspective emphasizes their *technical* environments, while the next one concentrates on the *institutional* environments of organizations.

The technical environments can be defined either broadly as all aspects of the environment potentially relevant to goal setting and goal attainment, or more narrowly as the sources for inputs, markets for outputs, competitors, and regulators (cf. Dill 1958; Thompson 1967; Scott 2003). In the academic literature, several dimensions of technical environments affecting organizational uncertainty and dependence have been proposed and examined, for example, the degree of homogeneity-heterogeneity, the degree of stability-variability and the degree of concentration-dispersion.

The technical environments of an organization are to a large extent determined by the type of tasks it performs. Compared to structure and culture, the importance of organizational tasks is a more recent topic in the study of organizations and of public administration, even though some of the ideas have been around for some time. As with the case for the other characteristics, the existing tasks may constrain and enable what an organization and its members are doing, and over time tasks may be changed as a result of instrumental action or appropriate behaviour.

The literature on organizations has for some time been interested in the importance of the type of tasks undertaken, for example, for strategy and structure. Thompson and Tuden (1959, cf. also Thompson 1967) categorize what they call *decision issues* along two dimensions: preferences about possible outcomes, and beliefs about causation. For both dimensions they distinguish between agreement and disagreement, thus forming the basis for four types of decision issues and corresponding strategies for handling them: computation for agreement on both, majority judgement for agreement on preferences and disagreement on causation, compromise for disagreement on preferences and agreement on causation, and, finally, inspiration for disagreement on both. They also relate the four types of strategies to certain structures: computation in bureaucratic structures, majority judgement in collegial structures, compromise in representative structures, and inspiration in 'anomic' structures. Applied to public administration, as noted by DeLeon (2003), these types of issues, strategies and structures may also be related to different forms of administrative responsibility, and thus to chances for autonomy and control of agencies.

Wilson (1989) gives a clear and extended analysis of the importance of the 'task' factor in public administration and of the measurability of tasks in particular. In his discussion on bureaucracies, Wilson takes as his point of departure the activities of public agencies. He distinguishes partly between *outputs* (the work or activities that the agency does) and *outcomes* (the result of their activities), and partly between whether outputs and outcomes can be observed and measured or not. By combining the two dimensions he identifies four types of organizations: *Production* organizations have both observable outputs and observable outcomes; *procedural* organizations are characterized by observable work but unobservable outcomes; *craft* organizations produce observable outcomes through unobservable work; and in *coping* organizations neither the work nor the outcomes is observable. As noted by Pollitt et al. (2004), these types of activities and organizations, and their corresponding degrees of observability and measurability, may also imply different chances for autonomy and control of agencies.

In general, characteristics of the tasks the agencies perform are of relevance for whether, and how, the agencies and their superior bodies take an interest in the autonomy and control of agencies. Discussions of these topics often emphasize how the choice of (formal) autonomy and control is based on a logic of consequentiality. This is done quite explicitly in some contributions based on economic organization theory and rational choice theory in political science. For example, Greer (1994) points out how the 'Next Steps Initiative' in the United Kingdom fits well into ideas in public choice theory on controlling bureaucratic self-interest. Moreover, her typology of agencies and their tasks along two dimensions is based on transaction cost theory, implying differences in the interest of superior bodies for agency autonomy and control.

The concept of *political salience* has also been used in relation to task features in several studies in public administration, and seems to be particularly important in understanding the autonomy and control of agencies (Pollitt et al. 2004). Hood and Dunsire (1981), for example, include this aspect in their systematic analysis of characteristics of British central government agencies.

The task-specific perspective, therefore, focuses on how task features affect organizational design and practice. According to Pollitt et al. (2004), this perspective is highly relevant in explaining the differences and similarities of autonomy, control and internal management in different countries and contexts. In Chapter 10 we develop this perspective further and formulate hypotheses, focusing on the measurability and political saliency of tasks.

3.5 An environmental perspective on public sector organizations: Institutional environments matters

The emphasis on the importance of the environment for organizational structure and behaviour has increased in the study of organizations and of public administration since the Second World War. At first, what has been called the technical (or task) environments were emphasized (see above). Since the 1970s, *institutional environment* has been added, stressing the importance of the symbolic aspects of environments (cf. Meyer and Rowan 1977; Scott 2003). Institutional environments are characterized by the development of socially created norms to which individual organizations must conform in order to receive legitimacy and support. Thus, in institutional environments organizations are rewarded for utilizing what are deemed as correct structures and processes, and not for the quantity and quality of their outputs, as in technical environments. As with the cultural-institutional perspective, the choice of (formal) autonomy and control is primarily based on a logic of appropriateness, but in this case the dominant norms and values in the environment are most important.

We begin by examining some potential effects of institutional environments. Like other organizations, agencies must try to incorporate and reflect the prevailing norms in the environment outwardly, even if they do not necessarily make the organization's activities more effective and efficient. Through these processes organizations become more similar to one another, at least on the surface, in stark contrast to the multiplicity described by a cultural-institutional perspective (cf. Christensen et al. 2007). Socially created norms in institutional environments are called *myths* or *standards*. They can spread quickly, through imitation, and they can be adopted by agencies without producing instrumental effects, that is, they may sometimes function as 'window dressing'. Agency leaders can, for instance, talk about reforms in a way that makes people believe they are putting reforms into practice, while in reality the leaders do little to make this happen (cf. Brunsson 1989; Pollitt 2001).

In addition to this decoupling between structure and practice in organizations, an institutional environment perspective emphasizes how the similarity between organizations gradually increases. Such isomorphism, however, is expected to be restricted to a particular institutional sphere, or organizational field, that is, 'those organizations that, in the aggregate, constitute a recognized area of institutional life' (DiMaggio and Powell 1983: 148). According to DiMaggio and Powell (1983), three different processes or mechanisms may produce isomorphism in an organizational field: coercive adoption, normative adoption and mimetic adoption (cf. also Christensen et al. 2007). *Coercive adoption* for agencies in an organizational field occurs when they are instructed to implement certain standards via laws or regulations. In such a situation the agencies have no other choice. This may apply, for instance, to some instructions on financial management or human resource management. *Normative adoption* refers to the kind of dissemination and adoption that arises in organizational fields from the common norms, values, knowledge and networks held, or engaged in, by various professional groups. Examples of this might include the contribution of economists in spreading some of the basic ideas associated with NPM. *Mimetic adoption* often occurs when agencies – in situations marked by great uncertainty – try to emulate others who are perceived to be successful and prestigious within their organizational field. Usually, this takes the form of imitation without much preliminary calculation and analysis.

Taking agencies as the point of departure, and assuming that, in a broad sense, they may be said to belong to the same organizational field, pressure from institutional environments implies that over time they will adopt the same standards with regard to autonomy, control and internal management. The exact type of standards adopted may change over time, depending on what is seen as modern and fashionable at any given time. Therefore, we expect organizations in certain organizational fields to tend to have similar levels and patterns of autonomy, control and use of management techniques. Like most studies of isomorphism, however, based on our cross-sectional data we are only able to measure the outcome while having to assume the process (cf. Mizruchi and Fein 1999: 664). Moreover, the standards adopted, for example formal organizational structures related to autonomy and control, may not always affect practice, and management techniques may also be used primarily to receive legitimacy in the institutional environments.

The delineation of the 'organizational field' can differ quite substantially. Thus, it can refer to organizations within a policy area, a state or an international sphere. For example, several scholars (for example, Pollitt et al. 2001, 2004) have observed that there is international pressure for governments to create agencies, since international organizations propagate autonomous agencies as an efficient organizational form for policy implementation. Also, as noted in Chapter 1, the NPM doctrines emphasize the ideal-type agency. Given this international pressure, we would expect an isomorphic process by which agencies with similar features in different states show similar levels and patterns of autonomy, control and the use of internal management techniques. We may argue that the states being examined here (Norway, Ireland and Flanders) belong to the same organizational field (OECD) and that the processes of isomorphism (through NPM doctrines) have been going on for some time. According to this method of reasoning, the idea of 'organizational field' is understood as the group of states, subject to the same pressure. But the concept of 'organizational field' and isomorphism can also be relevant at a lower level: agencies with similar tasks, or in a similar formal-legal position may model themselves or be modelled like agencies with similar features, within the same state or abroad, because of coercive, normative or mimetic pressure.

Our discussion of institutional environments has until now been strongly focused on processes of decoupling and isomorphism. However, institutional environments also have other dimensions. Public sector organizations are embedded in a wider politico-administrative environment, which will also constrain and enable agencies. The dynamics of this environment at the state level, and its influence on organizational behaviour, are determined by the structure (polity), and (administrative) culture at this level. However, as several students of comparative public management reform argue (Christensen and Lægreid 2001a; Pollitt and Bouckaert 2004; Pollitt et al. 2007), internationally diffused NPM ideas and concepts may result in quite different contents, effects and implications in different settings or states. Similar doctrines on organizational forms are transferred and adopted in several states, but in most cases they are translated to the specific context in which they are supposed to operate. Thus, like in the cultural-institutional perspective, ideas of path-dependency are important, but in this perspective we refer to the institutional environments at the state level as creating historical paths that shape current choices. How the three states being examined score on relevant dimensions of politico-administrative environments is outlined in Chapter 5.

This perspective emphasizes the importance of the institutional environments in explaining organizational design and functioning. Since we are comparing agencies in different states, the perspective is highly relevant in explaining differences and similarities of autonomy, control and internal management among states. In Chapter 7 we further develop this perspective and formulate specific hypotheses, focusing on the influence of the politico-administrative context as institutional environments for state agencies.

3.6 An integrated heuristic model

In our theoretical framework for comparing and explaining autonomy, control and internal management of agencies in the three states we try to combine the four theoretical perspectives which explain similarity and dissimilarity. The model involves three analytical levels, which fit into each other like Russian dolls: the international level, the level of the state, and the level of the individual agency.

In this framework we include pressures (factors) for similarities or dissimilarities at each of these levels. These pressures represent different explanatory factors which may interact in order to explain similarities or dissimilarities of autonomy, control and internal management of agencies in the three states studied. The model is to a large extent based on ideas in the *transformative perspective* of Christensen and Lægreid (2001b, 2001c, 2007a). We discuss three different levels of analysis (international, state and agency) and make clear which theoretical perspectives we use. The model is presented in Figure 3.1.

Our point of departure is the pressure for conformity that comes from international NPM doctrines on optimal structure of public administration and the related 'ideal-type agency' image. As noted in Chapter 1,

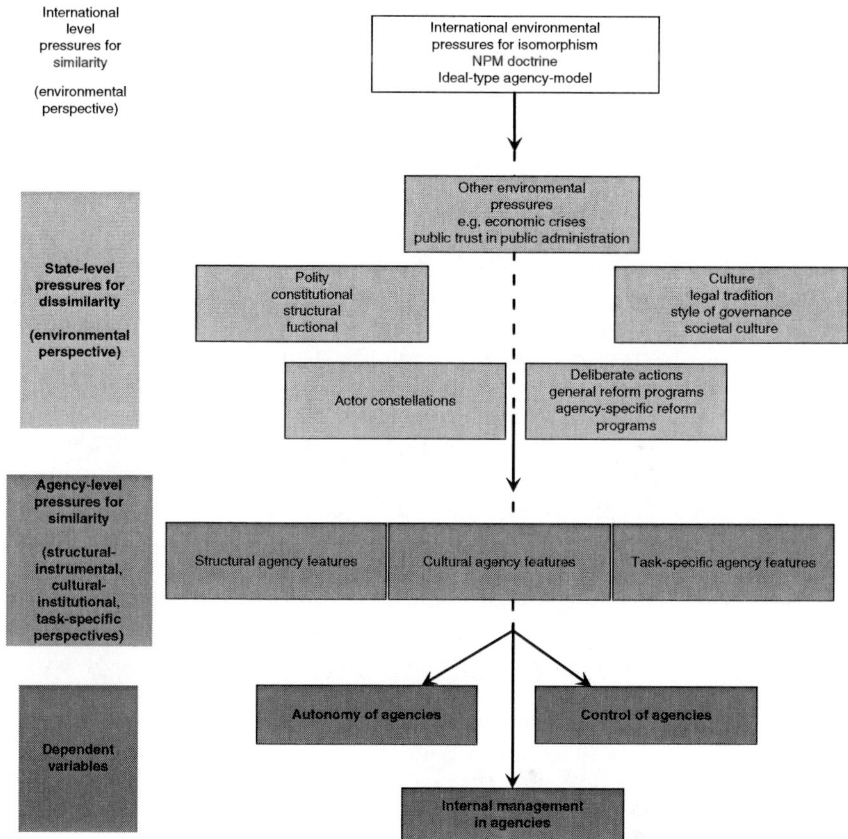

Figure 3.1   A model for comparing and explaining agency autonomy, control and internal management in different state

agencification as a result of structural disaggregation (increased vertical specialization) in central government is a crucial component in the NPM doctrine (Hood 1991), and the ideal-type agency form has for some time been prescribed by the OECD (Pollitt et al. 2004).

This international-level pressure for convergence is expected to lead to isomorphic organizational forms and similarity in behaviour of political principals and administrators. Thus, in all states there will be external isomorphic pressure to adjust the organizational structure of agencies towards the internationally propagated NPM ideal-type agency image. According to our model, these doctrines are being transformed when they meet state-specific environmental factors, polity, administrative culture and actor constellations, which may lead to different responses and deliberate actions in the form of reform programmes (that is, *state-level pressures for divergence and dissimilarity*). These state-level factors imply that states with different polity features and cultural features are expected to adopt NPM doctrines on ideal-type agencies in different ways. Theoretically, this idea of transformation is partly rooted in historical institutionalism: reforms and changes of organizational design within states are path-dependent, and international doctrines have to align with past history of organizational structure and culture. Although the 'talk' about agencies may reflect internationally proclaimed NPM doctrines, the organizational forms chosen and the behaviour of politicians and administrators may differ (Pollitt 2001). As a consequence, agency autonomy, control and internal management across such states are expected to show important dissimilarities.

Moreover, these potentially different reform programmes may be reformulated and adapted when they are applied to agencies with different features, such as organizational structure, organizational culture and tasks. Taking tasks as an example, on the one hand, we will expect that agencies with different types of tasks will have different levels of autonomy and control (that is *agency-level pressures for divergence and dissimilarity*). This could be due to variations in the demands of agencies based on their tasks, or variations in the interests of political principals for autonomy and control of agencies according to their tasks. On the other hand, however, we expect that agencies with similar types of tasks will have somewhat similar levels of autonomy and control across states (that is *agency-level pressures for convergence and similarity*). This could be due to demands of agencies with these tasks, to judgements and views of the political principals, or to internationally proclaimed myths.

This example also shows that the state-level pressure for divergence and dissimilarity can be counterbalanced by, or may interact with, pressures at the agency level which are pressing for greater similarity. From that agency-level angle, agencies with similar structural, cultural and task features are expected to show similar levels of autonomy, control and use of management techniques within and across states.

How does this model and its three levels relate to our four theoretical perspectives? At the *international level* we emphasize the environmental perspective, with special reference to international normative and mimetic isomorphic processes, stemming from international doctrines and fashions. In general, the importance of institutional environments is examined by regarding a high extent of similarity across states and agencies as a null hypothesis, but this will not be discussed in depth. At the *state level* we emphasize other elements of the environmental perspective, where we distinguish between three main types of factors: polity, administrative culture and actor constellations/instrumental actions. At the *agency level* we distinguish between three main types of factors: organizational structure, organizational culture and tasks, which are emphasized in, respectively, the structural-instrumental perspective, the cultural-institutional perspective and the task-specific perspective. In the structural-instrumental perspective we also include ideas on instrumental actions, which is a separate factor at the state level. In the cultural-institutional perspective the focus is on organizational characteristics, in contrast to administrative culture at the state level. Agency tasks have no equivalent at the state level. For agency level, too, the importance of tasks is linked to certain theories (for example different strands of organization theory).

3.7 The model and the book outline

Taking this theoretical framework as the point of departure, in Part II we describe the agencies and their contexts in the three states: the politico-administrative regimes, the general reform programmes and the agency reform programmes, and main aspects of the agencies (structure, culture and tasks).

In Part III we compare states, examining whether agencies in the three states or agencies with similar features in the states (including selected indicators of structure, culture and tasks) show similar or dissimilar levels and patterns of autonomy, control and use of management techniques. Here, state-level factors are independent variables, that is, different aspects of polity, administrative culture and reform programmes. If the NPM doctrines are dominant, we will expect similarities in autonomy, control and internal management of agencies across states. Likewise, we will expect similarities in autonomy, control and internal management of agencies across states if the states are similar on important independent variables. However, we will expect dissimilarities in autonomy, control and internal management of agencies across states if the states are dissimilar on important independent variables. In this part we examine agency-level pressures for similarity by analysing whether, across states, agencies with similar features show the same levels and patterns of autonomy, control and use of management techniques as all agencies. If there is agency-level pressure for similarity, we will expect that the differences across states are smaller for agencies with similar features than for all agencies.

In Part IV we compare agencies, examining whether agencies with different features show similar or dissimilar levels and patterns of autonomy, control and use of management techniques. Here, agency-level factors are independent variables, that is, different aspects of agency structure, culture and tasks. If the NPM doctrines are dominant, we will expect similarities in autonomy, control and internal management among agencies. Likewise, we will expect similarities in autonomy, control and internal management among agencies if they are similar on important independent variables at the agency level. However, at this level too, we will expect dissimilarities among agencies in autonomy, control and internal management if they are dissimilar on important independent variables. Thus, in this part we examine agency-level pressures for dissimilarity by examining differences in autonomy, control and internal management among agencies.

4
Data and Methods

4.1 Introduction

This chapter addresses the basic characteristics of our comparative research design; the subjects studied (population), the measurement instruments used (survey and document analysis) and procedures chosen for analyses (types of statistical techniques used). The first part describes the survey populations in Flanders, Norway and Ireland, based on the understanding of what constitutes a public sector agency as outlined in Chapter 2. Choices made for the purposes of enhancing the comparability of our three samples are described. We then focus on the design of the surveys in the three states, their particularities and similarities, and how we proceeded in constructing a common data set comprising similar information for all three states stemming from these surveys. This process included the conscious identification and selection of comparable data, and the exclusion of data that were not considered to be directly comparable. Lastly, the chapter addresses the various types of statistical procedures undertaken when comparing agencies in the three states, and their inherent strengths and shortcomings.

4.2 Research design: Developing and administering the surveys in Flanders, Norway and Ireland

The study is a cross-state comparison of agencies in Flanders, Norway and Ireland, drawing on joint research efforts by Flemish, Irish and Norwegian research teams in the context of the COBRA research project (COmparative public organization data Base for Research and Analysis: www.publicmanagement-cobra.org). Under the umbrella of COBRA, research teams from different states conducted surveys in their respective states. The aim of these surveys was to collect data from agencies in these states, with a focus on their autonomy vis-à-vis their oversight authorities (minister and parent department), the way in which they are controlled by their oversight authorities, the extent to which they use modern management techniques, and some organizational characteristics such as their task, age, size, budget and source of income, as well as culture. Each survey contains key questions that are the same for each individual survey, so that data are comparable across states (information about this common survey is available at: www.publicmanagement-cobra.org/survey/index.htm).

This book is the result of cooperation between the Norwegian, Irish and Flemish research teams, and presents the comparative analysis of data on autonomy, control and management techniques that were collected using virtually identical questions in the three states within the period 2002–2004. These three states are interesting to compare for several reasons. They share some similar features with respect to the politico-administrative system. All three are small European parliamentary democracies. Their electoral system is proportional, and since 1980, their cabinets are mostly of a consensual kind (coalitions or minority cabinets). And although Norway is not an EU member, unlike Ireland or Flanders (as a member state of Belgium), its affiliation with the EU is substantial and on many policy areas Norway aligns itself with European norms. Moreover, all three states are known as 'NPM-laggards', having introduced NPM-like reforms only recently or in a very piecemeal manner. Notwithstanding these similarities, the politico-administrative systems of Norway, Ireland and Flanders do differ in other respects, for example, Flanders is a regional member state of a federal state. They also differ with regard to their politico-administrative culture. We return to this particular aspect in later chapters.

For the empirical part of this study, we rely largely on the survey-data that were collected, but also on other more state-specific data sets. When we describe the history of administrative reform and prevalence of agencies in the three states (Chapter 6), we also utilize state-specific databases on public sector organizations and agencies, which were constructed using analyses of documents and yearbooks. In subsequent chapters where we focus on the autonomy, control and use of management techniques of agencies in the three states (Chapters 8–13), we narrow the scope and rely exclusively on the survey data.

The types of organizations addressed by the surveys in the three states match the definition of state agencies, as elaborated in Chapter 2, and are as such public sector organizations outside core departments, directly reporting to a minister or parent department. The population of agencies to which the survey was targeted was exhaustive, meaning that all organizations that fit our definition of 'state agency' were addressed to fill in the questionnaire. In case of Flanders and Ireland, some additional types of public sector organizations were addressed, such as core government units or private law agencies, in case of Flanders. As expected, however, not all organizations responded, resulting in a response rate of 55 per cent in Flanders for the total survey (2002–2003), 70 per cent in Norway (2004) and 43 per cent in

Ireland (2004). The organizations that responded proved to be quite representative for the total populations in each state. In the Flemish survey, we were able to collect data from a representative sample of the different kinds of states agencies, vested in public law, in terms of agency type and parent department (Verhoest et al. 2003). For the Irish survey, the sample is also representative of the total population of agencies, and distribution in the response sample across different agency tasks and different parent ministries, compared with the total population, is fair (McGauran and Humphreys 2004). As far as the representativeness of the Norwegian sample is concerned, when compared to the total population of Norwegian agencies, we can again draw similar conclusions. Moreover, here too, all types of agencies (different formal-legal status, functions and parent departments) are well represented in the sample, compared with the total population (Lægreid et al. 2006a, 2006b).

All three surveys reveal similar questions with regard to the way organizations perceive different forms of autonomy and control, and in each state the CEOs of the organizations were asked to fill in a web-based questionnaire. The data collected through these web-based surveys and used in this book are thus reporting the perception of senior agency managers. The rationale behind this is that the perception of senior managers about the actual autonomy and control of their agency will determine their actions and the way in which they manage their agency. It became clear from extensive case studies preceding the surveys (Verhoest 2002) that the de facto autonomy and control perceived by the CEOs may differ from the formal autonomy and control of agencies, as set out in enacting legislation and other regulations. This point has since been confirmed in other research (for example, Verhoest et al. 2004a; Yesilkagit 2004a). Moreover, the behaviour of senior management was guided by these perceptions (see for example Verhoest 2005). Therefore, perceptions of autonomy, control and managerial practice give us insights about the room for manoeuvre that senior managers think they have, and hence about the actual functioning of agencies.

Though the data were collected in the period 2002–2003 in the case of Flanders, and 2004 in the case of Norway and Ireland, the data is relevant to compare agencification in the three states. At the time of writing, it may be supposed that the survey data still give a fair picture of the current position and roles of agencies in the three states, since no major changes to autonomy and control arrangements have occurred since the data collections. Flanders has seen a structural agency reform in 2006, but without drastic consequences with regard to the autonomy of agencies. Moreover, the analyses in this book aim mainly to test expectations derived from theoretical perspectives. The primary aim of this work is not to describe agencification in these three states as such, but to look for factors that help to explain the perceived autonomy, control and internal management of state agencies in small European states. The principal objective of the book is explanatory and theory-testing, in order to improve our understanding of the functioning of agencies.

4.2.1 Developing and administering the survey in Flanders

The first survey was developed by a Flemish research team from the Public Management Institute (KU Leuven), and was administered to 149 Flemish public sector organizations in 2002–2003. This survey has served as the point of departure for designing later, similar surveys in Norway (University of Bergen) and Ireland (Institute of Public Administration, Dublin). All three state-specific surveys have been developed and adapted by nationally-based research teams. The Flemish survey contained questions on organizational characteristics of the agencies, their autonomy, the way they are controlled by the oversight authorities, their organizational culture and some aspects of organizational performance. The draft questionnaire was then piloted, by asking three selected agencies to review the questionnaire. In the next step, and based on the comments of the pilot-reviews, the questionnaire was refined and sent to the state agencies and to some other types of organisation. After a few rounds of (email and telephone) reminders, the response rate increased to 55 per cent for the total survey. Data for 82 organizations were collected, which can be clustered along their legal–formal characteristics (N = number of organizations that responded):

- core government organizations that are part of the legal person of the Ministry of the Flemish Community (N = 24, from a total population of 41)
- internally autonomous public sector organizations with no legal identity (N = 12, from a total population of 27)
- internally autonomous public sector organizations with a legal identity vested in public law (N = 7, from a total population of 13)
- externally autonomous public sector organizations with a legal identity vested in public law (N = 29, from a total population of 34)
- externally autonomous public sector organizations, which have a hybrid legal identity vested in both public and private law and which invest risk capital in private firms as a tasks (*'participatiemaatschappijen'*) (N = 0, from a total population of 16), and externally autonomous public organizations having a legal identity vested in private law (N = 10, from a included population of 18). On this latter subgroup, with a total population of 120, another survey was done in 2004, but these data are not used in the analyses in this book.

Those organizations that belong to the clusters of 'core government organizations' and 'externally autonomous public organizations with a hybrid and a private legal status' are excluded, because they do not fit the definition of 'state agencies' adopted for this book. As there were, in total, 74 state agencies as public law bodies in the total population, the 48 state agencies that responded to the survey make up a 64 per cent response rate with respect to the total population of public law agencies.

4.2.2 Developing and administering the survey in Norway

By March 2004, the Norwegian research team at the University of Bergen had translated and adapted the Flemish survey, and it was distributed to all civil service organizations reporting directly to a department. The survey comprised five clusters of questions relating to organizational characteristics, autonomy characteristics, steering and control characteristics, organizational culture and other factual information. Much effort was put into both sticking to the Flemish questionnaire, but also adapting questions so that they were relevant to Norwegian conditions and context, and to the specific organizations in question (that is, organizations which are part of the state as a legal entity). In this way, the core issues from the original Flemish survey were kept, but some state-specific adjustments were made. The main differences between the Flemish and the Norwegian questionnaires relate to the exclusion or additions of some questions in the Norwegian survey. In particular, since the Norwegian State Administration database (NSA) includes information on some organizational characteristics such as formal status, organizational history and parent department, some questions on these issues were excluded from the Norwegian survey. The NSA database contains information on (changes in) the formal structure of Norwegian state organizations from 1947 onwards, and is accessible through the Internet (see the website of the Norwegian Social Science Data Services (NSD): http://www.nsd.uib.no/civilservice/). However, questions on control of agencies (mainly questions on informal steering, steering meetings, performance indicators, reporting and auditing) were added. In addition, some of the Norwegian questions included different alternative answers although the questions were similar to the Flemish ones. This is mainly due to state-specific differences concerning formal structural arrangements in the two states.

The existence of the NSA database means that the Norwegian survey population could easily be extracted. The organizations targeted by the survey are part of the state as a legal entity and had existed for at least a year. The survey was distributed in March 2004 to a total of 215 organizations. All single national bodies, without any subordinate units (107 organizations) were included, as well as all integrated/regional organizations with subordinate units (40 organizations). All single units in groups of similar civil service organizations in different geographical areas, reporting to one or more department were included (68 organizations). After several rounds throughout the year, a response rate of 70 per cent (150 organizations) was eventually achieved in February 2005. The distribution is as follows, according to sub-types of civil service organizations:

- central agencies/directorates (N = 43, from a total population of 54)
- other ordinary civil service organizations (N = 83, from a total population of 125)
- civil service organizations with extended authority (N = 18, from a total population of 28)
- government administrative enterprises (N = 4, from a total population of 5)
- financial institutions (N = 2, from a total population of 3)

In the analyses for this book, those organizations that belong to groups of similar civil service organizations in different geographical areas (that is, duplicate agencies) are excluded, because they are not covered in the two other states.

4.2.3   Developing and administering the survey in Ireland

In Ireland, the survey was developed in relation to a wider project commissioned by the Committee for Public Management Research (CPMR), comprising representatives of eight Irish government departments. The project had had two key objectives: (a) to map the development of Irish public service agencies over time and (b) to view/arrange this information in a wider international setting. As a first step in the mapping process, a database was constructed comprising existing agencies in Ireland at both national and sub-national levels, by using authoritative secondary sources. This database was constructed during 2003 and consisted of 601 bodies. The second step in the project was the survey, and it was decided to survey only those agencies that operated at the national level and that were non-commercial in character. In the absence of an accepted categorization as to what constitutes a public sector agency in Ireland (see the discussion in Chapter 6), the research team relied closely on the definition of an agency as described in Chapter 2. This resulted in a list of 211 state agencies that were identified as the relevant survey population. The Irish questionnaire had different clusters of questions focusing on identification data, autonomy, accountability and responsibility. The questionnaire was piloted in eight organizations, and a number of minor amendments subsequently made before it was finalised. After two rounds of mail and telephone contacts, 93 organizations responded, giving a response rate of 43 per cent. The organizations in the sample are representative of the total population of non-commercial agencies operating at national level (McGauran et al. 2005: 246–8). A comparison between the total population (N = 211) and the sample of agencies that completed the survey (N = 93) on some variables, such as parent department, function, and so on, shows that agencies of all parent departments and agencies with all kinds of functions are represented in the sample (McGauran and Humphreys 2004).

4.3 Comparability of organizations and information across states

In each state, the results from the surveys were stored in the form of state-specific databases (using SPSS). For responding organizations in all states where similar information on some of the variables was available, a joint database comprising a total of 335 organizations was constructed. When attempting to compare the data across states, it was necessary to first identify what should be considered as comparable organizations (that is, state agencies), and second; what were considered to be comparable data/information.

Of the 335 organizations in the joint database, a total of 226 organizations have been identified as comparable units based on a set of general criteria, resulting in the exclusion of some organizations originally included in the state-specific samples. Some organizations were excluded because they do not meet the requirements necessary to be considered as a state agency as defined in Chapter 2 (for example military operative units, central banks, advisory bodies/committees without their own legal status, non-autonomous units within core departments and agencies founded in private law or hybrids, such as charities, trusts or companies under private law, agencies directly and solely accountable to Parliament, organizations without their own budget). In addition, duplicate organizations in the Norwegian database were excluded owing to the lack of equivalent types of organizations in the other state-specific data sets. Lastly, a few cases were omitted because they showed a lot of missing data on the autonomy and control variables, which are central to our analysis. This resulted in a restricted database that consists of 226 organizations (46 in Flanders, 103 in Norway and 77 in Ireland). This database forms the basis for analyses undertaken later in this book (Chapters 8–13). Even if the formal-legal types of these 226 organizations vary within and across states, their basic characteristics are similar enough to make comparisons meaningful.

Steps were also taken in order to increase the comparability of the data itself. Even if the questions on different forms of autonomy and control in the three surveys were quite similar, in some instances different categorizations of answers were used for each state. For these variables, a careful recoding and standardization of values was undertaken, ranging from '0' for organizations perceiving no or low autonomy (or control) to '1' for organizations perceiving full or high autonomy (or control). For variables with intermediate values, proportional intervals were used ('0.5' for variables having three values in total, and '0.33' and '0.66' for variables having four values in total). This recoding has been done mainly for the variables on organizational autonomy and the combined variables on control. It is worth noting here that these variables and values were treated as being ordinal in kind.

Additional checks on the validity of the response (essentially, the perceptions of the individuals in the organizations) were done on identification data related to mere factual variables, such as task, budget size, staff size and source of income, and by using other sources such as administrative year-books and budgets. This resulted in a limited number of minor corrections to our database. Moreover, we created some simple indices which combined the answers of different survey questions in single variables. This was mainly the case for variables relating to autonomy, rewards and sanctions, and result control (see Appendix A for variables and indices).

4.4   Types of analyses and statistical procedures

Different forms of analyses are performed throughout this book. The choice of suitable analyses or statistical procedures is guided by our research questions (outlined in Chapter 1), but also by methodological requirements stemming from the data itself (the ordinal or dichotomous nature of dependent variables), or the number of observations made in each state (different sizes in state-specific samples of organizations).

In the descriptive parts of the study (Chapter 6) we rely mainly on cross tables (in either whole numbers or percentages) when describing the agency landscape in general, and the organizations that we include in comparative analyses later in the book. When we compare states (Chapter 8), in addition to frequencies, distributions and cross tables, we use the non-parametric Mann-Whitney test to look for significant different patterns between Flanders, Norway and Ireland, comparing them in pairs. The Mann-Whitney test compares two independent groups of sampled data, and allows for samples which differ substantially with respect to the number of observations. Unlike the parametric t-test, this non-parametric test makes no assumptions about the distribution of the data (for example normality), and is an alternative to the independent group t-test, when the assumption of normality or equality of variance is not met.

The Mann-Whitney test, like many non-parametric tests, uses the ranks of the data rather than their raw values to calculate the statistic, and can be used to compare independent samples (of different sizes) for their score on variables of an ordinal nature. The Mann-Whitney test helps us to establish a ranking of the three states for each sample when comparing agency autonomy, control and internal management. For example, with regard to autonomy on salary issues we could find a rank pattern like N > (I = F), meaning that Norwegian agencies tend to have significantly more autonomy than Irish and Flemish agencies, and that there are no significant

Part II

Describing Agencies and Their Contexts

5
Politico-Administrative Regimes in Norway, Ireland and Flanders

5.1 Studying politico-administrative regimes: Relevant dimensions

In their comparative work on public management reforms, Pollitt and Bouckaert (2004: 40) refer to politico-administrative systems as those fundamentals of political and administrative systems that change only gradually or infrequently, and which may therefore be regarded as rather stable characteristics of the environment in a given polity. A politico-administrative system, in their view, includes structural, cultural and functional elements. Drawing from this and other sources (Christensen and Lægreid 2001b; Wollmann 2003b), we identify and distinguish here between different levels of politico-administrative analysis, which will serve to illuminate later chapters both theoretically and empirically. The emphasis in this chapter is on characterizing the politico-administrative regimes in Norway, Ireland and Flanders across a range of relevant dimensions. The implications of these regimes for agency autonomy, control and internal management are then discussed in Chapter 7.

As Table 5.1 details, we propose five different levels for the analysis of politico-administrative regimes. The levels are not mutually exclusive and the aspects of each are influenced by the interrelationships between them. With environmental pressures as the first level, the second level entails those elements of politico-administrative systems that are the most enduring and least subject to reform and change. Legal tradition is one of the most enduring elements of second-level issues, as are key characteristics of politico-administrative culture. Issues at the third level are less susceptible to reform and change, and occur infrequently and usually in response to institutional failure or a crisis in public confidence. The key variables here include the distribution of power between levels of government and the form of democratic engagement and government that emerges. Finally, issues at the fourth and fifth level in this context consist of political and administrative matters that are subject to the most frequent change and

Table 5.1 Relevant elements of environment, politico-administrative culture, polity, with respect to actor constellations and deliberate actions

---

Relevant elements of environment and politico-administrative systems

---

First level – Environmental pressures

Affiliation with and openness to international and European supranational authorities
Economic and budgetary-fiscal crises
Trust of citizens in governments

Second level – Politico-administrative culture: Fairly stable and fundamental cultural aspects of politico-administrative systems
Legal tradition (Rechtsstaat versus Common Law tradition)
Cultural traits (Hofstede 2001), like uncertainty avoidance and power distance

Third level – Polity: Rather stable and fundamental structural and functional aspects of politico-administrative systems
Relation public-private sectors – Type of welfare regimes (Esping-Andersen 1999)
Relative size – Task division – Private involvement in service delivery
State structure
Vertical dispersion of authority (Lijphart 1999)
Relation central-local authorities
Relative size – Task division – Power distribution and control relationship
Political system: Type of democracy: consensualist versus majoritarian (Lijphart 1999)
Parliamentary/presidential system
Electoral system: majoritarian electoral systems versus proportional representation
Executive government (Lijphart 1999)

Cabinet structure: degree of consensualism
Cabinet lifespan – cabinet stability
Cabinet composition – dominant political parties
Parliament
Executive-legislative relationships: degree of dominance of executive power (Lijphart 1999)
Ex post control mechanisms for parliaments towards the executive and agencies
Degree of corporatism
Extra-parliamentary checks on agencies' action (Ombudsman, Freedom of Information and judicial review)

Fourth level – Actor constellations: Relative power positions of main actors and their attitude towards reform. Aspects which are changeable, at least in a long-term perspective
Minister – senior civil servant relations
Division of roles and responsibilities – Integrated or separate careers – Politicization of senior civil servant positions – Cooperative or adversarial relationships
Ministerial capacity for control
Parent departments: capacity for control
Position and reform ideas within central departments
Number and most important central departments – Power distribution between central and line departments

Fifth level – Instrumental actions and deliberate decisions (taken by political and administrative leaders to further collective goals through administrative design and active administrative policy)
Deliberate decision with regard to
General public administration reform programs – Specific agency reform programmes

reconfiguration. They include the relative position and reform attitudes of the main actors as well as deliberate decisions taken with regard to administrative reform programmes. The latter do not really form part of politico-administrative regimes but are, instead, the outcome. However, these deliberate decisions regarding administrative reform programmes do influence perceived autonomy, control and management of agencies. Beginning, therefore, with environmental pressures, for each of these levels we consider the distinguishing characteristics in Norway, Flanders and Ireland.

5.2   Environmental pressures

It is worth noting here that all three states have relatively small populations – Flanders has approximately 6 million citizens, Norway just over 4.5 million while the Republic of Ireland has 4.2 million citizens at time of writing.

All are member of the OECD. In addition, the European Union (EU) plays an influential role in each state. Ireland and Belgium are both very active members within the Union, from the creation of the EU onwards in the case of Belgium, and since the 1970s in the case of Ireland. Norway is not a member of the EU but, nonetheless, retains very strong links, especially through the European Economic Area Agreement, since 1994, and since 2001 through an association agreement concerning the Schengen treaty on border control.

The three states have, in different degrees, experienced economic crises as a trigger for administrative reforms. Looking at the period since 1980 (the period in which NPM reforms spread globally), Norway was the only state under review that did not face periods of severe national fiscal pressure. The discovery and exploitation of large petroleum reserves brought the state large budgetary surpluses, reducing the need for large public sector reforms in order to yield substantial efficiency gains (Listhaug 2007). During the 1980s, Ireland struggled considerably to balance its domestic budget, and relied on significant transfers from the EU. From the early 1990s onwards, Ireland witnessed a period of unprecedented economic growth, with the highest average annual rate of real gross domestic product (GDP) from 1995 onwards exceeding 7 per cent, compared to 2.7 per cent in the OECD area (OECD 2008: 48). As a result, per capita income was propelled above the OECD average in 2005, but still remained below Norwegian per capita income (OECD 2008: 50). Moreover, the economy in Ireland is highly globalized and is one of the most open in the OECD. Belgium, and by consequence Flanders, faced a severe economic crisis in the 1980s, leading to major budgetary debts. During most of the 1990s, the Maastricht norms put severe fiscal pressure on Belgian governments, which had to cut the public sector budgets substantially (Bouckaert and Auwers 1999).

Another important element, which may potentially explain administrative reforms, is external pressure stemming from citizens and media regarding the legitimacy of government and administration. The extent to which citizens trust government or have positive attitudes towards public services may be considered as a proxy measurement of the relative strength of such legitimacy pressures. In a recent article, Van de Walle et al. (2008) analyse the extent to which there is a decline of trust in government across OECD states. Using data from World Values Studies and European Values Studies the authors show the evolution during the 1981–2000 period of confidence in the civil service for the three states under study. Ireland scores highly on the share of respondents expressing 'a great deal' or 'quite a lot' of confidence in the civil service, ranging from 54 per cent in 1981 to 59 per cent in 1999–2000. Norway observes a sharp decline however, between 1981 (58 per cent) and 1997 (51 per cent) with only a 44 per cent share in 1990. The share of respondents having confidence in the civil service in Belgium remains remarkably stable over this period, with values ranging at around 45 per cent, ranking 17th on the total sample of 29 states. Norway ranked tenth and Ireland third.

5.3 Politico-administrative culture

The essential features comprising this level are the legal tradition of the territory and the cultural traits that define its political and administrative identity. In terms of legal traditions, a distinction is normally drawn between the European *Rechtsstaat* (mainly civil law) tradition of continental Europe and the 'public interest' (mainly common law) tradition more closely associated with the Westminster/Whitehall systems (De Jong et al. 2002; Wollmann 2003a; Pollitt and Bouckaert 2004). Looking at Norway, Flanders and Ireland, respectively, reveals important differences in legal tradition, as summarized in Table 5.2. Norwegian public administration is not exclusively characterized by either public interest or Rechtsstaat traditions, and instead displays elements of both, although according to Lijphart, the Norwegian constitution is relatively rigid (Lijphart 1999: 220–6). While power was substantially devolved in Belgium following constitutional changes in 1993, Flanders retains a legal system closely aligned to the Rechtsstaat tradition, as visible in relatively high levels of constitutional rigidity (Lijphart 1999: 220–6). The Irish legal tradition is that of the public interest model with its roots in the English common law system. Irish law (including administrative law) draws on a combination of the 1937 Constitution, which is relatively less rigid, EU law, statute law and judicial decisions.

Turning to the other principal characteristic of politico-administrative cultural traits, we draw on the work of Hofstede (2001) and Hofstede and Hofstede (2005) on national cultures. They identify five key dimensions. The first dimension is power distance, that is, the difference between the extent to which a boss can determine the behaviour of a subordinate and vice versa. The second dimension, 'uncertainty avoidance', refers to the extent to which

Table 5.2 Legal tradition and Hofstede's cultural values in Norway, Ireland and Flanders

	Norway	Ireland	Flanders
Rechtsstaat or public interest	Elements of both *Rechtsstaat* and public interest	Public interest	Mainly *Rechtsstaat*
Flexibility/Rigidity of Constitution (Lijphart 1999: 220)	Score 3 out of 4 for rigidity	Score 2 out of 4 for rigidity	Score 3 out of 4 for rigidity (Belgium)
Power Distance (PDI)	Low (score 31, rank 67 out of 74)	Low (score 28, rank 69 out of 74)	High[*] (score 61, rank 39 out of 74)
Uncertainty Avoidance (UAI)	Moderate (score 50, rank 57 out of 74)	Low (score 35, rank 67 out of 74)	High[*] (score 97, rank 5 out of 74)
Individualism (IND)	High (score 69, rank 16 out of 74)	High (score 70, rank 15 out of 74)	High[*] (score 78, rank 8 out of 74)
Masculinity (MAS)	Low (score 8, rank 73 out of 74)	High (score 68, rank 9 out of 74)	Moderate[*] (score 43, rank 47 out of 74)
Long-term orientation (LT)	Moderate (score 44, rank 13 out of 74)	Moderate (score 45, rank 15 out of 74)	Moderate[*] (score 38, rank 20 out of 74)

*Note that Hofstede and Hofstede (2005) refer to 'Flemish Belgium' in their categorizations.

members of a culture feel threatened by uncertainty or unknown situations. When individualism is high, such societies experience loose ties between individuals. Masculinity versus femininity refers to the distinction between organizations or societies where gender roles are distinct and where they are more blurred. The final dimension is long-term versus short-term orientation, that is, encouraging virtues geared towards future rewards or virtues aimed at satisfying a more immediate need.

Table 5.2 provides a summary of their findings for our three states. In terms of power distance and uncertainty avoidance, Norway and Ireland achieve a relatively low score and Flanders a comparatively high score (Hofstede and Hofstede 2005: 43–4). Masculine values are much more prominent in Ireland, followed by Flanders, compared to Norway where distinct gender roles are much less developed. On the two other dimensions, the three states do not differ substantially. Table 5.2 suggests that Norway, Belgium (total) and Ireland all achieve relatively high levels of individualism as well as moderate results on 'long-term orientation'.

5.4 Polity

Having considered the key elements of legal tradition and cultural characteristics for our three states, we examine here the structural and functional aspects of polity. These are the state structure – including welfare regime – and the type of democracy as described by Lijphart (1999).

5.4.1 Relationships between public and private sectors

First, we consider the relative task division between the public and private sectors in each state, since this may be expected to affect the number and features of agencies created. There are several indicators which may be used to determine the relative task division between public and private sector, such as the size of the public sector within the economic system of a state, as measured by public expenditure or by public employment. Another indicator could be the welfare regime employed by the states under review (Esping-Andersen 1999).

In terms of both expenditure as a percentage of GDP and public employment as a percentage of the total workforce, the Irish public sector is much smaller relative to that of Norway and Flanders. Whereas in 1970 all three states used about one third of their GDP for public expenditure, in 2005, public expenditure in Belgium took up 50 per cent of GDP, with 42 per cent in Norway, compared with 34 per cent in Ireland (OECD 1997, 2007). In terms of employment, in 2005 about 28 per cent of the Norwegian workforce worked in the public sector. The Irish public sector employs approximately 14 per cent of the total labour force (OECD 2008: 21), whereas for Belgium and Flanders this share was about 17 per cent (OECD 2007: 161). According to the recent OECD report on the Irish public services (OECD 2008), Ireland has been able to deliver public services with a public sector that is relatively small compared to other OECD states, given the size of its economy and labour force.

Moreover, the structure of public expenditure differs between the three states. Government expenditures for the production of goods and services in the public domain, as well as other non-productive transfers to other economic actors, take up a larger share of GDP in Belgium and Norway than in Ireland (OECD 2007; Lonti and Woods 2008). This data suggests that both Norway and Belgium have a public sector of substantial size, which provides many services to the citizens. In addition, in Belgium, many public services are delivered to users through market corporations and quasi-corporations, financed by public funds. The Irish state has a relatively small public sector, with considerable outsourcing and relatively few services and goods provided by publicly funded market corporations.

This empirical picture aligns, to a great extent, with the distinction made between Nordic, Anglo and Continental-European style welfare regimes by Esping-Andersen (1999; cf. also Esping-Andersen and Myles n.d.). He found that the Nordic and Continental European systems tend to favour higher levels of government expenditure on social services, with relatively small private sector contributions to such services. As an example, par excellence, of the Nordic model, Norway has an extensive welfare state and government social expenditure accounted for approximately 25 per cent of GDP in 2003 (OECD Social Expenditure Database 2008). In Belgium, 26 per cent of GDP in 2003 was allocated to social expenditure. Esping-Andersen includes Belgium (and hence, Flanders) in the group of continental 'conservative' welfare states. By contrast, in Anglo systems levels of spending on social services by the state is lower, with the figures practically matched by funding from non-state sources. In Ireland, government social expenditure accounted for approximately 15 per cent of GDP in 2003 (OECD Social Expenditure Database 2008) and the welfare regime is more 'liberal', built on 'the assumption that the majority of citizens can obtain adequate welfare from the market' (Esping-Andersen and Myles n.d.: 6–7).

5.4.2   State structure and central-local relationships

The structure of the state and the dispersion of power between levels of government are defining characteristics of polities (Christensen and Lægreid 2001b; Lalenis et al. 2002; Pollitt and Bouckaert 2004). As Chapter 7 shows, levels of public authority centralization or decentralization may play an important role in determining the type and form of agencies used.

Vertical dispersion of power is a defining feature of Flemish government, at least with respect to the interaction between the federal and regional levels. Following a series of constitutional reforms in recent decades, political power in Belgium has been divided between regions and linguistic communities. As a region, legislative power in Flanders is constitutionally similar in status to that of the federal Belgian government. However, the Flemish government does not have authority over such issues as defence, social security, finances or justice, but it has full competence in other areas, including the economy, labour market policy, education, health and foreign affairs. Moreover, within the Flemish region, the status and power of local authorities is in line with the so-called Franco system of local government (Hesse 1991). Flemish local authorities have mainly a political role but to a substantial degree are functionally dependent on higher levels of government in a form of tutelage relationship. The Flemish government has regulatory and financial control over 308 municipalities, which are grouped into five provinces. However, there has recently been an increased emphasis on decentralization of competencies as well as a partnership approach between the levels of government. The majority of public sector employees in Flanders work at the local level, approximating 70 per cent in 2005 (OECD 2007: 166). This points to a considerable level of involvement on the part of local authorities in service delivery, such as primary education.

Norway is a unitary state, but authority is more dispersed than within Ireland and Flanders. Since the 1970s, there has been considerable political decentralization to Norwegian sub-national government. Despite this decentralization, however, between 70 and 80 per cent of the national tax share is retained at central level. The Norwegian system of local government belongs to what Hesse (1991) refers to as the North European type, in which local government has a strong constitutional status, a strong political function of local democracy, general functional competences as well as a high degree of policy-making autonomy and financial independence. There are currently 430 municipalities in Norway, which have a considerable range of functions, such as social services, zoning, primary and lower secondary education. There are 19 counties, which are primarily concerned with issues such as upper secondary education and roads. According to *Statistics Norway*, in 2004 two-thirds of a total of approximately 725,000 public sector employees were working at the local governmental level, a share somewhat similar to Flanders.

Ireland, which is also a unitary state, is arguably one of the most centralized in the EU. Local government displays many of the features of Anglo-American systems (Hesse 1991), including limited discretion and weak financial independence. Irish local government is often criticized for being more akin to a system of local administration than a separate tier of democratic governance (Callanan 2003; OECD 2008), and this is reflected in the fact that local authorities retain less than 5 per cent of the national tax share (OECD 2008). The primary local authorities are the 29 county and five city councils covering the whole national territory. A smaller tier of local government – town and borough councils – has even less autonomy. Whereas in Norway many important services are funded or delivered predominantly by sub-national authorities, in Ireland this is only the case for a small number of key services. In 2004, approximately 11 per cent of public sector employees were working in local authorities (Institute of Public Administration 2005). Only in 2008 did the Irish Government appear to move in the direction of more service delivery decentralization, but the relationship remains one in which central government retains strong control over local authorities.

5.4.3   Types of democracy

One of the most important dynamics affecting a democracy is the type of political system it has. Elements identified by Lijphart (1999), which affect political systems include: whether or not it is a parliamentary or presidential system, the form of electoral system used, the existence of corporatist interest groups arrangements, executive-legislative relations and parliamentary control of public services. Lijphart's two-dimensional conceptual map of democracy types clusters the three states relatively close together (1999: 248). All three are Western parliamentary democracies. Moreover, all use proportional electoral systems. However, while consensus politics characterize Norwegian and Flemish democracy, the form of engagement in Irish democratic life is held to be strongly informed by classic Westminster-style adversarial politics (MacCarthaigh 2005).

The nature of executive government is clearly important for understanding the context of the decision-making framework. Again, Lijphart's analysis is instructive, particularly in relation to his categorization of democracies according to the concentration or sharing of executive power in governments, ranging from single party majority cabinets to broad multi-party coalitions (1999: 110–1). Norwegian cabinets from 1945 to 1996 score an average of 63 per cent (47 per cent minimal winning cabinets and 79 per cent one-party cabinets) on an index of majoritarianism, while Irish cabinets achieve a similar score of 59 per cent (64 per cent minimal winning cabinets and 54 per cent one-party cabinets). Interesting additional data is provided by Strøm et al. (2003a: 661), which suggest that Ireland and Norway are quite comparable in terms of majoritarian-type cabinet structures. They clearly show that Ireland has seen during the period 1945–1999 30 per cent single-party majority cabinets, 26 per cent single-party minority cabinets and 44 per cent coalition cabinets. Norwegian cabinets were 31 per cent single-party majority cabinets, 49 per cent single-party minority cabinets and 20 per cent coalition cabinets.

The score for Belgium is quite different, with 91 per cent coalition cabinets, suggesting a much more consensual cabinet structure. Cabinets in Flanders have predominantly been minimum-winning or oversized grand coalitions. As our analysis extends to 2004, and as the period since 1980 has been particularly important in terms of administrative (NPM) changes, we need to check whether this general picture holds during the 1980–2004 period. Therefore, we briefly analyse the major characteristics of cabinets in the three states during this period, including the number of cabinets, their form in terms of single-party or coalitions governments; their parliamentary support in terms of majority, minimal winning, minority or oversized; as well as the cabinet lifespan during this period. In terms of lifespan, we consider the broad measure suggested by Lijphart (1999: 131), including the following events as the end of a cabinet: parliamentary elections, change in party composition, in premiership and in status of the cabinet.

In Norway, there have been 11 cabinets between 1980 and 2004, whereas in this period six elections were held. Of these cabinets, six have been minority single-party Labour governments, with the remaining five being minority centre or minority centre-conservative coalitions – though the conservative-centre government (1983–1986) had a majority until the election of 1985. Considering this dominance of minority cabinets, even if they are one-party governments, the Lijphart index on majoritarianism seems to be an overestimation in case of Norway, at least for the period since 1980. As Lijphart (1999: 105) points out, minority governments are very much like oversized coalitions in terms of their dominance. In total, of the 24 years in question, 14 were dominated by Labour governments and the remainder by either centre or conservative-centre coalitions. The average cabinet duration during this period was according to the broad definition 1.92 years (compared to 2.11 years in the period 1945–1996), since 13 cabinet or PM changes happened. Party composition changes in terms of changes along the left–right continuum happened eight times during this period.

Unlike Norway, Irish political parties do not lend themselves to easy categorization along an ideological spectrum. However, there is some agreement among analysts (see Mitchell 2003) that the two largest parties (Fianna Fáil and Fine Gael) traditionally occupy the centre/centre-right, with the Labour Party the largest party on the left. There have also been 11 governments between 1980 and 2004; eight of these were coalitions while of the remaining three governments two were single-party minority and one a single-party majority held by Fianna Fáil. Of the eight coalition governments, one was a minority centre-left and one a minority centre-right government. The remaining six majority coalitions consisted of three which were centre-right leaning and three which were centre-left. In total, there have been 14 years of centre-right governments in Ireland interspersed by ten years of centre-left government during the 1980–2004 period. In Ireland, the average cabinet duration during this period according to the broad definition was 2.27 years (compared to 2.42 years in the period 1945–1996). Party composition changes happened six times during this period, in which the two main centrist parties alternated with other coalition partners. As was the case for Norway since 1980, the cabinet instability seems to be higher overall, compared to the 1945–1996 period.

In Flanders, the story is quite different, with seven cabinet changes throughout the period. Because of intergovernmental arrangements following from the state reforms of 1980 and 1988, several subsequent cabinets were composed proportionally, rather than by majority, leading to oversized grand coalitions containing parties from the centre, centre-left and centre-right. In the period between 1980 and 2004 only three cabinets, encompassing eight years, were minimal-winning coalitions, with the rest being oversized coalitions. Until 1999, the centric Christian-democratic party was dominant in all cabinets. One cabinet was centre-right and one was centre-left, but all other cabinets included left-wing and right-wing parties at the same time. Moreover, the anti-Christian democratic cabinet formed in 1999 again contained parties from both the left and right of the political spectrum. Overall, stability of Flemish cabinets was relatively high, when measured with the Lijphart's broad measure: The average cabinet lifespan is for this period 3.57 years, which is much higher than on the federal level (Lijphart 1999).

As is shown above, all three jurisdictions have had a dominant political party providing a majority of these cabinets. In Norway, the Labour Party have held power for a considerable number of years, as have the populist and also centrist Fianna Fáil in Ireland either alone or, more recently, with a variety of coalition parties from both sides of the political spectrum. In Flanders, the Christian Democratic Party has traditionally dominated in the coalition cabinets, except for the period since 1999. Recently, their electoral dominance has come under pressure with competition from other parties.

Another aspect to consider is the influence and power of parliament vis-à-vis the cabinet, with regard to policy in general and with regard to agency control in particular. Using Lijphart's criteria for measuring aspects of democracy, Lane and Ersson (1998: 235–6) find that the Irish executive is one of the more dominant, and more so than Norway or Belgium. Indeed, the extensive veto powers held by Irish governments over the parliamentary agenda is not reflected in Norwegian or Flemish cases where the legislatures enjoy greater influence (Mitchell 2003). All three states adhere to a doctrine of ministerial accountability to Parliament. While parliamentary *ex post* control of cabinet actions' and public services tends to be traditionally not strongly developed in all states (see Table 5.3), in Ireland parliamentary scrutiny and monitoring is particularly weak (MacCarthaigh 2005), and giving answers to parliamentary questions can be avoided quite easily. The parliamentary committee system has recently been developed, with new committees being re-established after each election since 1992, albeit with varying jurisdictions. However, they remain relatively weak in terms of agenda setting. Before the mid-1990s they tended not to focus on monitoring specific departments and their remains considerable variance between committees in terms of sitting frequency and reporting. Only since the late 1990s can sectoral committees compel Irish CEOs and

Table 5.3 Parliamentary and extra-parliamentary control on agencies' actions in Norway, Ireland and Flanders

Ex post parliamentary controls	Norway	Ireland	Flanders
Parliamentary questions permitted? Are parliamentary questions of different kinds on cabinet and administrative actions permitted? (Bergman et al. 2003: Table 4.14)	Moderate to strong	Weak to moderate, because government can avoid answering questions in many ways	Strong
Committees: Power of parliamentary committees to supervises governments' organizations (Bergman et al. 2003: Table 4.14)	Moderate to strong (quite stable jurisdictions to monitor departments)	Weak (committees with changing jurisdictions did not routinely monitor government departments until the late 1990s)	Strong (standing and permanent committees)
Accountability of CEO before committees: Can parliamentary committees question directly the senior management of agencies?	Absent (only minister)	Moderate (CEOs may be called before committees but may decline, most only formally accountable as financial officers to Committee on Public Accounts)	Weak (only exceptionally and mainly informally)

Table 5.3 (Continued)

Ex post parliamentary controls	Norway	Ireland	Flanders
Annual reporting by agencies: Are agencies obliged to report annually to the Parliament?	Strong (all agencies, through the parent department)	Moderate (majority of agencies)	Strong (quasi all agencies)
Audit office: Does the audit office (auditor-general) have the opportunity to carry out regular financial and performance audits within the agencies and does it report these audits to Parliament?	Strong since regular financial audit on all agencies. Moderate – strong performance audit (guidelines since 1981 and strengthened since 1996)	Moderate because regular financial audit by the C&AG, with several agencies exempted Weak to moderate because of Value for Money audits since 1993, but not focused on single organizations	Strong because regular financial audit on all agencies. Weak to moderate because performance audit since 1991; intensification after 1998
Extra-parliamentary checks on agency actions *Ombudsman:* Can citizens appeal against agency decisions to an Ombudsman, who reports regularly to Parliament, and since when?	Strong (since 1962 and on all agencies)	Weak (since 1984, but minor share of older agencies and agencies within departments is covered)	Weak (only since 1998, applicable on all agencies)

Freedom of Information Act: Does the Freedom of Information Act apply to actions by agencies, since when, and what are grounds for exemptions?	Strong (FOI act since 1970, covers all state agencies)	Relatively weak Tradition of executive secrecy (FOI act since 1997, but many agencies exempted)	Moderate (FOI act since 1991, amended in 1999 and 2004)
Judicial review of administrative actions: Can citizens appeal to the courts against agency decisions (what kind of courts)? What is the degree of judicial review by courts (Lijphart 1999)?	Weak to moderate. Appeal is possible through normal civil court system. Weak degree of judicial review	Weak. Appeal is possible through the normal civil court system. Weak degree of judicial review	Moderate to strong Appeal is possible to specialized administrative courts. Moderate degree of judicial review

senior management teams to appear before them, though in most cases parliamentary accountability is pursued through the minister responsible. Many agency CEOs must appear before the Committee on Public Accounts in respect of their role as accounting officers. Regular financial audits by the Comptroller and Auditor General (C&AG) could help to overcome information asymmetries, but as Clancy and Murphy (2006: 39–41) assess, several public bodies, including many state agencies, are excluded from the ambit of the C&AG.

The Norwegian Storting is comparatively well-equipped for *ex-post* parliamentary control, because of a central oversight committee working alongside permanent standing committees linked to the remit of government departments, and with an extensive remit for parliamentary questioning. Annual reports, delivered by all agencies to their parent department and included in the state budget, have a standardized content, outlining objectives, results, activities and resources. The Auditor General conducts regular financial audits and, since the 1980s, increasingly comprehensive performance audits on specific agencies, which are discussed in the oversight committees in the Storting. In general, parliamentary activism and scrutiny increased in the 1990s (Strøm and Narud 2003: 539). However, with regard to formulating administrative policies, the Storting has not played an active role. Political control over reform of the civil service has traditionally been general and passive, allowing the executive a lot of leeway (Christensen et al. 2002). The parliamentary committee handling the organization of government administration has been regarded as among the least prestigious among the legislators themselves, in contrast with the Committee on Finance and Economic Affairs (Roness 2001a).

Formally, the Flemish Parliament has somewhat similar scrutiny powers as the Norwegian Storting, but as in the Federal Parliament, 'the majority's duty to promote government stability has undermined Parliament's control function' (De Winter and Dumont 2003: 266). Committees are permanent and largely structured according to government departments, and the Committee for Finance and Budget, as well as the Committee for Administrative Affairs, provide for some overarching forums to discuss administrative policy. Besides parliamentary questioning, interpellations provide for a more powerful tool of parliamentary control as well as ad hoc committees for inquiries. Ministers are obliged to lay down a policy note for the whole legislature and update this every year in an annual policy brief. Annual reporting of agencies is obligatory, but these reports are hardly discussed. Since the early 1990s, the Court of Audit conducts increasingly critical audits, and has motivated Parliament to vote some resolutions, calling for better control of autonomous agencies. Although parliamentary control in Flanders has its limits, partisan control over the civil service and agencies is substantial, as will be discussed below (see De Winter and Dumont 2003; Pelgrims 2008).

Corporatism – the active involvement of interest groups in policy-making processes – also affects the style of democracy in a state. Drawing on Lijphart (1999; cf. Loughlin and Peters 1997: 46) we conceptualize corporatism as coordinated action aimed at compromise between social actors as distinct from free-for-all pluralist competition. Both Norway and Belgium/ Flanders produce a relatively low score in Lijphart's comparative overview on interest-group pluralism (0.44 and 1.25, respectively, on a maximum of 4), demonstrating the relatively strong presence and involvement of corporatist interest-group structures (Lijphart 1999: 177). However, Ireland scores somewhat higher (2.94), meaning that Ireland experiences relatively more interest-group pluralism, and hence less dominance of a few well-structured interest groups. Nevertheless, the rise of a formal corporatist bargaining structure in Ireland (known as social partnership), which is facilitated by the government, has placed more emphasis on consensus-building between government and the main economic and social representative bodies since the late 1980s.

When it comes to extra-parliamentary checks on agencies' actions (see Table 5.3), Norway has a long and strong tradition with regard to Ombudsmen's offices and the accessibility of government information for citizens. Lægreid et al. (forthcoming) refer to a high degree of transparency and an open attitude to critical scrutiny by the media. Traditionally, Norway has not had any type of administrative court. Appeals are directed to the parent department, which can also instruct agencies. However, Flanders has an elaborate system of administrative courts, which allow for appeal on administrative decisions, and a Freedom of Information (FOI) Act with a quite extensive remit, although the number of exemptions for application is higher than in Norway. Compared to Norway and Flanders, Ireland has quite weakly developed extra-parliamentary checks. Moreover, although the post of Ombudsman has existed since 1980, a major number of agencies are not under its remit (Clancy and Murphy 2006: 39). The same holds for the FOI Act which was only issued in 1997 and for the application of the Code of Practice for the Governance of State Boards, issued in 2001 (Clancy and Murphy 2006: 39–43).

5.5   Actor constellations

The final level for analysing politico-administrative regimes encompasses those issues that are subject to the most frequent changes. One principal dimension to be considered here are actor constellations at the state level.

A main issue concerning actor constellations in each state is the relationship between ministers and their civil servants. Appointments to the senior administrative levels within departments in Norway and Ireland are not political and civil servants are not removed when the cabinet or individual ministers resign. Strøm et al. (2003b: 661) report that partisanship as a basis for appointments to leading and other civil service positions is absent in Ireland, and only moderately present in Norway in the case of appointments to the management of state enterprises. In Belgium and Flanders however, partisanship as a basis is strong for appointments to most kinds of senior positions, which influences considerably relations between the minister and his or her senior civil servants (Strøm et al. 2003b: 661).

In Ireland, the senior civil service is explicitly non-political and civil servants are precluded from joining political parties. Traditionally, the role of top civil servants has been to provide impartial advice and policy options to government. There is considerable emphasis on cooperation at the political-administrative interface and resignations of senior civil servants are rare. An important development in Ireland has been the growing number and role of special advisers employed by ministers to ensure the successful implementation of political programmes in recent coalition cabinets, which involve considerable interaction between these political appointees and civil servants (Mitchell 2003: 436–8).

In Norway, political partisanship is also absent from the administrative levels of ministries and civil servants enjoy strong and protected tenure. The consensus-based Norwegian political-administrative system implies that the relationship between politicians and administrative leaders has traditionally been cooperative and based on mutual understanding and shared values (Christensen and Lægreid 2005). Considerable emphasis is placed on partnership between ministers and senior civil servants in the implementation of policy programmes.

In Flanders the position of senior civil servants is quite different. Traditionally, the senior civil service has been quite weak and its roles unclearly delineated. Individual ministers have very substantial political secretariats – called 'ministerial cabinets' (*cabinet de Ministre*) – which they use 'for more than the usual purpose of providing politically sensitive advice to ministers as they ensure the political oversight of executive bodies' (OECD 2007: 24). As it is the case at the federal level, 'the excessive use of ministerial cabinets is partially due to the politicization of the civil service, which often creates tensions when top civil servants belong to a different party than their minister' (De Winter and Dumont 2003: 271–2). Despite rhetorical changes, the allocation of former 'cabinetards' or other candidates, who are politically affiliated to one of the governing political parties, to senior management positions in departments and agencies, as well as the distribution of these positions among the political parties in power is still an ongoing practice (Pelgrims 2008).

Because of this politicization, ministers fear 'that they could not unconditionally rely on the loyalty of their civil servants, hence most policy development, verification of policy implementation and mediation with interest groups is done by the personal staff' (De Winter and Dumont 2003: 273). The existence of large ministerial 'cabinets' increases substantially the capacity of individual ministers to micro-manage policy implementation by agencies (Huber and Shipan 2002), compared to Norway and Ireland. Matheson et al. (2007: table 16) report that in Belgium politicians tend to interfere in the management responsibilities of senior civil servants rather frequently, and legal limitations on administrative actions by politicians are low. Ministerial capacity to control externally decentralized agencies is enhanced by the presence of two government commissioners, who are politically appointed and solely accountable to the portfolio minister and to the Minister of Finance, in the governing boards of such agencies (De Winter and Dumont 2003: 273). These government commissioners may annul all decisions taken by the agencies before they take effect, if they do not seem to accord with the general interest, the law, the budget and the political will of the minister. Traditionally, the relationship between ministers and senior civil servants in Flanders has been based less on consensual interaction than on subordination and close supervision of the latter.

Another important determinant of agency autonomy and control is the size and capacity of parent departments. In Norway, departments are in general very small and account only for about 5 per cent of the civil service at national level (cf. Lægreid et al. forthcoming). In 2004, about 4100 full-time employees (FTE's) worked in departments, whereas about 130,000 civil servants were employed outside departments. In contrast to the two other states, Norwegian departments act merely as political secretariats for the political leadership and are heavily involved in policy formulation, whereas the implementation occurs through agencies. In contrast, and excluding health services, police forces and defence forces, Irish departments accounted for 77 per cent of the civil service workforce (approximately 37,000 civil servants) in 2004, whereas non-commercial bodies only count for 23 per cent (approximately 11,000 civil servants). Flanders holds a middle position with 31 per cent of the workforce working in departments (OECD 2007).

A key issue is the relationship between the central and line departments in each state. Line departments, like the Department of Health, are responsible for the design and implementation of policies, that are externally oriented towards society. Staff departments, or central departments as we call them, provide policies and services, that are internally oriented towards the other departments. Central departments are usually responsible for budget, finances, human resources and coordination of policies. In Ireland, the constitution limits the number of ministerial portfolios to 15, including the Department of the *Taoiseach* (prime minister). This department, along with the Department of Finance, are referred to as the 'central' departments, with all others being regarded as 'line' departments. All major policy decisions normally require the approval of the two central departments in order that they be successfully implemented. The *Taoiseach* is also pre-eminent at cabinet and holds extensive veto and agenda setting powers that, in many respects, are unrivalled in the EU, with perhaps the exception of the British prime minister (Mitchell 2003: 436). The Irish prime minister, in contrast to his Norwegian and Flemish equivalents, holds the formal right to decide ministry jurisdiction, and holds full control over the cabinet agenda (Bergman et al. 2003: 186–7), besides the right to steer and coordinate other ministers. The Minister of Finance is very powerful vis-à-vis the line departments (Mitchell 2003: 436).

In Norway, since 1980 there have been 16–18 departments (called ministries), normally with one minister each. While all departments have equal legal standing, the Prime Minister's Office and the Ministry of Finance have some coordinating authority. However, in a comparative perspective the role of the prime minister is very limited and his powers are very weak, since he does not even have formal rights to steer and control the other ministers (Bergman et al. 2003: 186–7). In relation to national administrative policy, the Ministry of Finance has been responsible for reforms in budget and financial management. What is now the Ministry of Government Administration and Reform (it has previously had different names) has handled reforms on wage and personnel policy, as well as issues of organizational design and administrative policy questions, in general. However, this ministry has less binding authority with regard to organizational design than the Ministry of Finance has concerning budgetary decisions.

In Flanders, the premier has relatively moderate powers within the cabinet, with the right to steer and coordinate other ministries, but without the formal right to decide ministry jurisdiction, and holds full control over the cabinet agenda (Bergman et al. 2003: 186–7). There are seven departmental portfolios, of which the two central departments, the departments of Coordination and of General Matters, can be considered relatively strong. Within a government-wide matrix structure, both central departments, and in particularly the Department of General Affairs (including administration of finances, budgets and civil service) have considerable controlling powers over the line departments with respect to input management. During the 1990s, the latter department was responsible for government-wide policy regarding financial management and HRM. It was usually led by several ministers holding the portfolio of Budget, Finance and HRM. The Department of Coordination was more involved in general administrative policy matters, and in particular matters of organization (Bouckaert and Auwers 1999).

5.6 Conclusion

This chapter has presented an analysis of the politico-administrative regimes in the three states by framing each within different levels of analysis – environmental pressures, politico-administrative culture and governance style, polity, and finally actor constellations. In conclusion, it is instructive to briefly recap on some of the key characteristics of each state, which will be used to expand on theories concerning similarities and dissimilarities in the process of agencification in Norway, Ireland and Flanders.

Ireland's position as a centralized, common law state, which has recently experienced an extensive phase of public sector reform, and which has high levels of private spending on social services, contrasts with Norway. There, the mixed system of public administration has a long history of reform programmes and the state has combined high levels of government expenditure on social services with considerable devolution of authority to local government. Like Norway, Ireland demonstrates a low level of power distance and uncertainty avoidance but while Ireland has high masculinity values these are correspondingly low in Norway. Also, the consensus-based Norwegian political system stands in contrast to the more majoritarian form of democratic politics practiced in Ireland. However, in both states considerable emphasis is placed on the non-partisan nature of the senior civil service. In contrast to both Ireland and Norway, as a regional state, Flanders operates in a federal context and has a public sector that cooperates strongly with private actors. Also, Flanders combines high uncertainty avoidance with high levels of power distance, and the senior levels of the civil service are more politicized than in the other states. Flemish public administration is strongly based on the *Rechtsstaat* legal system. However, like Norway, it has a strong corporatist tradition.

These dimensions of the politico-administrative systems in each state will inform the theoretical and empirical analysis in Parts III and IV. The last element mentioned in Table 5.1 refers to instrumental actions and deliberate decisions taken by political and administrative leaders to further collective goals through administrative design and active administrative policy. All three states have recently undertaken considerable public sector reforms. These reform programmes, for the public sector in general, and targeted at agencies in particular, are considered in detail in Chapter 6.

6
Agencification in Norway, Ireland and Flanders: History, Reforms and Types

This chapter maps the development of agencies in the three states, with a particular focus on 'waves' or agencification and related administrative reforms. We respond to the first empirical research question, setting the background of this study:

RQ 1:   *To what extent are agencies created by the governments of the three states, in what form, with what legal-structural status, and in which policy domains? What tasks are they performing? How is the creation of agencies evolving over time?*

While clearly delineating what does or does not constitute an agency differs according to politico-administrative regimes, the definitions discussed in Chapter 2 provide a compass for our inquiries. Each state is considered in turn, beginning with Norway. The last part of the chapter compares the actual agency landscapes in the three states in terms of task, size, budget, governance structures and other characteristics.

6.1   History of agencification and public sector reform in Norway

6.1.1   Types of agencies in Norway

In Norway, the concept 'agency', as defined in Chapter 2, largely corresponds to what is called civil service organizations outside ministries. For state organizations in general, considerable emphasis is placed on the form of affiliation to central political authorities, be that in legal or ownership terms. A main distinction is between civil service organizations and state-owned companies (Roness 2007; Lægreid et al. forthcoming). A significant difference is also seen between state-owned companies and governmental foundations. While state-owned companies and governmental foundations are separate legal entities, civil service organizations outside the ministries are, legally speaking, government entities subject to ministerial directions and directly subordinated to ministerial control. In contrast to state-owned companies, the state budget, the state collective wage agreement, the state pension scheme, the Freedom of Information Act, the Public Administration Act and the Civil Servants Act regulate civil service organizations.

Within the civil service, while strict legal definitions do not exist distinguishing between different types of agencies, it is nevertheless possible to rank some types according to formal autonomy from parent departments. Since 2003, these have included the five types listed in Chapter 4 in increasing order of distance from the parent department, in total encompassing 215 bodies (cf. Lægreid et al. forthcoming).

Central agencies (called 'directorates') normally carry out tasks related to the exercise of public authority or policy formulation, while other ordinary civil service organizations normally have tasks related to service delivery (see below). Civil service organizations with extended authority have formally been delegated autonomy (primarily managerial autonomy) beyond the standard regulations, and government administrative enterprises have even more formal autonomy.

With some few exceptions, Norwegian agencies are established by a normal statute emerging from the legislature, by royal decree or by a ministerial act. Central agencies can be identified as far back as the mid-nineteenth century. Norwegian reform attempts have largely focused on the internal structure and organization of central government, its function and tasks, work procedures, decision making and steering structures. We first describe the history of agencification, before turning to the recent reform programmes.

6.1.2 History of agency creation in Norway

The first wave of what can be termed agencification occurred around the 1850s when governments under pressure from professional groups agreed to create independent professional bodies (such as central agencies or directorates) outside of ministries, primarily in the communications sector. A second wave occurred in the 1870s with the establishment of independent agencies similar to the 'Swedish model'. However, following initial experiments, it was not until the 1920s that the use of central agencies, albeit with closer links to departments, became more widespread.

The third wave began in the mid-1950s and emerged from a proactive attitude towards reform. This wave, which coincided with the development of the Norwegian welfare state, lasted for several decades, until the early 1970s, and witnessed successive Labour governments engaged in a programme of delegating a wide range of tasks, both technical and routine, from departments to central agencies. This was done in order to allow ministers and departments to engage in more strategic issues. Departments were supposed to be become more like secretariats for political leadership. While central agencies continued to be created, the focus from the early 1970s, however, began to shift towards the decentralization from central government to the (new) regional level and local government. Since then the number of central agencies has increased only slightly.

Looking at all civil service organizations outside the ministries, there was an increase in the number of units until the mid-1980s. Since then, the number of units has declined (cf. Figure 6.1). Rather than the reabsorption of functions into departments or privatization, this decline is caused by a significant merging of civil service organizations (for example, higher education organizations) into larger bodies from 1990 onwards (cf. Lægreid et al. 2003, forthcoming). Moreover, major public activities like railways, telecommunication, power, postal services, forestry, grain selling, public road construction and airport administration were organized as central agencies or government administrative enterprises until the early 1990s. Since then, the commercial parts of these enterprises have been converted into state-owned companies. Regulatory parts have remained within the central agency form. As a result, more autonomous regulatory and controlling agencies have been established. In contrast to the decreasing number of civil service organizations, the number of state-owned companies and (governmental) central foundations has increased over time, particularly from 1983 onwards in the case of the latter, and from 1990 onwards in case of the former. That means that

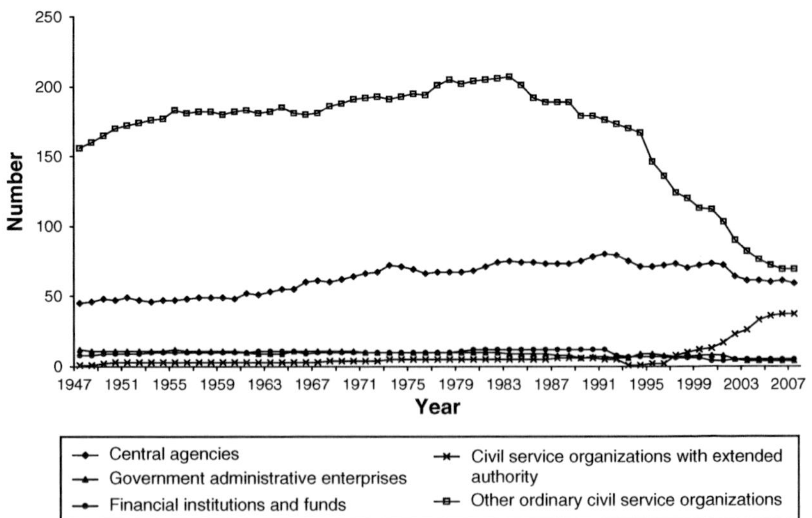

Figure 6.1   Number of units within sub-types of civil service organizations 1947–2007. (Source: Norwegian State Administration Database.)

the extent of internal devolution towards agencies, which has declined since 1980 has been accompanied by an increasing degree of external devolution towards commercial and non-profit forms outside the legal entity of the Norwegian state.

6.1.3 Public sector reforms in Norway

From the 1980s onwards, these structural changes were accompanied by different kinds of administrative reform programmes. A series of influential reports and programmes by successive governments (or commissions appointed by them) were issued (cf. Lægreid and Roness 1999, 2003; Lægreid et al. forthcoming). They included: The Willoch government's modernization programme (1986); the Brundtland II government's renewal programme (1987); the report of the Hermansen Commission on a better organized state (1989); the Bondevik I government's programme on a 'Simplified Norway' (1999); the Stoltenberg government's programme for innovation of the public sector in Norway (2000); the Bondevik II government's programme entitled *From Words to Action* (2002) and the White Paper on regulatory reform (2003).

A first set of reforms had principally a managerial focus. The modernization programmes from the mid-1980s emphasized that the public sector had to make better use of resources and increase efficiency. Proposals were made for less input control and greater managerial autonomy. Following up on the recommendations of the Haga-Commission (NOU 1984: 23), the mid-1980s witnessed the start of a comprehensive budget reform, resulting in a more flexible general budgetary framework for civil service organizations. These reforms allowed for greater discretion over the use of financial packages for civil service organizations, including the ability to move budgets between functional areas (for example, between personnel and running costs, as well as between running costs and investment budgets). The budget reforms of the mid-1980s aimed at granting all Norwegian civil service organizations a general freedom for shifting resources. Moreover, the reforms included a general permission for shifting budgets between years, limited to 5 per cent of unused funds allocated to running costs. Additionally, the opportunity to exceed the funds related to running costs by offsetting it against an equivalent amount of self-generated income, was granted after approval from the parent department.

A similar gradual relaxation of central control over HR issues also supported this budget reform. Following a number of pilot programmes, the general personnel statute and the framework specifying the maximum numbers of staff in the agencies were abolished in June 1997. Since 1998, the number of personnel is no longer meant to be used as a steering instrument connected to the budget for Parliament. This means that, from that time, parliamentary control over personnel limited itself to decisions on funding, and there was no longer an overarching frame or decision specifying the maximum number of personnel in the agencies. Before these changes, Parliament allocated funds through a specific budget reserved for personnel, while the organizations' running costs were funded from a separate budget. After the changes, personnel costs and running costs were meant to be funded from the same budget, allowing the organizations to see these two input factors as a whole and to achieve the allocations best suited for their individual specific situation.

The programmes initially had a strong management approach using management-by-objectives-techniques and structural devolution, and the slogan 'letting the manager manage' was popular. Since then, control components through the use of performance management have been emphasized more strongly. A formalized performance-assessment regime, known as 'management by objectives and results' (MBOR), was introduced as a main tool for regulating relations between departments and subordinate bodies (Lægreid et al. 2006a). Initially, the budget reforms of the mid-1980s stressed the inclusion of objectives and expected results in the budget documents. MBOR was particularly emphasized later on by the Bruntland II government and their reform programme from 1987. In 1991, MBOR was made mandatory for all civil service organizations, and encompassed three reform measures: activity planning, budget reforms and pay reforms, all of which later became integral parts of the governmental financial regulatory system (Lægreid et al. 2006a). One part of this system was the establishment of a quasi-contractual control ('*styring*') model, whereby the parent department allocates resources and specifies targets and goals for the various agencies by means of an annual steering document known as the letter of allocation. The agency was in turn expected to report on performance through formal reports and a formalized 'dialogue' in the form of one or more formal steering meetings with the parent department per year. Additionally, a pay-for-performance system for top managers was introduced in 1991, and substantially changed in 1997. But at the same time, its objectives and incentives were reduced (Lægreid 2001). Since 2000, this system of result control was combined with more explicit market-like pressure on managers, through the use of contracts, marketization and outsourcing, and has become a major strategic priority.

Besides these managerial reforms, the Norwegian government also focused on reforms affecting the structure of government (cf. Roness 2007). Of all the reform packages, the Hermansen commission's report on the organization of the state (NOU 1989: 5) was of particular significance for agencies as it paid particular attention to the relationship between tasks and organizational form. The Commission encouraged greater consideration in the choice of form used by governments, suggesting that various standardized forms of state-owned companies should be used more actively. Governmental foundations were not recommended, because of accountability and steering problems connected to this form of affiliation. This report was a plea for more specialization in single-purpose organizations with appropriate degrees of autonomy. Since this report, the external devolution of tasks to state-owned companies and other forms has increased. Moreover, the reforms under the Bondevik II government (2001–2005) did include more radical aspects of NPM, as the focus was on improving substantive outcomes rather than the symbolic aspects of administrative reform (Christensen and Lægreid 2003). This was particularly evident in respect of the creation of highly independent regulatory agencies, combined with an emphasis on competitive tendering, efficiency measures, consumer choice and the decentralization of service provision (Christensen and Lægreid 2003, 2007b). These more radical NPM-like reforms were highly contested with intense parliamentary debates.

6.2   History of agencification and public sector reform in Ireland

6.2.1   Types of agencies in Ireland

In the absence of an established legal framework for the classification of agency types in Irish administrative law, as well as the circumstances surrounding the creation of many agencies, it is not easy to comprehensively categorize Irish agencies (McGauran et al. 2005). As Hardiman and Scott (forthcoming) identify, most (but not all) Irish agencies are owned by government on a statutory basis and are granted various forms of public authority. However, the legal form of this ownership can vary considerably, ranging from those created on a statutory basis (with or without corporate form), to those incorporated as companies under company legislation. The type of legislation creating agencies can also vary, from primary or secondary (delegated) legislation, to administrative circular. National public sector wage agreements also apply to the staff of these agencies.

However, some broad groupings emerge from the survey conducted in 2004 (McGauran et al. 2005: 52–3). At least half are bodies established by statute (as corporate or non-corporate bodies, public or private companies), and with the bulk of their funding coming in the form of an annual grant-in-aid from their parent department (Agency Type A). They normally have a governing board and their staff may enjoy similar terms and conditions to the general civil service, but, in the main, they are not civil servants. The remainder consists of two types of entity. The first type consists of what are traditionally referred to as 'executive agencies', meaning units of departments with some autonomy but often without a governing board and staffed by civil service and under the direct control of the minister (Agency Type B). The second consists of statutory (or constitutional) bodies, which are funded by their own 'vote' in the general budget and which are also staffed by civil servants but do not have a governing board (Agency Type C). The latter type are known as government offices and are directly represented in the

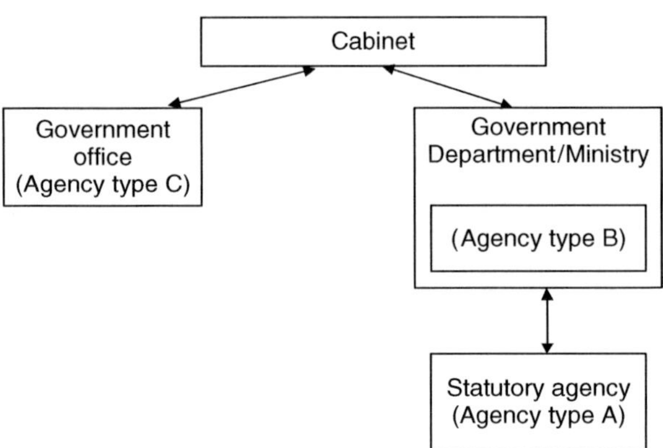

Figure 6.2   Relationship between cabinet and agencies in Ireland

cabinet. Our analysis focuses on Type A and B agencies, since no comparable agencies of type C can be found in the other two states. Figure 6.2 represents the delegation and accountability links for the Irish agencies.

The vast majority of these bodies are subject to the audit by the Office of the Comptroller and Auditor-General, either directly or through their parent departments. About 37 commercial state-sponsored bodies exist alongside these three types of non-commercial agencies, but the focus of our analyses is on non-commercial agencies.

6.2.2   History of agency creation in Ireland

Waves of agencification are not as easily discernible in Ireland as for Norway, not least because agencies since the middle of the nineteenth century have tended to appear and accumulate in an ad-hoc manner. In fact, the development of Irish agencies during this period is perhaps better conceptualized as one of gradual acceleration from a slow start. It is only since the 1990s that a 'wave' of agency establishment has occurred in Ireland. State agencies were no innovation of the post-independence state, of course, and the Whitehall administrative tradition has scope for a range of types of agency, commissions, boards and other forms of non-departmental structure. Upon independence in 1922, the new Irish Free State moved swiftly to abolish the majority of inherited non-departmental bodies and to transfer their functions into nine ministries. A small number of existing non-departmental bodies sustained their existence. As the 1920s and 1930s progressed, a further number of statutory and non-statutory agencies were created to fulfil a number of the state's financial, economic and cultural duties. While most were non-commercial, they included some commercial or trading enterprises established under statute in areas such as energy, aviation and banking. As was to later characterize the state's use of the agency structure, there was no uniformity in the form of affiliation used. The quarter century following the Second World War witnessed an expansion of the public service and also saw a relatively modest number of agencies, increasingly referred to as 'state-sponsored bodies', being established, and those in existence at the end of this period were mainly concerned with health, enterprise and culture (McGauran et al. 2005: 43). These decades also saw the state establish a further number of commercial enterprises in order to develop its infrastructure, as well as in response to market failure, unemployment and wider economic malaise.

The Public Service Organisation Review Group worked through 1966–1969 to produce the pioneering 'Devlin' report, which included an analysis of existing agency-department relationships in the context of how government policy was being implemented. It noted the heterogeneity of state-sponsored bodies due to the ad-hoc nature of their establishment and of financial, HR, legal autonomy arrangements (Institute of Public Administration 1970: 3–21). It also suggested that the creation of such bodies was 'an abandonment…of the concept of the Minister as a corporation sole'. Among other things, the Devlin report recommended the separation of policy design from implementation within ministries, and proposed the establishment of multiple 'executive offices' to which non-commercial state sponsored bodies (to be re-cast as 'executive agencies') would be accountable, in order to reinforce ministerial control. In spite of attempts within some departments to develop policy units free from implementation tasks, and the short-lived creation of a Department of Public Service, little ultimately came of the Devlin report's recommendations, particularly in respect of executive agencies and departmental restructuring.

The two decades post-Devlin saw a small increase in the number of non-commercial agencies established, most notably in social services, as the modern Irish welfare state began to take shape. In part, this coincided with Ireland's accession to the then EEC, but greater political volatility also translated into increased organizational activity within the public service. With coalition (rather than single party) government becoming more common, there was a tendency for functions to move between departments and, in some cases, outside of them to new agencies. Also, while the international trend towards privatization of network industries did lead to the state divesting its interest in some commercial enterprises during the 1980s, during this period a number of commercial enterprises were also created, particularly in the transport and communications sectors.

While the recommendations of the Devlin report had not been warmly received by the public service, another reform agenda in the mid-1980s held out better hope of success. The 1985 Government White Paper, *Serving the Country Better*, was published with a view to introducing new management systems into the public service, including greater responsibility for budgets and performance. Significantly, and in many ways mirroring Devlin's proposals, the White Paper proposed the creation of 'executive offices', which could lessen the burden of executive responsibility on ministers and which would enjoy considerable autonomy from departments in the pursuit of better results. However, economic circumstances conspired to ensure that budgetary considerations dominated all matters relating to the public service for the rest of the decade.

While the 1980s witnessed an increase in the number of agencies being established, it was not until the early 1990s that a veritable wave of agencification occurred. Indeed, a study by McGauran et al. (2005: 51) estimated that over 60 per cent of agencies were established post 1990 (the equivalent figure for this period for sub-national agencies rises to 80 per cent (MacCarthaigh 2007: 24)). Significantly, many of these agencies were concerned with 'soft' policy areas, including social services, equality, safety, health and education. Rather than being a response to a defined set of criteria, the decision to create agencies was in reaction to a variety of stimuli. Political responsiveness played an important role in agencification as governments in an expanding economy wished to demonstrate their commitment to new emerging policy issues and public tasks by creating agencies. Compared to other OECD states, most agencies in Ireland have thus been created *ex nihilo*, that is, to fulfil a new function (OECD 2008: 296). No substantive ideological differences emerged over the issue of agencification until government revenues began to contract. A related emphasis on the political independence of agencies also enhanced their policy autonomy. The EU also played a role in their creation, and particularly those with regulatory functions. A number of commercial enterprises were also created during this period.

This wave of agencification continued into the early years of the twenty first century and by 2004, McGauran et al. (2005) estimated that 211 non-commercial state agencies existed. A number of mergers in recent years (particularly in the health sector, with the creation of one very large agency – the Health Services Executive) combined with the creation of several new agencies has resulted in a stabilisation in the number of agencies. A review by MacCarthaigh in 2007 counted 199 national non-commercial agencies. An OECD review of the Irish public service (2008), including its agencies, criticized the ad-hoc manner in which agencies were established, which it argued 'had decreased the overall accountability of the Public Service while increasing fragmentation and complexity' (OECD 2008: 39). The report called for 'performance dialogues' between departments and agencies and recommended greater use of departmental or 'executive' agencies rather than non-departmental state agencies. In the context of this report, as well as contracting public revenues and public and media criticism of the number and performance of agencies, the wave of agencification that began in the 1990s had ended by 2008. At the time of writing, the elimination of at least 40 agencies was envisaged under proposals outlined in the national budget for 2009.

6.2.3 Public sector reform in Ireland

The post-1990 wave of agencification coincided with, and was heavily influenced by, the launch of the NPM-styled Strategic Management Initiative (SMI) in 1994 (Collins et al. 2007; MacCarthaigh 2008: 75–84). While some important developments preceded the SMI, they had done so in a piecemeal fashion. For example, multi-annual 'administrative budgets' were introduced in all departments in 1991, and legislation in 1993 empowered the Comptroller and Auditor-General to initiate 'value-for-money' audits. SMI however was envisaged as being a more wide-ranging and systemic programme. Based on analysis of administrative reforms in New Zealand, SMI proposed to address three key issues: the enhanced contribution of the public service to national development; the provision of top quality services in a timely and efficient manner; and the effective use of available resources. It supported the creation of executive agencies for the performance of certain tasks. Later stimuli towards 'agencification' arose from sectoral policy reports, like the Cromien report for the education sector, and the Brennan report on the health sector.

SMI led to a variety of sector-specific programmes, including *Delivering Better Government* (DBG) for the civil service. This report stressed the need for greater performance orientation and for increased flexibility in the management of personnel, including a reduction in central regulation and control of the human resource function, and the development and introduction of effective performance management, measurement and appraisal systems (OECD 2008). Table 6.1 shows some different initiatives emerging out of SMI and DBG related to issues of autonomy, performance management and result control.

One of the key goals of the reform agenda was to transform the public service into a more strategically-focused organization, and in order to provide a statutory basis for this, the Public Service Management Act 1997 was passed by the *Oireachtas*. The Act obliged departments to prepare three-year strategic plans, and provided for the vertical devolution of authority and accountability within departments. Many of the state agencies that emerged during this period also had provisions for creating strategic plans included in their founding legislation, as well as mechanisms for regular reporting to their parent departments.

Furthermore, in response to wider international developments in corporate governance, in 2001 the Department of Finance published its *Code of Practice for the Governance of State Bodies*. While an earlier version (published in 1992) had been designed to support board members on state-owned commercial enterprises, the Code was quickly adopted by non-commercial

Table 6.1   Timeline of some selected public sector reform initiatives in Ireland

1994	Launch by Prime Minister of the Strategic Management Initiative (SMI). Departments start to produce Strategy Statements.
1996	Publication of Delivering Better Government (DBG).
1997	*Public Service Management Act 1997.* Quality Customer Service Initiative and first publication by departments of individual Customer Service Action Plans. *Freedom of Information Act.*
1998	Government Approval given for Multi-annual Budgets and enhanced Administrative Budgets.
1999	Design of new Civil Service policies and systems on HRM and Performance Management. Government approval of Financial Management system.
2000	Launch of Performance Management and Development System (PMDS) for the civil service.
2002	Independent Evaluation on SMI (PA Evaluation). Independent Evaluation on Quality Customer Service (Butler). Review of Partnership within the Civil Service (National Centre for Partnership and Performance).
2003	Publication of Social Partnership Agreement *Sustaining Progress.*
2004	PMDS Evaluation (Mercer): main recommendation to integrate PMDS with wider HR system, including assessment systems. *Public Services Management (Recruitment and Appointments) Act.* Civil Service Code of Standards Agreed.
2006	Publication of Social Partnership Agreement *Towards 2016* contains further commitments in relation to modernisation of the public service.
2008	Publication of the OECD's Review of the Irish Public Service.

Source: Hardiman and Mac Carthaigh (2008: appendix 1).

bodies. Though not legally binding, it became a key document in detailing the financial and legal responsibilities of board members. The Code was also of considerable use to departments as it detailed their role in ensuring that agencies under their remit had adequate monitoring and reporting systems in place. Also, new 'Public Financial Procedures' produced by the Department of Finance placed responsibility for the financial performance of agencies with their parent departments.

6.3   History of agencification and public sector reform in Flanders

6.3.1   Types of agencies in Flanders

As described below, the 1954 law rationalising the different agency types in Flanders provides a framework for understanding their different forms of affiliation. Unlike Ireland, each agency has its own enacting legislation. There are several types of agency in Flanders under the 1954 law, largely referring to the broad classification of departmental, public law and private

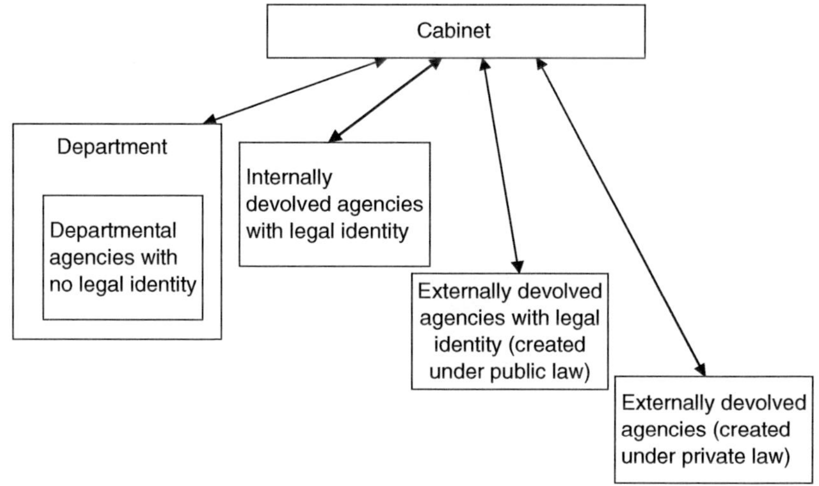

Figure 6.3 Relationship between cabinet and agencies in Flanders

law agencies (OECD 2002a). Chapter 4 lists the types of agencies at the time the survey was conducted, together with their number in the total population, and in the database used for this study.

The 2003 framework law on better governmental policy referred to largely similar formal-legal types of agencies, but changed their governance arrangements. Existing agencies were reformed according to the 2003 framework law in 2006–2007.

A typical characteristic concerning the governance of Flemish agencies under both 1954 legislation and the 2003 legislation is that agencies are controlled by, and accountable to, the cabinet directly, in particular the involved portfolio minister and, under the 1954 law, the Minister of Finance. Formally and in practice, the role of parent departments in the control of agencies in the same policy area is very unclear, and usually interpreted in a minimal way. In that way, departments and agencies are de facto considered to be on the same hierarchical level. In contrast, almost all Norwegian and Irish agencies report to their parent department. Figure 6.3 represents the nature of the delegation and accountability links between the Flemish agencies and government.

As with Ireland and Norway, Flemish private law agencies (state-owned companies and government foundations) and agencies with a hybrid legal basis (both public and private law) are excluded from the analysis.

6.3.2 History of agency creation in Flanders

The complex federal governing arrangements within Belgium, mentioned in Chapter 5, has also been responsible for considerable activity in the development of Flemish agencies. Until 1970, before the process of regionalization in Belgium began, public sector organisations were all federal. As agencification at the regional level of the Flemish government was closely linked to the regionalization of federal competencies, we start this overview with the history of agencies at the federal level of Belgium. We focus on the *'Openbare Instellingen'*, so-called 'parastatal' organizations with their own legal personality under public law, and which are the most important group of agencies.

In the latter half of the nineteenth century, and specifically after 1860, the central government started to create such agencies in order to perform more industrial or commercial services, such as banking. By 1913, their numbers were still quite limited; only five public law agencies were active at that time (Verhoest 2002). Their numbers increased steadily in the interwar years, but multiplied at a faster rate after the Second World War, in large part because of the development of the social security system. By 1955, there were 95 public law agencies.

However, because of this proliferation in agencies and the enormous heterogeneity in forms and control arrangements, public opinion feared an increasing fragmentation and weakening of state authority. Moreover, it was perceived that the public agencies were financially uncontrollable (Verhoest 2002). Parliament, describing the situation as 'a complete chaos', issued the Law of 16 March 1954 concerning the control of some institutions with a public function. In order to rationalize the control and oversight of these agencies, this law defined four types of public institutions with different control regimes for most of the existing public law agencies.

The first type (Category A organizations) referred to public law agencies without a board and under the hierarchy of the minister, but having their own legal identity. The other categories referred to public law agencies with a governing board, where the functional minister had an oversight function only. The focus of the control regime under the 1954 Law was strongly *ex ante* on administrative, financial and budgetary issues, giving much controlling power to the responsible minister and the ministers of Finance and of the Civil Service. Later amendments of the Law made the control arrangements even stricter and increased its remit. The Law was increasingly subject to a double criticism: proponents claimed a failure to enforce compliance to the law, whereas opponents stated that the strict nature of the law limited the management autonomy of agencies to the extent that they could not work efficiently (Verhoest 2002). However, the law did not slow down the pace of agency creation. By 1976, 249 public law agencies were active.

The history of agencification at the Flemish regional level begins with the first state reform in 1970, with four public law agencies being decentralized. The second state reform in 1980 gave the Flemish government the right to create public law agencies under the 1954 law in the, now, regionalized policy areas (welfare, health, environment, tourism, housing and employment).

This led to 11 more public law agencies, of which some replaced the pre-1980 agencies. However, the 'big' state reform of 1988, involving the regionalization of major competences (education, public works and mobility, economic policy) led to a boom in the number of Flemish public law agencies. Twenty-six public agencies were created in the period 1988–1992 of which the majority were *'sui generis'* agencies with control arrangements partially diverging from those under 1954 law. In the period 1992–1999, another 18 organizations were established with Category A status.

Three different types of agency emerged during the period of regionalization – agencies that previously had a federal remit but were now succeeded by an equivalent for Flanders; agencies that were created for the Flemish community but which became the responsibility of the new Flemish government; and agencies that were newly established (Verschuere 2006: 35). The majority of Flemish agencies were of the first type, and hence federalization can be identified as a major driver for agencification in Flanders. That does not mean, however, that agencies were transferred without reconsideration or organizational changes.

At the time of the survey (see Chapter 4), 74 agencies based on public law existed. Under the new 2003 framework law, these agencies, as well as parts of departments, were reorganized into a similar number of agencies. The periphery of the Flemish public sector contained about 120 private law agencies in the form of not-for-profit associations or companies of limited liability. These private law agencies, although very numerous, were kept outside most of the public sector reforms in the period 1990–2003, to which we now turn.

6.3.3 Public sector reforms in Flanders

The history and form of agencification at the Flemish government level is not only strongly intertwined with the different phases of regionalization, but also heavily influenced by general public sector reforms, as well as by recurrent debates on the controllability of agencies. The state reform of 1988 provided a stimulus for the new Flemish government to reconsider the structure of the Flemish public sector, in order to be able to take over the large number of federal competences and civil servants in an efficient way. One Ministry of the Flemish Community was created, which functioned as a matrix organization with, on the one hand, seven line departments and, on the other, two powerful central departments. In particular, the Department of General Affairs, which included within its remit the administration of the state budget, finances and civil service, was very active in regulating for resource management by line entities. During 1993–1996 the departments were subjected to a set of organization-related reforms, including the development of missions, objectives, processes and supporting systems (such as ICT and staff planning).

Strategic planning was also introduced. A reform with considerable impact on the public law agencies was the adoption in 1993 of the new personnel statute for Flemish civil servants, which substituted the (stricter) federal 1937 statute. The new Flemish personnel statute emphasized modern HRM policies and new HR instruments, such as the setting of individual objectives, evaluation, promotion based on merit and seniority, a rather weak form of result-oriented pay (in the form of acceleration of pecuniary career), and the possibility for personnel dismissal.

In a critical report in 1996, the Court of Audit pointed to the ever-increasing financial and budgetary importance of the public law agencies, and several problems associated with the governance arrangements stipulated in the 1954 law. First, the creation of *sui generic* public law agencies led to a new variety of governance mechanisms. Moreover, many of the regulations and standards set by the 1954 law were never implemented because of a lack of action by the involved ministers or by the agencies. The *ex ante* control mechanisms, and in particular the figure of the *Commissaire de Gouvernement*, were considered to function ineffectively because of a shortage of expertise and capacity. The 1954 law stipulated the presence of two *Commissaires de Gouvernement* representing the functional minister and the minister of Finances in the governing board of the agencies. These *Commissaires* had the right to *ex ante* veto decisions by the agencies which they considered to be acting contrary to the 'general interest', the law, and the budgetary context. Moreover, the functional minister had the right to intervene in agency decisions if the governing board exhibited problematic decision-making behaviour.

The Parliament proposed to develop a new framework legislation to substitute the 1954 law and form the basis for a new governmental landscape. At the time of the Court of Audit report, the government, and particularly the Department of Finance, had already drafted such a framework law in 1994–1995, based on a problem analysis similar to that of the Court of Audit. The 1995 Declaration of the new government also stressed the development of such a framework law and a scrutiny of the agency landscape. The proposal for a new framework law emphasized clearer governance mechanisms as well as less input control if agencies negotiated a performance contract. However, this framework law did not survive the deliberations of the coalition government. Nor did the planned review of the agency landscape occur.

Nevertheless, in the subsequent years the Minister of Finance managed to have several elements in that framework law approved through separate regulations related to issues such as cash management and insurance. From 1994 onwards, organizations could develop voluntary budget implementation plans, which implied less *ex ante* file-specific budget controls in exchange for more planning and monitoring by budgetary tables, indicators and audits.

From 1998 onwards public law agencies were required to have an accrual accounting system with facultative analytical dimensions besides a cash-based budget reporting (ESER '95), with a common and uniform accounting and reporting scheme. In addition, during that period several agencies were granted exemptions from punctual financial and budgetary regulations on an ad hoc basis because of the specificity of their task or because they agreed a performance contract with their portfolio minister.

In the 1990s, the Flemish administration piloted and launched several initiatives related to performance control, such as the development of performance indicators, effect indicators, efficiency analysis, performance objectives for senior managers, performance budgeting and reporting, zero-based budgeting and strategic planning. Some of these initiatives were only indirectly targeted at the agencies, but they created at least a growing awareness of performance management. The 1995 Declaration of the Vandenbrande II government stressed the contractualization of the relationship between government and agencies in order to shift the control of agencies towards outputs. Some experiences with performance contracting had already produced learning results for designing good performance contracts, but now a general introduction of performance contracts was aimed for. In such multi-year performance contracts, the minister and the agency board or CEO agreed upon the performance objectives and targets for a period of three to five years, as well as the financial resources for the agency. From the 1990s onwards, the agencies' CEOs could be held accountable for the achievement of individual yearly performance objectives, and evaluation could affect their salary. During this period, both government and Parliament became more reluctant to establish new public law agencies with their own governing boards. Emphasis shifted towards the creation of departmental agencies and public law agencies in the form of budgetary funds.

After a period of multiple partial initiatives, the new Liberal-Socialist-Green government decided in 1999 to implement the parliamentary resolution in its entirety. The 'Beter Bestuurlijk Beleid' (BBB) reforms were implemented in 2006 and integrated many of the reform elements, which had been partially adopted in the 1990s: the agencification of policy implementation tasks; the restructuring of existing agencies into four clear types of agencies; a radical shift to *ex post* and result-oriented control by a further introduction of performance contracts; an overall introduction of accrual accounting and increased budgetary flexibility for departments and agencies, and the marketization of management support tasks. This resulted in a structural reorganization of the agency landscape with about 70 departmental and public law agencies being created in 2006–2007. However, several of the announced reforms concerning result control, managerial autonomy and marketization are not yet implemented. Financial management autonomy is still regulated by the 1954 law, and HRM autonomy by a general personnel statute. At the time of writing, media and pressure groups increasingly vent concerns about over-fragmentation in government policy, caused partially by this large-scale reorganization. This study however focuses on the pre-BBB agency landscape.

6.4   The agency landscape in the three states

Now that we have described for the three states the agency types, the history of agency creation and the public sector reforms which might affect agencies, we ask: What does the agency landscape in the three states look like in terms of task, policy area, governance structure, size and other key features? We focus on the agencies included in our joint database of 226 organizations. In preparation for later sections in this book where the various dimensions of autonomy, control and internal management are examined, we provide here some of the basic descriptive features of these agencies. For each state, the following characteristics are considered:

- the primary tasks of the agencies
- the policy area in which the agencies operate
- the governance structure of the agencies
- the territorial structure of the agencies
- the age of the agencies
- the size of the agencies (as measured by staff numbers)
- the size of agency budgets
- the sources of the agencies' income

Whether, and how, these features are expected to affect the autonomy, control and internal management of agencies is discussed in Chapter 10.

6.4.1   Primary task

In the academic literature, several classifications of agencies have been launched, based on tasks, state activities and functions or roles (cf. Roness 2007). For example, the point of departure for Dunleavy (1991) in his 'bureau-shaping model' is the different types of budgets (that is, expenditures) that agencies have (see also James 2003). He distinguishes between five basic agency types: 1) delivery agencies, 2) regulatory agencies, 3) transfer agencies, 4) contract agencies, and 5) control agencies. He includes some additional categories to achieve comprehensive coverage: 6) taxing agencies, 7) trading agencies, and 8) service agencies. Alternatively, Bouckaert and Peters (2004) differentiate between different types of activities and functions that autonomous agencies may perform: 1) implementation (direct service delivery or transfer of funds), 2) regulation, 3) advice and policy development, 4) information, 5) research, 6) tribunals and public enquiries, and 7) representation. Since our starting point is primarily related to the NPM ideal-type model, we need a classification that emphasizes the types of tasks that are particularly important for this model: regulatory and service delivery tasks. Thus, based on the answers in the surveys and other available information on agencies in the three states, we differentiate between four types of primary task, which are:

- Policy formulation: encompassing activities of policy design, policy advice and policy evaluation that are directed towards political authorities (cabinet, Parliament).
- Service delivery: referring to production and direct delivery of general public services on a not-for-profit basis for free, or partly financed by the user. It includes several activities directed towards citizens, and/or private or public organisations: direct service provision; counselling or advisory tasks; informative and guidance tasks; administrative services of different types; equipment and delivery services; training and competence building. Public sector organizations with commercial activities as primary tasks are not included in our database.
- Regulation: encompassing activities of scrutiny/regulation/control that are closely connected to either the follow-up of or regulation/control in accordance with regulations, rules, laws, contracts or agreements. It does not refer to making or concretizing rules or laws (see below, other kinds of exercising public authority). A vital criterion is that regulatory functions are directed towards other public or private agents or institutions outside the organization which maintains the function.
- Exercising other kinds of public authority: referring to the execution of tasks according to, on behalf of or based in law, regulations or precepts. Such tasks are normally subordinate to rules for procedure. It encompasses the legitimate use of violence by states and by parts of public administration, such as policing and prisons; interest-mediating and conflict-resolving and processing in accordance with law, such as arbitration committees; administration and evaluation of precepts; and transfer of funds, such as taxes and subsidies.

When comparing states in Part III we examine the subgroup of service delivery agencies, while in comparing agencies in Part IV we make two distinctions: service delivery agencies versus other agencies, and regulatory agencies versus other agencies. As with the other relevant agency characteristics, the distribution of agencies in the three states according to primary task is presented in Table 6.2. In this table we have also included the exact codes of the categories of the independent variables being used in Part IV.

In the whole population, almost every second agency (47 per cent) has service delivery as a primary task. The share of service delivery agencies is highest in Flanders (61 per cent) and lowest in Ireland (35 per cent). In all states, the number of agencies having regulation as a primary task is lower than for service delivery, ranging from 7 per cent in Flanders to 21 per cent

Table 6.2 Agency features in Flanders, Norway and Ireland. Percentages of agencies with different types of characteristics

Agency characteristics		Flanders	Norway	Ireland	Total
Primary tasks					
0	Policy formulation	7	4	9	6
0	Other kinds of exercising public authority	24	27	35	29
0/1	Regulation	9	18	21	17
0/1	Service delivery	61	50	35	47
N		*46*	*103*	*77*	*226*
Policy area					
0/1	Economic policy	48	19	27	28
0/1	Welfare and social policy	39	49	51	47
0	Other	13	32	22	25
N		*46*	*103*	*77*	*226*
Existence of a board					
0	No	46	52	28	43
1	Yes	54	48	72	57
N		*46*	*101*	*74*	*221*
Agency type					
0	Single national organisation without territorial sub-units	67	73	83	75
1	Single national organisation with territorial sub-units	33	27	17	25
N		*46*	*103*	*77*	*226*
Agency age					
0	1990 or later	59	35	51	45
1	Before 1990	41	65	49	55
N		*46*	*103*	*75*	*224*
Agency size					
0	Small (less than 50 FTEs)	40	36	61	45
0.5	Medium (50–199 FTEs)	22	29	25	36
1	Large (200 or more FTEs)	38	35	13	28
N		*45*	*103*	*75*	*223*
Budget size					
0	Small (<5 m)	33	32	55	40
0.5	Medium (5–40 m)	26	40	32	27
1	Large (>40 m)	41	29	12	26
N		*46*	*98*	*74*	*218*
Source of income					
0	Solely government budget allocation	41	43	54	46
0.5	Mixed	41	49	30	41
1	Other sources than government dominant	17	9	16	13
N		*46*	*101*	*76*	*223*

in Ireland. Moreover, in all states, less than 10 per cent of agencies have policy formulation as a primary task. Finally, exercising other kinds of public authority as a primary task is a bit more common in Ireland (35 per cent) than in Norway (27 per cent) and Flanders (24 per cent).

Although we focus our analyses on the primary task which the agencies report performing, we should not forget that agencies may perform more than one task. For example, about half of the agencies in the total database reported having service delivery as a primary task, but about 10 per cent perform an additional task. Moreover, about 25 per cent of agencies report having service delivery as a secondary task. Also, regulation is combined with other tasks, mostly exercising other kinds of public authority. The same holds for policy formulation, where 6 per cent of all agencies perform this as a primary task, but about 14 per cent of all agencies report that they perform this task as secondary task. When compared across states, the majority of service delivery agencies and regulatory agencies in Norway are multi-functional, combining several tasks, compared to half or less than half of such agencies in Flanders and Ireland. Overall, many agencies combine their primary task with other tasks, an issue to which we return at the end of the book.

6.4.2 Policy area

The classification of agencies according to policy area has been undertaken by academics as well as by practitioners. Our starting point is the United Nations *Classification of Functions of Government* (COFOG), which has emerged as an international standard (cf. Roness 2007). This classification lists ten main types of activities (each having between five and nine sub-types): (1) general public services, (2) defence, (3) public order and safety, (4) economic affairs, (5) environmental protection, (6) housing and community amenities, (7) health, (8) recreation, culture and religion, (9) education and (10) social protection. We have simplified this by distinguishing between three more encompassing types of policy area:

- welfare and social policy (categories 6–10)
- economic policy (category 4)
- others (categories 1, 2, 3, 5)

Overall, there are more agencies in the welfare and social policy area (47 per cent) than in the economic policy area (28 per cent). This is particularly the case in Norway, but also in Ireland, where half of the agencies are active in the welfare and social policy area. On the other hand, in Flanders about half of all agencies are active in economic policy.

6.4.3   Governance structure

Governing boards provide a key steering and oversight mechanism for agency control. In the absence of a board, other mechanisms (such as regular reporting, external audit or meetings with parent departments) may need to be employed. Overall, for the three states, just over half of the agencies have a board, with Ireland having the highest number (72 per cent), as Table 6.2 demonstrates.

A more detailed analysis, not shown here, identifies that agencies which are primarily involved in policy formulation are most likely to have a board, as are the majority of those involved in service delivery. However, for agencies involved in regulation and exercising other kinds of public authority, the picture is less clear and almost half of the agencies surveyed in this category do not have a board.

The composition of the board may also be relevant in considering whether, and how, it can be a mechanism for agency control. We find that two out of three of the agencies with a board have central government representatives among their board memberships, and this share is even higher in Flanders (88 per cent). Two out of three of the agencies with a board have independent experts among their board memberships, and mostly so in Norway and Ireland. Interest groups and other stakeholders (64 per cent), employees (44 per cent) and other groups (37 per cent) are also represented on many boards. It is of particular importance for the role of the board as an instrument for government control whether the boards consist solely of government representatives, have no government representatives, or have a combination of government representatives and representatives from interest groups or other stakeholders. Overall, for agencies with a board, only a small part (4 per cent) have government representatives alone, about one third (32 per cent) have no government representatives, while a majority (64 per cent) has a mixture of government and non-government representatives on their boards. For agencies with a governing board, boards with solely non-government representatives are quite rare in Flanders (12 per cent), while they are more common in Ireland (32 per cent) and in Norway (44 per cent). Besides stakeholder involvement, in Flanders, governing boards seem to have a stronger controlling role, while in Norway and Ireland the emphasis seems to be on bringing in independent expertise.

6.4.4   Agency type

Agencies may or may not have subordinate units, normally organized according to territory. Of the agencies in our data set, 75 per cent have no territorial component while the remainder do. The breakdown by state in Table 6.2 reveals that having a territorial component for agencies is most common in Flanders, where one third of agencies do so. This is also true for over a quarter of Norwegian agencies, but is a less common phenomenon in the highly centralized Irish state.

6.4.5 Agency age

As this chapter details, the three states differ in relation to periods in which most agencies were created. Using 1990 as a key stage in the development of agencies, our data demonstrates that overall, 45 per cent of agencies examined were established in 1990 or later (cf. Table 6.2). That year saw the beginning of a strong 'wave' of agencification in Ireland, as well as in Flanders. In Norway, most agencies were created prior to 1990. We may also add that agency age does not vary much across type of primary task in Norway. In Ireland there is a somewhat larger share of regulatory agencies among pre-1990 agencies, while in Flanders there is a somewhat larger share of service delivery agencies among pre-1990 agencies.

6.4.6 Agency size

We use the number of full-time employees (FTEs) as our prime indicator of agency size. A small agency is defined as one with fewer than 50 FTEs, a medium agency as one with between 50 and 199 FTEs, and a large agency as one with 200 FTEs or more. We find that, overall, almost half of the agencies (45 per cent) were of small size while 27 per cent were of medium size and the remainder (28 per cent) employed a large number of staff. Table 6.2 also demonstrates that while Ireland has the largest proportion of small agencies (61 per cent), Norway and Flanders respectively had a considerable proportion of large agencies (35 per cent and 38 per cent).

6.4.7 Agency budget

As with the number of staff, we differentiate here between agencies according to whether their budget is small (less than €5 million), medium (€5 to €40 million) or large (more than €40 million). Budget sizes ranged from €20,000 to €1240 million with the average being €68 million (and the median €9.6 million). Forty per cent of agencies are in the small category, while 34 per cent are considered to be of medium size. The remainder (26 per cent) have large budgets. When we break this down by state in Table 6.2 we find that as with the staff numbers, Ireland has the largest proportion of agencies with small budgets (55 per cent) and Flanders has the highest proportion of those with large budgets (41 per cent).

6.4.8 Source of income

The vast majority of agencies in our database rely heavily on budgetary allocations from the government to perform their work. Overall, for 46 per cent of the agencies, a budget allocation from government is their sole source of income, while a further 41 per cent have a mixed source of funding, albeit with government funding remaining the dominant source. Only 13 per cent receive either all or the majority of their income from sources other than the government. Table 6.2 also demonstrates that over half of Irish agencies (54 per cent) are completely reliant on government funding, while in Norway almost half (49 per cent) generate their income by supplementing a central budgetary allocation with other sources of revenue. The proportion of Irish and Flemish agencies depending on sources other than government for the major part of their income is approximately double that of Norway. It may also be added that not relying solely on a budgetary allocation from government is most common among service delivery agencies.

6.5 Conclusion

Although state agencies have existed for a considerable time in all three states, only Norway has a long-standing tradition of state agency governance, combined with clear rationales for agency creation, such as professionalization and the need for a strategic focus within parent departments. Moreover, state agencies in Norway, which are within the civil service, and which belong to quite clearly defined agency types, lack their own legal identity and are under control of parent departments, which represents an overall ambition of integration of the state apparatus (Lægreid et al. 2003, forthcoming). Subsequent waves of agencification throughout the last two centuries have been followed since 1980 by a decrease and consolidation of state agencies. In contrast, in Ireland, agency creation was slow but has accelerated towards a boom since 1990. Agency types are not clearly legally defined and their creation occurs in an ad hoc manner, and mainly to host new tasks that the government takes on. In Flanders, agencification is heavily linked to the regionalization of competences. The agency types which are defined in framework laws, refer to similar federal types. Although the governance of the different agency types is defined in law, no clear rationale has existed for agency creation which has occurred mainly in an ad hoc and pragmatic way. Typical for Flanders is that parent departments play hardly any role in supervising and controlling state agencies. This is seen as the role of the minister and his or her political secretariat.

All three states have seen several reform initiatives during the last three decades, Norway since the mid-1980s and Ireland and Flanders mainly after 1990. Reform strategies in all three states have been incremental, and with a combined focus on sectoral and government-wide initiatives. Although in all three states there was some rhetorical reference to NPM (Lægreid et al. 2003, forthcoming; Verhoest et al. 2004b; Hardiman and MacCarthaigh 2008), they may be considered as rather slow and non-radical reformers. In Norway, administrative reform before the late 1990s was mainly oriented towards predominantly managerial aspects of NPM, like structural devolution, increasing managerial flexibilities and MBOR. After that, more market-oriented aspects of NPM were included in reform initiatives, which were much more contested. Under the umbrella of SMI, the Irish government has focused its reform initiatives on issues such as strategic management, performance measurement and reporting, new accountability systems, HRM and pay for performance, financial flexibilities, efficiency reviews, quality customer service and regulatory reform. Similarly, in Flanders, internal reorganization, the introduction of modern HRM with incentives, strategic planning, initiatives for performance measurement, result-oriented financial management and contractualization of government-agency relationships were at the forefront. These initiatives in all three states share a common orientation towards managerial modernization and performance management systems, which may be considered as core managerial aspects of NPM, that is, 'letting managers manage' and 'making them manage' (Pollitt and Bouckaert 2004). How do these announced reform initiatives influence the autonomy, control and internal management of agencies in the three states? Do they bring about more similarities between agencies in the three states? This question is central to Part III.

As to the characteristics of agencies, we find some similarities as well as some differences in the agency landscape across the three states. Among the differences are the fact that Ireland has fewer service delivery agencies, more agencies with a governing board, more agencies without territorial sub-units, more small agencies (according to staff and budget size) and more agencies which rely solely on government budget allocations than Flanders and Norway. Flanders, on the other hand, has fewer regulatory agencies, more agencies in the economic policy area, more young agencies and more agencies with a large budget than the others. However, and even more importantly, in all states, a number of agencies are included in all relevant categories with regard to primary task, policy area, (the existence of a) governing board, agency type, agency age, agency size, budget of the agency and source of income. This facilitates the forthcoming analyses in Parts III and IV.

Part III
Comparing States

7
Theories on Similarities and Dissimilarities Between States

7.1 Introduction

In Chapter 3, we briefly formulated our model for comparing agencies within and across states. We described a model of conflicting pressures for similarity and dissimilarity at international, state and agency level. Figure 3.1 presents this model in a schematic way. In this chapter we ask what kind of state-level factors/pressures for divergence may influence the actual autonomy and control of agencies in the three states. As outlined in Chapter 5, these factors may be clustered in five main sets with different levels of change-ability: environmental pressures, dimensions of politico-administrative culture, structural and functional elements of polity, actor constellations and deliberate action (for example, general reform programmes).

As several students of comparative public management reform argue, internationally diffused NPM ideas and concepts may have different content, effects and implications in different settings or states. Pollitt and Bouckaert (2004, Chapter 2) explain the different emanations of public management reform in 12 OECD states by presenting reforms as products of elite decision making, which are inspired, triggered or restrained by international public management ideas, socio-economic forces and environmental events (like scandals), existing administrative structures and cultures and characteristics of main actors in the political system. In their model, all these factors may create a considerable distance between, respectively, international reform ideas, the content of an announced reform programme, its subsequent implementation and its actual outcomes. Wollmann (2003b, 2004) presents six explanatory factors for public-sector reforms: the socio-economic and budgetary context, including external influences (for example, the EU); the starting conditions; the institutional and cultural traditions; the institutional (polity) setting; actor constellations, intentions, interests, 'will and skill' of the relevant political, administrative and socio-economic actors; and national and international discourses. In a somewhat simpler model, which we utilize in this book, Christensen and Lægreid

(2001b: 24) emphasize how external reform concepts and programmes are filtered, interpreted and modified by a combination of the national political-administrative history and culture, as well as national polity features. They also mention environmental factors, such as the economic situation. In later variants, this model is made more dynamic by making reference to how political leaders have varying amounts of leeway to launch and implement NPM and post-NPM reforms via administrative design and an active administrative policy (Christensen and Lægreid 2007a: 6).

In summary, internationally propagated NPM doctrines on the optimal public administration structure and the related ideal-type agency create homogenizing pressures for governments in different states. However, the extent to which governments are receptive of these ideas, and their actual translation, is influenced and moulded by state-level factors. Based on Pollitt and Bouckaert (2004) and other comparative studies (Lijphart 1999; Christensen and Lægreid 2001a; Lalenis et al. 2002; Wollmann 2003a), we selected a number of relevant aspects of politico-administrative systems. Table 5.1 provides a full listing of these elements. While in Chapter 5 we outlined how these state-level factors manifest themselves in the three states, here we emphasize whether, and how, they may affect the adoption and translation of international NPM ideas. We now discuss their expected influence on agency autonomy, control and management at length and formulate hypotheses referring to the relative ranking of states. We refer the reader to Chapter 5 for more details about the politico-administrative systems in the three states.

Two lines of reasoning provide our points of departure to formulate hypotheses. The first builds on a change management approach in public sector reform (see Pollitt and Bouckaert 2004; Elgie 2006). It considers the influence of environmental, cultural and polity features, and actor constellations on the degree of leeway available to politicians to launch and implement internationally propagated NPM reforms in a radical way, or not. In some political systems, politicians are much more powerful in pursuing radical reforms, and may respond much more easily and quickly to international reform pressures.

According to a second line of reasoning, we consider the autonomy and control of agencies as being related to the more general issue of delegation in parliamentary democracies from a principal-agent approach. According to Strøm (2003: 64), delegation within a parliamentary democracy can be conceived as a chain of principal-agent relations, encompassing delegation from voters, to legislators, prime minister and cabinet, individual ministers, to civil servants and agencies. Within this chain of delegation our focus is on the autonomy of agencies as an act of delegation from ministers to agency heads. The level of agencies' autonomy and, as such, the level of decision-making power delegated to agencies, are deliberately decided upon by risk-averse rationally acting political actors, who are confronted with potential agency problems of adverse selection and moral hazard. The feasibility of delegation within a parliamentary system is heavily influenced by a number of environmental and polity features, as well as specific actor constellations. For instance, building on North-American theories of structural choice (Moe 1990; Horn 1995; Huber and Shipan 2002; Elgie 2006; Yesilkagit and Christensen forthcoming), many scholars assert that the autonomy and control of agencies are dependent on the level of policy conflict between different actors and policy uncertainty at the time of agency creation. The levels of policy conflict and political uncertainty within a parliamentary politico-administrative system are determined by different power relationships as well as institutional factors (Strøm 2003: 72–3). In this principal-agent delegation approach, autonomy of agencies is the result of an interaction of democratic and extra-democratic checks and balances in a game with the responsible minister, other cabinet ministers, Parliament, political parties, interest groups and citizens, as the main actors.

As we elaborate in this chapter, these two approaches result in hypotheses which are mostly mutually contrasting and sometimes supplementary (cf. Roness 2009). However, it is not relevant to elaborate both approaches for all features. For example, cultural features only lead to hypotheses in the change management approach, as the principal-agent delegation approach does not account for cultural differences between states.

Additionally, both approaches focus partially on different dependent variables. In the change management approach, state-level features would induce politicians to adopt NPM reforms, implying the creation of NPM ideal-type agencies with high levels of managerial autonomy, result control and modern management. However, the principal-agent delegation approach focuses mainly on the autonomy of agencies, but does not say much about the expected level of result control, or use of management techniques. Implicitly, the control of agencies by the minister and parent department is considered in this approach to be the inverse of agency autonomy. Therefore, hypotheses in the principal agent delegation approach will only refer to the expected influence on the agencies' autonomy.

Lastly, the two approaches differ with regard to the time period included in the analysis. The change management approach principally considers expectations of what has happened since 1980, that is, when NPM doctrines started to become globally spread. The principal-agent delegation approach focuses on the full period of agency creation. For this approach we use data for the relevant state-level factors which, if available for each state, go back as far as possible.

We first elaborate the hypotheses based on the change management approach. The principal-agent delegation approach and its related hypotheses are presented in the second part of the chapter. In the conclusion to this chapter we list all formulated hypotheses and cluster them according to the approach used.

7.2   A change management approach to state differences

7.2.1   Environmental factors in a change management approach

A first and crucial environmental factor influencing the creation of agencies is the relationship with relevant international and supranational organizations (for example the OECD or EU), which are active in propagating the NPM ideal-type agency form (Dimitrakopoulos and Passas 2003). The extent of the link between the states under review and these international bodies will determine to some extent the openness of the state elite to the international discourse on agencification. All three states are active member of the OECD and World Bank and hence they are confronted with international propaganda on NPM reforms in general, and on ideal-type agencies in particular. However, also the EU puts normative pressure on the domestic administration and also more directly demands certain ways of organizing and controlling state apparatus to secure competition in the internal market, like the establishment of autonomous control and regulatory agencies (Jacobsson et al. 2004). Studies on the Europeanization of state administrations provide evidence for a substantial influence (Goetz 2000; Knill 2001). Hence, the isomorphic pressure stemming from the rather late EEA accession and EU doctrines on the public administration structures in Norway may be expected to be less profound, when compared with Ireland and Flanders, who are long-standing full members of the EU.

Hc1   Time and high intensity of EU adhesion fosters agency
reforms along NPM lines. *Therefore, we expect that agencies
in Ireland and Flanders will have relatively more management
autonomy, more result control and will use more management
techniques, compared to Norwegian agencies*

Public sector reforms in many states have been triggered by other external pressures, like economic and budgetary fiscal crises (Wollmann 2003b; Pollitt and Bouckaert 2004). As one of the forerunners in implementing radical NPM-like reforms, New Zealand did this when facing the most severe economic crisis in its existence. In line with the evidence of comparative studies on NPM reforms (Pollitt and Bouckaert 2004), budgetary-fiscal pressure may be expected to have a stimulating effect on the creation of NPM ideal-type agencies. Reforms which stimulate managerial flexibility and private-sector type management are assumed to lead to more efficiency (cf. New Zealand). Furthermore, in some states, agencification helps to keep financial resources outside the official state budget, resulting in virtually lower state debts. As shown in Chapter 5, Norway was the only state under review which had not faced times of national fiscal pressure since 1980, in contrast to Flanders and Ireland.

Hc2   High intensity of economic and budgetary-fiscal crises
since 1980s leads to agencies which are more NPM-like,
*Hence, we expect agencies with high managerial autonomy,
result control and management techniques being relatively more
present in Flanders, and to a lesser extent Ireland, compared to
Norway.*

A last source of environmental pressure contributing to public sector reform could stem from a lack of perceived government legitimacy by citizens and the media. Low or declining trust in government and public services could stimulate politicians to act and reform, either effectively or symbolically. In the period 1980–2000, Belgian and Flemish citizens' confidence in their civil service appears to be the lowest of the three states. Such confidence declined in Norway, whereas in Ireland it remained quite high over the whole period.

Hc3   Relatively low level of trust in government fosters agency
reforms along NPM lines. *Hence, we expect agencies with
high managerial autonomy, result control and management
techniques being relatively more present in Flanders, followed
by Norway, compared to Ireland.*

7.2.2   Politico-administrative culture in a change management approach

As the most enduring and stable element of politico-administrative regimes, our model addresses the politico-administrative culture of states in order to understand and explain similar or different levels and patterns of agency autonomy and control. Internationally propagated images of agencies will be pursued in agency reform programmes within states, as long these images fit – or are adapted to fit – the existing politico-administrative culture, historical-institutional tradition and legacies, and dominant styles of governance (Christensen and Lægreid 2001b; Lalenis et al. 2002; Wollmann 2003b; Pollitt and Bouckaert 2004, Chapter 3; Schedler and Proeller 2007).

As shown in the analytical framework (see Table 5.1), politico-administrative culture is operationalized in two ways. A first important element is the legal tradition of a state, and more specifically, the dominance of administrative law in politico-administrative interactions. As outlined in Chapter 5, two major legal traditions may be distinguished: the *Rechtsstaat* tradition or model and the common law tradition, which aligns with the public interest model (Pierre 1995; Kickert and Hakvoort 2000, table 11.1; Lalenis et al. 2002: 36). Depending on their historical-institutional past, most states belong quite clearly to the one or other tradition, but some states (for example, The Netherlands) appear to have a mixed tradition, or to move away from this dichotomy (Lalenis et al. 2002; Pollitt and Bouckaert 2004: 53–4). We shall elaborate on the possible consequences for agencification in states that adhere to these legal models.

In the continental system and the corresponding *Rechtsstaat*, administrative law is the basic guiding principle for public administration, and the legality of all administrative actions is at the core of accountability systems. Administrative culture is deductive and rationalistic, and bureaucratic action is based on respect for the authority of the law. Considerable attention is given to precedent and a concern with equity, at least in the sense of equality before the law (Kickert and Hakvoort 2000; Peters 2001; Pollitt and Bouckaert 2004). Generally, *Rechtsstaat*-based states are more accepting of bureaucracy as an appropriate form of social organization (Peters 2001). In contrast, in those states with a common law tradition, where the public interest model is central, there is a more pragmatic attitude towards administrative action and individual entrepreneurs within public administration are valued (Peters 2001). Key values for administrative action in such states are fairness and independence of the play of sectional interests, with pragmatism and flexibility as qualities. Overall, public interest states are more open to the basic ideas of NPM, which stress entrepreneurial and pragmatic values (Peters 2001).

Agencies in *Rechtsstaat* systems would need a clear legal basis in law or statute because of their legitimacy and accountability requirements. Moreover, their functioning would be regulated in rather uniform legal frameworks. Because of these regulations, one can expect that the level of autonomy will be more uniform across agencies and relatively low. Control of agencies, as well as their internal management will be bureaucratic in kind. In contrast, agencies in public interest states may be expected to be closer to the NPM ideal-type model, combining high levels of (managerial) autonomy, and exhibiting higher levels of result control, including accountability for results and the existence of performance-related rewards or sanctions. Overall, internal management within agencies will be more geared towards their private sector equivalents. The need for a firm legal basis for agencies is much less in 'public interest models'. A clear example is demonstrated in the creation of numerous next steps agencies in the UK without changing a single statute (Pollitt and Bouckaert 2004).

A second element of politico-administrative culture included in our framework is in the different dimensions of organizational and societal culture, according to Hofstede (2001). Although these dimensions refer rather to standard cultures in organizations in general and in wider society, these dimensions and tendencies are mirrored in the structure and procedures of the public administration system (cf. Peters 2001). As outlined in Chapter 5, Hofstede (2001) distinguishes between five different dimensions. He applies these to different societal levels and identifies how specific cultural dimensions reveal themselves in family life, at school, in the workplace, in political, legal and belief systems. We focus here solely on three dimensions: power distance, uncertainty avoidance and masculinity, for only on these three aspects do the three states under review show clear differences. As identified in Chapter 5, the scores of the three states on individualism and on long-term orientation are respectively high and moderate for all three states.

When power distance scores high, centralization and tall organization pyramids are preferred (Hofstede 2001: 107–8). Hierarchy in organizations reflects the existential inequality. Managers rely on formal rules and subordinates are directed by formal authority and sanctions. Authoritative leadership and close supervision leads to satisfaction, performance and productivity. Control systems are based on 'political' rather than 'strategic' thinking and trust in subordinates is lacking (Hofstede 2001: 382). In work situations with a high uncertainty avoidance culture (Hofstede 2001: 169–70), there will be also a preference for larger organizations and for hierarchical control. Top managers are involved in operations rather than strategy, and their power depends on the control of uncertainties. There is a need for more detail in planning and more short-term feedback (Hofstede 2001: 382). Legal systems are characterized by numerous precise laws and regulations (Hofstede 2001: 180). High power distance and high uncertainty avoidance lead to quite similar hypotheses. Hofstede (2001: 377 exhibit 8.1) uses these two dimensions to define four types of functioning of organizations (adhocracy, personnel bureaucracy, work-flow bureaucracy and full bureaucracy) and links them with states. When this is applied to public administration, it is clear that governments in states with high values of power distance and uncertainty avoidance, such as Flanders, would prefer rather centralized, large bureaucracies, in which work processes are strictly prescribed by regulations or by law. Moreover, the combination of high power distance and uncertainty avoidance inhibits the empowerment of lower organizational levels (Hofstede 2001: 388–9). This implies lower levels of autonomy for agencies and less use of management techniques. In contrast, in states with low to medium levels of power distance and uncertainty avoidance, such as Ireland and Norway, a structure in which autonomous agencies are common, with wide diversity in forms and with less detailed control would be preferred (in other words, the positions of adhocracy or divisionalized form).

A society with high masculinity considers money, material things and performance orientedness as more important (Hofstede 2001: 299), than quality of life. A performance and punitive society is seen as ideal (Hofstede 2001: 323). In work situations, emphasis is placed on mutual competition and performance and there is a preference for higher pay (instead of fewer working hours) (Hofstede 2001: 318). According to Hofstede (2001: 391), the adoption of Management by Objectives and individual pecuniary rewards and sanctions seems to be most appropriate in cultures with rather low values of power distance, low values of uncertainty avoidance and high masculinity values. This is of relevance with regard to result control of agencies.

Based on these considerations of the importance of legal tradition, the (separate and combined) cultural dimensions of Hofstede (2001), and the relative score of the three states being examined, we may formulate a hypothesis with respect to dominant patterns of agency autonomy and control across states.

Hc4   A legal tradition in common law, combined with a public
       interest model, low values with regard to power distance
       and uncertainty avoidance and high values with regard to
       masculinity foster agency reforms along NPM lines.
       Therefore, we expect agencies with relatively higher levels of
       managerial autonomy, result control and use of management
       techniques in Ireland, followed by Norway, compared to
       Flanders, where there is a relative preference for bureaucratic
       organizational forms.

7.2.3   Structural and functional elements of polity in a change management approach

Different elements of a state's polity can influence the autonomy, control and internal management of agencies. In Chapter 5 we list some relevant elements. Here we discuss whether, and how, they may make a difference for agency autonomy and control, building on the change management perspective.

The extent to which a government uses agency-type organizational forms and grants their agencies autonomy, depends first on the kind of tasks that the central government engages in on the one hand and the kind of tasks taken up by the private sector or by lower levels of government on the other hand. General ideas and models concerning task allocation between the public and private sectors in a state differ. Some states adhere to liberal ideas of the minimal state, with many tasks devolved to the market, whereas other states see a more encompassing role for the public sector, including the provision of numerous services and goods to citizens. There is a global tendency towards the core business of a state being 'steering rather than rowing'. Nevertheless, even within Europe states still differ quite strongly on the relative involvement of the public or private sectors in economic life in general. In systems where the public sector takes on a large number of tasks, compared to states with a minimal role, the size, number and kind of tasks may allow for the creation of relatively more agencies, as well as agencies which need extended autonomy to fulfil these tasks. When governments are extensively involved in providing services or commercial and industrial services and

goods, agencies will have particular need for extended managerial autonomy in order to provide those goods and services in an efficient way. On
the other hand, in states where most of the policy implementation or service delivery is privatized or contracted out, there is less need for agency
creation, or for agencies with extended autonomy, for reasons of efficiency.
Moreover, since NPM reforms are mainly grounded in managerial-type ideas
of private sector enterprises, public sector organizations that focus on service
provision are much more conducive to the introduction of NPM-like reforms
than public sector organizations with other tasks such as policy design or
regulation.

As shown in Chapter 5, the task allocation between public and private
sectors is quite different in Norway, where the public sector provides many
comprehensive services, unlike Ireland, which adheres more to the ideal of a
minimal state in areas such as welfare policy. Flanders has a public sector that
cooperates strongly with private actors, at least in the fields of education and
welfare policy. In other sectors, the Flemish public sector is still quite comprehensive in its service provision. One may also expect that states with a
liberal market economy, which is very much reliant on foreign investments
and trade, like in Ireland, is relatively more attuned to market-based disciplines in the state sector, and that it would have been to the forefront of
NPM experiments (Hardiman and MacCarthaigh 2008: 4).

Hc5   A relatively strong involvement of public sector in
      economic life, in public service delivery and policy
      implementation fosters agency reforms along NPM lines.
      We expect Norway to have more autonomous, result-controlled
      and well managed agencies, compared to Flanders, and
      certainly Ireland.

A further element is the very basic feature of state structure, and more
specifically, the level of vertical dispersion of authority between the central,
regional/provincial and local levels of government. As outlined in Chapter 5,
the state structure can be labelled, on the one hand unitarist – regionalist –
federalist, depending on the division of authority between national and
regional levels, and on the other hand, centralized – decentralized, depending on the relations between central and local levels (Loughlin and Peters
1997; Christensen and Lægreid 2001b; Lalenis et al. 2002; Pollitt and
Bouckaert 2004).

One can think of several ways in which the state structure may affect
agency autonomy and control. First, the very division of competences
between the different levels of government will also influence the tasks and
number of agencies – and, consequently, their autonomy and control – at
the central level. In a state where policy implementation and service delivery is principally devolved to the local level, public sector organizations at

the central level will focus primarily on policy design and regulation. As such NPM-oriented reforms leading to higher autonomy and result control for public sector organizations at the central level will take root less easily in a strongly decentralized state than in a highly centralized state. According to Pollitt and Bouckaert (2004: 43), the state structure may also influence how radical the pace and scope of public sector reforms will be. In centralized states, public management content and trajectories are expected to be much more encompassing in scope, and uniform, compared to highly federalized or decentralized states because of the multiple veto points in the latter states (Wollmann 2003b; Pollitt and Bouckaert 2004: 43). Moreover, the reform programmes are expected to focus more heavily on issues concerning service delivery, rather than on a more strategic concern with policy impacts and overall outcomes (Pollitt and Bouckaert 2004: 43).

Hc6   A strong centralization of service delivery and policy
      implementation fosters agency reforms along NPM
      lines (at central level) compared to states where local
      government levels are strongly involved in service delivery
      and policy implementation. *Hence, we expect Ireland as a
      strong centralist state to have many agencies at the national
      level performing service delivery tasks, which would be reflected
      in high levels of managerial autonomy, result control and use of
      management techniques, compared to Norway and Flanders
      where decentralization leads to less radical agency reform
      programmes.*

As noted in Chapter 5, a further element of polity is concerned with the structural and functional elements of the political system and the executive government. It can be summarized by referring to the extent to which a democracy is perceived as being consensualist or majoritarian (cf. the executives-parties dimension of Lijphart 1999: 248; Weaver and Rockman 1993). Overall, in a change management approach, one can expect that in a majoritarian political system public sector reforms will be more encompassing, radical and 'sweeping', than in more consensualist democracies (Wollmann 2003b; Pollitt and Bouckaert 2004). In the latter, bargaining and compromise between multiple actors (for example, political parties and interest groups) is a dominant (and necessary) pattern of decision making (Lijphart 1999; Strøm et al. 2003b). According to Christensen and Lægreid (2001b: 28), the two-party Westminster system makes the forceful implementation of NPM-like reforms more likely than in states with a multi-party system and minority governments. This implies that the electoral system and the nature of executive government plays a role in the extent to which states will be able to restructure existing agencies (and create new agencies) along the lines of the ideal-type agency model, with a high level of managerial autonomy, result control and use of modern management techniques (see Zuna 2001; Pollitt et al. 2004). A continuum with regard to the nature of executive government could move from the more majoritarian single-party government, to minimal-winning coalitions and minority cabinets, to strongly consensual oversized executives or 'grand coalitions' (Wollmann 2003b; Pollitt and Bouckaert 2004).

When considering the period 1980–2004, in Ireland most governments were multi-party coalitions, with some minority cabinets. All but one Norwegian cabinet in this period were minority cabinets, while Flanders has mainly had oversized coalitions.

Hc7   A more majoritarian cabinet structure (in the period 1980–2004) fosters agency reforms along NPM lines. *As in all three states consensual cabinet structures were omnipresent in the period 1980–2004, we cannot expect any major differences in the level of managerial autonomy, result control and management techniques between the different states.*

Despite these similarities in having predominantly consensual cabinet structures, cabinets in the three states differed in their stability and party composition. Indeed, how radical reforms are may also be affected by cabinet duration. When there is a high turnover of cabinets and, consequently, substantial parliamentary turbulence, the stability necessary to employ substantial administrative reforms is lacking (Christensen and Lægreid 2001b).

Hc8   Longer cabinet lifespan (in the period 1980–2004) fosters agency reforms along NPM lines. When considering the period of 1980–2004, average cabinet lifespan is substantially higher in Flanders than in Ireland or Norway, *which lead us to expect Flemish agencies to have relatively higher levels of managerial autonomy, result control and modern management than in the other two states.*

Moreover, partisan composition in these coalition and minority cabinets could make a difference when it comes to radical NPM-like changes. NPM reforms are rooted in a rationalistic, economic view of government, emphasizing the superiority of the private sector and the market in terms of efficiency. It may be expected that right-wing oriented political parties are more inclined to align with such view on government (Lonti 2005), whereas left-wing political parties would place more emphasis on the merits of the public sector in its own right and with its traditional Weberian features. In the period 1980–2004 Ireland had 14 years of centre-right cabinets, whereas Norway experienced a dominance of Labour cabinets.

Hc9   More dominance of right-wing political parties in cabinet
(in the period 1980–2004) fosters agency reforms along
NPM lines. *Therefore, agency reform in Ireland is expected to
be more radical and more NPM-like, compared to Norway.
Flanders with its grand coalitions encompassing left and right
oriented political parties would hold the middle position.*

As noted in Chapter 5, the level of involvement of societal interest groups
in political and administrative decision making is another important element of the political system. Lijphart (1999) distinguishes between plural
and corporatist interest group systems, where Loughlin and Peters (1997: 46)
see the first mainly in Anglo-Saxon states and the latter in, for example,
Germany and Sweden. In states with a corporatist tradition, one would
expect that during the enactment of reform programmes, the main societal
interest groups, like labour unions and employer organizations, will be consulted and play an important role. Most likely, this consultative tradition
will result in less radical agency reform programmes. A related element is
the strength of civil service unions (Christensen and Lægreid 2001b, Roness
2001b). Industrial relations, particularly in the public sector, also play a
strong influence on the extent to which agencification can occur, and the
manner in which this happens. For example, in Norwegian administrative
policy-making the manner of working with civil service unions has traditionally been one of cooperation and mutual understanding, in contrast to
the more confrontational style of Anglo-American reforms with respect to
these unions.

Hc10   A comparatively less corporatist state tradition and less
involvement of strongly organized interest groups in
policy design and implementation fosters agency reforms
along NPM lines. *Therefore, we expect that Ireland with its
pluralistic interest representation tradition will have agencies
with relatively higher levels of managerial autonomy, result
control and modern management, than in both Norway and
Flanders with their strong corporatist state tradition.*

7.2.4   Actor constellations in a change management approach

Until now we have focused mainly on elements of the politico-
administrative regimes as potential state-level factors to explain the features
of agencies in different states. These elements are fundamental, in the sense
that changes are effected over a long period. However, the actual autonomy
and control of agencies is also influenced by more dynamic aspects, which
are related to actor constellations as well as the instrumental actions taken by
political and administrative leaders (Christensen and Lægreid 2001b). Actor
constellations deal with the intentions, interests, discourses and the 'will

and skill' of the relevant political, administrative and socio-economic actors (Wollmann 2003b) with regard to public sector reforms. In their model of public management reform, Pollitt and Bouckaert (2004) refer to the concept of politico-administrative elite perceptions of what management reforms are desirable, as well as feasible. We will focus on the perception of different actors within the administrative system with respect to the functioning of public administration, as well as the relative power position.

A specific actor constellation is the kind of relationship between political executives and senior civil servants, the so-called 'mandarins'. Several scholars (Pierre 1995; Christensen and Lægreid 2001b; Pollitt and Bouckaert 2004) point to this important interface in explaining the scope and pace of public management reform initiatives. Relevant dimensions are the extent to which career patterns are integrated and the extent of politicization of senior civil service functions. Both features enhance the ownership of public management reforms, but can cause instability in their extreme forms, as in the case of the US spoil system (Pollitt and Bouckaert 2004). Also, the division of labour, and roles, between ministers and senior civil servants, and the extent to which the relation is cooperative or adversarial, is important. In a cooperative relationship, senior civil servants are acknowledged as expert in policy design and implementation. In their analysis, Aberbach et al. (1981; cf. Peters 1987; Horn 1995) assert that senior civil servants tend to be rather conservative and aim to preserve the status quo, whereas politicians tend to emphasize radical changes. Therefore, cooperative relationships will reduce the radicalness of reforms.

Hc11   Politico-administrative relations (between ministers and senior civil servants) that are relatively adversarial and distrusting, with limited involvement of senior civil servants in policy making, fosters agency reforms along NPM lines. *Hence, we expect that Flanders, where senior civil servant positions tend to be politicized and relations adversarial, will have agencies with relatively higher levels of managerial autonomy, result control and modern management, compared to Norway and Ireland, where politico-administrative relationships are cooperative.*

The institutional position of central departments and their ministers, in particularly the prime minister, matters too, because the reform ideas and the relative power of these central departments towards the line departments will influence the dynamics of government-wide administrative reform to a great extent. Strong central ministers and departments exert pressures for uniformity of management reforms and may be the drivers for more radical NPM-based changes government-wide. For example, in New Zealand radical reforms were driven by the Treasury and the State Service Commission. In the UK agency reforms were initiated and enforced by the prime minister and the Treasury.

Hc12   A relatively stronger position of the prime minister and central departments vis-à-vis line ministers and line departments fosters agency reforms along NPM lines. Both Irish and Flemish prime ministers and central departments hold particularly strong positions, compared to Norway. *Therefore, we expect that Irish and Flemish agencies to have higher levels of managerial autonomy, result control and use of managerial techniques, than Norwegian agencies.*

The positions, discourses, power and resources of politico-administrative actors will influence the dynamics within an administrative system. Embedded in the politico-administrative regime, they will shape the content, normative frameworks and implementation of reform programmes as well as past and current experiences with those programmes. In turn, these reform programmes and related deliberate actions will shape the actual autonomy, control, internal management of agencies that we observe.

Hc13   The general and government-wide agency-specific reform programmes explain the actual levels of agency autonomy, result control and use of management techniques in the three states.

Hence, talk of reform, such as announced reform programmes, should be in line with the effective reform actions that are happening in reality, and which are, in turn leading, to effective reform results (Pollitt 2001). As described in Chapter 6, Norway, Flanders and Ireland have all announced several general initiatives to increase the autonomy of agencies, and to control agencies on results. In all three states we would expect to see the specific effects of these particular reforms on the actual perceived levels of autonomy, control and internal management.

7.3   A principal-agent delegation approach to state differences

Before proceeding further, we require some additional information on the principal agent delegation approach, in order to understand the formulated hypotheses on agency autonomy based on this theoretical framework. Structural choice theorists argue that there are essentially two logics that rationally acting politicians may follow when creating agencies (Horn 1995; Yesilkagit and Christensen forthcoming). The logic of agency problems, in which political principals do not trust their agents to execute their decisions correctly, will induce principals to create agencies with low levels of autonomy in which information asymmetry is easily bridged (Van Leerdam 1999). On the other hand, the logic of the commitment problem, referring to long-term policy uncertainty as to whether or not future enacting coalitions will subvert the current coalitions' policies, will lead to the creation of highly autonomous agencies, which are insulated from political changes and interference (Yesilkagit 2004a). Which logic prevails depends on a number of factors and the level of the transaction costs incurred. By default, the enacting coalition will prefer the creation of public sector organizations with low levels of autonomy, in order to minimize the agency problem. Formulating detailed regulations and procedures which curb *ex ante* the autonomy of the agency increases legislative costs for politicians. Reducing information asymmetry by *ex ante* and *ex post* control mechanisms increases control costs for the controlling politicians and the controlled agency experiences efficiency losses because of red tape (Horn 1995; Huber and Shipan 2002).

The feasibility of such autonomy-reducing rules and regulations, as well as control mechanisms, depends largely on the capacity, resources and instruments of ministers and Parliament to enhance compliance and performance by agencies, as well as the kinds of task the agency performs (in terms of measurability) and the extent of clear goals (Horn 1995). In specific situations commitment costs are potentially high, and hence the commitment logic might prevail. In situations where policy conflict between politicians is high, agencies will be more insulated from political oversight than those established in situations with lower levels of policy conflict (Yesilkagit 2004a; cf. Huber and Shipan 2002 for an opposite conclusion). Similarly, political uncertainty refers to the threat for enacting cabinets that agencies created by them will be drastically changed or abolished by other cabinets in the future. Moe (1990; see also Yesilkagit and Christensen forthcoming) stresses that political uncertainty urges politicians to design public bureaucracies so that they have the capacity to pursue their policy goals in a world in which their enemies later may achieve the right to govern. In this logic, agencies established by governments in contexts of high political uncertainty will be more insulated from political oversight than those established in regimes with low political uncertainty (Yesilkagit and Christensen forthcoming). In the case of a change of cabinet coalition, highly autonomous agencies provide more procedural and institutional safeguards for policy continuity.

The level of policy conflict and political uncertainty within a parliamentary politico-administrative system is determined by different power relations and institutional factors (Strøm 2003: 72). First, there are the relations within the executive government, as determined by the cabinet structure, the partisan composition of government, and the cabinet stability. For instance, policy conflict is considered to be higher within a coalition or minority government than in single-party majority governments. Second, the relations between the legislative and executive power play a role. The enacting coalition in Parliament will prefer agencies with low autonomy, except where parliamentary *ex post* control mechanisms are sufficient on cabinets' or agencies' actions. Third, political actors will allow for substantial autonomy for agencies if there are sufficient extra-parliamentary checks and constraints on agency actions, such as the corporatist involvement of interest groups (Horn 1995), potential appeals by citizens to agency actions, judicial review, or freedom of information obligations (Strøm 2003). Last, the autonomy of agencies vis-à-vis their minister and cabinet within a principal-agent relationship is largely influenced by the politico-administrative interface and specific actor constellations. These include the division of labour between ministers and civil servants and their mutual trust, the capacity of individual ministers and departments to control agency behaviour, and the role and power of central departments and their ministers as multiple principals. As previously noted, in this principal agent delegation framework, the autonomy of agencies is, as such, the result of an interaction of democratic and extra-democratic checks and balances.

7.3.1   Environmental factors in a principal agent delegation approach

One environmental factor which can be considered as an alternative to a principal agent approach is the occurrence of economic and budgetary fiscal crises. In a world in which political actors are risk-averse, one would expect that budgetary fiscal stress would trigger a recentralization of (specific kinds of) formerly devolved managerial flexibility in terms of budget and personnel. On the other hand, huge budgetary surpluses make devolution of managerial autonomy less risky for politicians.

Hp1   Economic and budgetary-fiscal crises cause risk-averse
       politicians to reduce (management) autonomy of agencies.
       Therefore, we expect that Norway has created more agencies
       with extended levels of autonomy, compared to Ireland and
       Flanders.

7.3.2   Structural and functional elements of polity in a principal-agent delegation approach

The prevailing type of executive government is not only expected to influence the degree to which reforms are radical, but may also be expected to affect the features of agency autonomy. When conceiving agency autonomy as a form of delegation in the principal agent delegation framework, we may ask ourselves in what way both cabinet structure and composition enhance policy conflict or political uncertainty. Scholars have linked both policy conflict and political uncertainty to the type of executive cabinet, by using measures like cabinet durability, cabinet size or portfolio turnover (Huber and Shipan 2002). Several authors (Huber and Shipan 2002; Yesilkagit and

Christensen forthcoming) assume that the level of policy conflict increases in executive cabinet systems ranging from single-party majority, single-party minority, coalition majority, coalition minority and oversized coalitions. Again, we have to take into account the extent to which parliamentary approval is needed for the creation and allocation of autonomy to agencies. Likewise, political uncertainty is assumed to pose a greater threat for minority cabinets than for majority cabinets, since 'the average cabinet duration of minority governments is substantially lower than the average life span of majority governments' (Lijphart 1999: 137).

In order to formulate hypotheses, we consider the time periods in which agencies were created in each state: 1945–2004 for Norway and Ireland, and 1980–2004 for Flanders. Looking at the kind of dominant cabinet structure, policy conflict seems to be much higher in Flanders, with its grand-sized coalitions and minimal winning coalitions. In the period 1945–2004 somewhat less than one third of both Norwegian and Irish agencies were single-party majority cabinets with the rest having more consensual cabinet structures.

Hp2   Higher policy conflict in more consensualist-type cabinet
       structures lead to more autonomous agencies. *Therefore, we
       expect Flemish agencies to have relatively higher autonomy
       levels than agencies in the other two states.*

Similarly, when looking at the longest possible period of agency creation for each state, political uncertainty as measured by cabinet instability (the broad conception measured by Lijphart 1999) is lower in Flanders than in Norway and Ireland. Therefore, we expect politicians in Norway and Ireland to have greater incentives to shield their agencies from political influence, in order to prevent other parties overruling the policies they have introduced.

Hp3   Higher policy uncertainty, as visible in shorter cabinet
       lifespans, lead to more autonomous agencies. *Therefore, we
       expect that the autonomy of agencies will be more substantial
       in Norway and Ireland, compared to Flanders.*

Principally, the enacting coalition will prefer public sector organizations with low autonomy and over which it has high levels of control, in order to reduce agency costs stemming from opportunistic bureaucratic behaviour. Policy conflict and policy uncertainty provide for two major exceptions. But there are also other conditions in which the enacting coalition may create agencies with higher levels of autonomy. Since costs for drafting detailed legislation and regulations, as well as for substantial ministerial or departmental control of agencies, are high, other forms of checks and balances may provide sufficient insurance for politicians to allow highly autonomous agencies. The politicians in Parliament will prefer agencies with low autonomy, except where *ex post* control mechanisms on cabinets' or agencies' actions are sufficiently present and functioning. In the latter case, autonomy for agencies will be more readily allowed by Parliament.

The controls that Parliament can exert *ex post* upon the actions of the executive powers in general, and of the agencies in particular, can take several forms. These include the extent to which parliamentary questions can elicit useful information; the power of parliamentary committees to scrutinize departments and agencies and to call agency heads personally to account; the presence of formal and regular reporting requirements for agencies to Parliament; the powers of an audit office, reporting to Parliament, to perform regular and ad hoc audits on financial and performance aspects of agencies (Bergman et al. 2003). As outlined in Chapter 5, *ex post* parliamentary controls are better developed in Norway and Flanders where parliamentary factions have rather effective formal or informal means to control administrative actor, compared to the less powerful Parliament in Ireland.

Hp4   The presence of more *ex post* parliamentary controls on
       the actions of the executive in general, and of agencies in
       particular, allows for more autonomous agencies. *Therefore,*
       we expect Irish agencies to have relatively lower levels of
       autonomy compared to Norwegian and Flemish agencies.

However, there are also extra-parliamentary controls on agencies in action. The involvement of well-organized constituents and interest groups in the management of policies and public sector organizations through corporatist structures assures the enacting coalition that the policy-implementing bureaucrats will not divert from the original policy objectives. Developing the ideas of Moe (1990) further in the context of parliamentary states, structural choice scholars assert that whereas politicians will stress the agency logic with respect to agency creation, leading to agencies with low autonomy and strong government control, interest groups will let the commitment logic of agency creation prevail (see also Horn 1995; Van Leerdam 1999; Van Thiel 2001; Yesilkagit 2004a; Moynihan and Pandey 2006; Yesilkagit and Christensen forthcoming). Creating highly autonomous agencies with little possibility for new coalitions to intervene in policy implementation reduces the uncertainty for interest groups (and for the enacting coalition) of radical policy changes. In states with powerful and concentrated interest groups, which are highly involved in political and administrative decisions making (Horn 1995), one would expect agencies to have relatively high levels of autonomy. However, the pure agency logic will prevail in political systems with dispersed interest representation structures, resulting in rather low levels of autonomy and elaborate control arrangements (Yesilkagit and Christensen forthcoming).

Hp5   More involvement of strongly organized interest groups in policy formulation and implementation (corporatist tradition) leads to more autonomous agencies. *Hence, we expect that both Norway and Flanders will have agencies with relatively higher levels of autonomy, compared to Ireland.*

Politicians may also rely on other kinds of 'fire alarms' and extra-parliamentary controls to keep highly autonomous agencies in check, similar to the instruments used to keep the executive and ministers in check (Strøm 2003). Citizens' appeal to a parliamentary or independent Ombudsman against the decisions of agencies, the application of the Freedom of Information Act to actions by agencies, as well as the level of judicial review of administrative actions, are all relevant here. In Norway and Flanders such extra-parliamentary checks seem to be relatively strongly elaborated, whereas in Ireland they are less well developed as a consequence of a tradition of executive secrecy (Mitchell 2003: 439).

Hp6   The presence of stronger 'fire alarms' and extra-parliamentary controls allows for more autonomous agencies. *Hence, we expect agency autonomy to be relatively higher in Norway and Flanders than in Ireland.*

7.3.3   Actor constellations in a principal-agent delegation approach

Structural choice theorists assume that ministers prefer micro-management of public sector organizations under their remit, in order to avoid moral hazard problems (Horn 1995; Huber and Shipan 2002). Such micro-management is less necessary when the ministers can trust their senior civil servants and agency heads to implement their policies without deviation. Where the relationships between ministers and senior civil servants are cooperative and trust-based, agencies may experience more autonomy and less control. If such relationships are more adversarial and distrusting, ministers must build capacity to control agencies intensively. The extent to which the positions of agency heads are politicized, may also make a difference. Strøm (2003), and also Horn (1995), refer to patronage and partisan influence over the appointment of officials as an important control mechanism to minimize principal agent problems between politicians and administrators. However, agency heads, appointed on the basis of their political affiliation with one of the political parties in power, may experience high levels of autonomy vis-à-vis the incumbent government, but will face distrust and substantial control once other political parties take over power (Horn 1995: 100).

As noted in Chapter 5, Flanders would fit this picture neatly with significant numbers of political appointments in the public administration, combined with a low turnover of senior civil servants. In order to overcome distrust in politico-administrative relations, Flemish ministers deploy large political secretariats, which perform substantial policy design and implementation functions. Moreover, government commissioners on the governing boards of agencies control all decisions of agencies *ex ante* (De Winter and Dumont 2003: 273). This leads to micro-management of the administration (Huber and Shipan 2002). In both Norway and Ireland relations seems to be much more cooperative.

Hp7   Politico-administrative relations between ministers and
      senior civil servants, which are relatively cooperative and
      trusting, with high involvement of senior civil servants in
      policy making, combined with low ministerial capacity to
      control agencies' actions, lead to more autonomous
      agencies. *Therefore, we expect agencies in Norway and Ireland
      to experience more autonomy, compared to Flanders.*

The capacity of individual ministers to control the behaviour of agencies is, of course, not only determined by personal staff, but also by the size and competences of the parent department which supports the minister. This crucial role of parent departments is proven in many instances: in Latvia, for example, the lack of departmental capacity to guide and monitor large groups of agencies resulted in 'undesirable financial practices' and other problems (OECD 2002; see also McGauran and Humphreys 2004). In states where parent departments are relatively large in size (in terms of FTEs) when compared with the size of the agencies, we expect parent departments to have a strong position and more capacity to control their agencies, in contrast to states where parent departments are relatively small.

Hp8   A weak position of the parent department with limited
      capacity to control agencies (in terms of FTEs) leads to
      more autonomous agencies. *Based on the capacity and
      relative size of the parent departments as described in Chapter
      5, we expect agencies in Ireland to have less autonomy
      compared to Norway and, to a lesser extent, Flanders.*

Furthermore, the relative power position and competencies of central departments of finance/civil service will affect the actual autonomy and control of agencies directly. For instance, a strong department of finance may have a dominant role in decision-making procedures for financial management transactions by agencies, like shifting budgets, or taking loans.

Table 7.1 Overview of hypotheses based on the change management approach and the principal agent delegation approach

Hypotheses based on change management approach	Hypotheses concerning: mn. autonomy, result control, mn. techniques	Hypotheses based principal agent delegation approach	Hypotheses concerning autonomy (mn./policy)
Environmental pressures			
Hc1. Time and high intensity of EU-adhesion fosters agency reforms along NPM lines	(F & I) > N		
Hc2. High intensity of economic and budgetary-fiscal crises since 1980s fosters agency reforms along NPM lines	(F > I) > N	Hp1. Economic and budgetary-fiscal crises causes risk averse politicians to reduce (management) autonomy of agencies	N > (I > F)
Hc3. Relatively low level of trust in government fosters agency reforms along NPM lines	(F > N) > I		
Politico-administrative culture			
Hc4. Legal tradition in common law, public interest model, low values concerning: power distance and uncertainty avoidance and high values concerning: masculinity foster agency reforms along NPM lines	I > N > F Less strict regulated Less uniform		
Polity			
Hc5. A relatively limited involvement of private sector in economic life, in public service delivery and policy implementation fosters agency reforms along NPM lines	N > (F > I)		

Table 7.1 (Continued)

Hypotheses based on change management approach	Hypotheses concerning: mn. autonomy, result control, mn. techniques	Hypotheses based principal agent delegation approach	Hypotheses concerning autonomy (mn./policy)
Hc6. A strong centralization of service delivery and policy implementation fosters agency reforms along NPM lines (at central level) compared to states where local governmental levels are strongly involved in service delivery and policy implementation	I > (F&N)		
Hc7. A more majoritarian cabinet structure (in the period 1980–2004) fosters agency reforms along NPM lines	N = (I = F)	Hp2. Higher policy conflict in more consensualist-type cabinet structures lead to more autonomous agencies	F > (N&I)
Hc8. Longer cabinet lifespan (in the period 1980–2004) fosters agency reforms along NPM lines	F > (N&I)	Hp3. Higher policy uncertainty, as visible in shorter cabinet lifespans, lead to more autonomous agencies	(N&I) > F
Hc9. More dominance of right-wing political parties in cabinet (parliament) (in the period 1980–2004) fosters agency reforms along NPM lines	I > (F > N)		

		Hp4. The presence of more *ex post* parliamentary controls on the actions of the executive in general and of agencies in particular allows for more autonomous agencies	(N&F) > I
Hc10. Less corporatist state tradition and less involvement of strongly organized interest groups in policy formulation and implementation fosters agency reforms along NPM lines	I > (F&N)	Hp5. More involvement of strongly organized interest groups in policy formulation and implementation (corporatist tradition) leads to more autonomous agencies	(N&F) > I
		Hp6. The presence of stronger 'fire alarms' and extra-parliamentary controls (ombudsman, FOI, judicial review) allows for more autonomous agencies	(N&F) > I
Actor constellations			
Hc11. Politico-administrative relations (between ministers and senior civil servants) which are relatively adversarial and distrusting, with limited involvement of senior civil servants in policy making, fosters agency reforms along NPM lines	F > (I&N)	Hp7. Politico-administrative relations (between ministers and senior civil servants) which are relatively cooperative and trusting, with high involvement of senior civil servants in policy making, combined with low ministerial capacity to control agencies' actions, lead to more autonomous agencies	(N&I) > F

Table 7.1   (Continued)

Hypotheses based on change management approach	Hypotheses concerning: mn. autonomy, result control, mn. techniques	Hypotheses based principal agent delegation approach	Hypotheses concerning autonomy (mn./policy)
		Hp8. A weak position of the parent department with limited capacity to control agencies leads to more autonomous agencies	N > (F > I)
Hc12. Stronger position of PM and central departments versus line ministers and line departments fosters agency reforms along NPM lines	(I > F) > N	Hp9. Weaker position of PM and central departments, with less capacity to control line ministers and line entities leads to more autonomous agencies	N > (F > I)
Deliberate action – reform programmes			
Hc13. General and government-wide agency-specific reform programmes (see Chapter 6) explain the actual levels of agency autonomy, result control and use of management techniques (talk about reform, reform actions and reform results are aligned)	In all three states reforms were announced		

Hp9   A relatively weak position of the PM and central
        departments, with less capacity to control line ministers
        and line entities leads to more autonomous agencies.
        *Therefore, Norway is expected to have relatively more
        autonomous agencies, compared to Ireland and (to a lesser
        extent), to Flanders.*

7.4   Summary

In this chapter we have discussed the potential relevance of five sets of
state-level factors for explaining state-level differences with respect agency
autonomy, control and management techniques. Based on two approaches –
a change management approach and a principal agent delegation approach –
we formulated expectations about the autonomy, control and use of
management techniques in the three different states. Table 7.1 lists these
hypotheses, which we formulated based on the two approaches. The next
chapter compares agencies in the three states with respect to their autonomy, control and internal management. In Chapter 9 we attempt to explain
the findings by referring to the hypotheses elaborated in this chapter.

8
Comparing Agency Autonomy, Control and Internal Management Between States

8.1 Introduction

In previous chapters we discussed the features of the ideal-type agency as elements within the NPM doctrine, and asserted that there are international pressures for similarity and convergence towards this NPM model. In our model, we expect that these doctrines are being transformed when they meet state-specific polity, administrative culture and actor constellations. This transformation may lead to different responses in different states (state-level pressures for divergence and dissimilarity).

In this part we analyse whether or not these international pressures have led to similarities or dissimilarities between agencies in the three states. Therefore, the following questions will be answered:

1) To what extent do the autonomy, control and internal management of agencies in the three states match with the NPM ideal-type agency model and its features (high levels of managerial autonomy, high levels of result control, and high use of management techniques)?
2) Do we find uniformity/similarities between agencies with regard to autonomy, control and internal management in the three states (particularly in the total sample of agencies); in subsamples of agencies with similar features (more specifically for agencies with the same size, age, task, governance structure and sources of income) or in the subsample of service delivery agencies with a governing board?
3) If we find similarities, are these consistent with NPM ideal-type prescriptions?

We compare the level of autonomy of agencies with similar features between the three states, in order to answer our second research question:

*RQ 2:   Do agencies in the three states or agencies with similar
features in the states (like governance structure and tasks)
show similar or dissimilar levels and patterns of autonomy,
control and use of management techniques? Are similarities
between agencies in the three states in line with the NPM
ideal-type agency model?*

This chapter focuses on the comparison of autonomy, control and the use of management techniques by agencies in the three states, as perceived by the senior management of these agencies. In order to achieve this, we analyse the data in search of similar and dissimilar patterns in the following way. Each kind of autonomy, control and management technique is compared between agencies in the three states at three different levels. A first level is a comparison of autonomy, control and internal management for all agencies. Second, agencies with similar features as regards size, tasks, source of income and governance structure are compared with respect to the level of autonomy, control and use of management techniques. More specifically, we compare agencies where we expect to find most reform initiatives in line with international practice, and with the greatest impact, because of their importance for the government or kind of task performed. Therefore, we compare agencies of a large size in terms of staff numbers, with service delivery as their primary task, agencies fully funded by the government budget, agencies with a governing board, and agencies created in 1990 or later. Third, we combine some of these features and form a subgroup, consisting of agencies with a board and with service delivery as a primary task. Again, for this subgroup we compare the level of autonomy, control and the use of management techniques, respectively. Besides comparing frequencies and distributions, we use the non-parametric Mann-Whitney test to identify any significant patterns between states. This test allows for samples which substantially differ with respect to the number of observations. The test, therefore, helps us to establish a ranking of the three states for each sample (for example on autonomy in relation to salary $N > (I = F)$).

By moving from comparison on the first level over the second, to the third level, we achieve an increasingly refined insight into the level of autonomy and control shared by agencies with similar features in the three states. The subsequent levels of analysis allow us to delineate subsamples with increasingly similar features. The central question in this part is:

Do we observe similar levels of autonomy, control or use of management techniques, respectively, when we compare the agencies in the three states, and does the level of similarity increase when we focus on the comparison of more specifically delineated subsamples with similar features?

By comparing the rankings of the three states for the total sample and the subsamples, we define a dominant pattern for each kind of autonomy, control and management technique. If the ranking of the total sample is different in more than half of the subsamples, we take the pattern observed in the diverging subsamples as the dominant one. In most cases the pattern of the total samples was to be observed in most of the subsamples also. In only some cases was the dominant pattern different from that found in the total sample. Similarities and dissimilarities are explained in Chapter 9 by referring to three different levels of aspects of politico-administrative regimes.

8.2 Agency autonomy

Two kinds of autonomy are distinguished here – managerial autonomy and policy autonomy. With respect to managerial autonomy, the focus in this book is on HRM and financial management autonomy. As shown in Chapter 1, the NPM ideal-type agency model would display high levels of managerial autonomy, since the relaxation of input controls in order to increase flexibility and efficient management is crucial to the NPM idea of 'letting managers manage' (OECD 1997). This high level of managerial autonomy would relate both to financial management autonomy (for example, budget flexibility) and HRM autonomy, since for most government organizations personnel is the most important production factor. However, the NPM doctrine would advise a rather low level of policy autonomy, for agencies are considered to be policy-implementing bodies with their objectives and policy instruments set in legislation and also in performance-based contracts with ministers. Policy design is a task for core departments, with ministers and Parliament deciding on policy. There is an organizational split between policy design and policy implementation, which is conducted by structurally disaggregated agencies in some kind of principal-agent relationship.

> Do agencies in some or all three states match these ideal-type levels of managerial and policy autonomy, and even more importantly, do we see similarities or convergence between the three states in line with this ideal-type image?

Table 8.1 shows the percentages of agencies in each state and their various levels of perceived autonomy.

8.2.1 Human resource management autonomy

As outlined in Chapter 2, human resource management autonomy is measured on both a strategic level (can they set general rules with respect to

Table 8.1 Extent of agency autonomy in Norway, Ireland and Flanders (percentages)

Kind of autonomy	Level of autonomy	Norway	Ireland	Flanders
HRM Autonomy – salary	No operational or strategic autonomy	13	86	75
	Operational, but not strategic autonomy	6	10	18
	Strategic autonomy	82	4	7
	N	*103*	*71*	*44*
HRM Autonomy – promotion	No operational or strategic autonomy	5	39	43
	Operational, but not strategic autonomy	5	11	41
	Strategic autonomy	90	50	16
	N	*103*	*70*	*44*
HRM Autonomy – evaluation	No operational or strategic autonomy	1	17	27
	Operational, but not strategic autonomy	5	14	52
	Strategic autonomy	94	69	21
	N	*103*	*71*	*44*
Financial management autonomy – taking out loans	No	98	59	63
	Yes, within limits or conditions set by the oversight authorities	0	38	35
	Yes, fully and without limits or conditions set by the oversight authorities	2	3	2
	N	*101*	*76*	*46*
Financial management – setting tariffs	No	39	39	39
	Yes, within limits set or conditions by the oversight authorities	36	39	48
	Yes, fully and without limits or conditions set by the oversight authorities	24	23	13
	N	*99*	*75*	*46*
Financial management autonomy – shifting budgets between years	No	29	71	67
	Yes	71	29	33
	N	*91*	*75*	*42*

Table 8.1   (Continued)

Kind of autonomy	Level of autonomy	Norway	Ireland	Flanders
Policy autonomy – choice of policy instruments	None – Minister/department takes most of the decisions independently of the organization	0	0	7
	Low – Minister/department takes most of the decisions after having consulted the organization	3	12	10
	High – when organization takes most of the decisions itself after having consulted minister/department or under explicit restrictions/conditions set by minister	63	36	50
	Very high – when organization takes most of the decisions itself, minister/department is not or only slightly involved and sets no or only minor restrictions	34	52	33
	N	*102*	*69*	*42*

that element of HRM?) and an operational level (can they take decisions in individual cases with respect to that element of HRM?). Three elements of HRM autonomy are included: autonomy with respect to salaries, promotion and evaluation. In the following sections we compare the extent of HRM autonomy between Norwegian, Irish and Flemish agencies.

Autonomy in relation to salary, pay and rewards is one of the most salient issues surrounding discretion for agency managers in HRM decisions, in view of the short- and long-term financial and budgetary implications. Table 8.1 shows that the Irish government, and to a lesser extent the Flemish government, are very reluctant to give agency managers flexibility in relation to salary. The vast majority of agencies in both states enjoy no freedom at all in terms of setting personnel salaries, and only about 5 per cent of the agencies have both operational and strategic autonomy. However, this situation contrasts clearly with that of the Norwegian agencies, where the vast majority (81 per cent) experience both operational and strategic autonomy in relation to salary. This means that they are able to set general regulations with respect to salaries, pay schemes and rewards to a large (or some) extent. The difference between Norway and the other two states proves to be statistically significant ($N > I$ and $N > F$). However, at the level of the total sample, Flemish and Irish agencies do not rank significantly different with regard to salary autonomy ($I = F$, see Table 8.2).

When we compare agencies with similar features, such as large size or the presence of a governing board, Norwegian agencies always rank significantly higher than Flemish and Irish agencies with respect to HRM autonomy in relation to salary. Agencies created in 1990 or later rank similarly in Ireland and Flanders, but much lower than Norwegian agencies. However, in most of the subsamples, Flemish agencies rank significantly higher than their Irish counterparts. This is the case for agencies of large size, with service delivery as a primary task, with their budget fully funded by government and with a board. Also, service delivery agencies with a board show similar differences ($N > I < F$). In this subsample, 94 per cent of Irish agencies have no autonomy at all, compared to 67 per cent of Flemish agencies and 12 per cent of the Norwegian agencies. Taking into account how the level of autonomy compares for similar subsamples in the different states, the dominant pattern suggests that Norwegian agencies place higher value on salary autonomy than Flemish agencies, which in turn display greater autonomy than Irish agencies.

Discretion in promotion of personnel is clearly a less salient issue than salaries. As Table 8.1 shows, the share of Irish and Flemish agencies with no such autonomy is around 40 per cent, which is considerably less than that for autonomy in relation to salary. Again, most Norwegian agencies have both strategic and operational autonomy, compared with half of the Irish agencies. Only 16 per cent of the Flemish agencies have full autonomy. Mann-Whitney tests show that the differences between the three states are statistically significant with Norway ranking higher than Ireland, and Ireland ranking higher than Flanders ($N > (I > F)$). However, focusing on the subsamples with similar features, the differences between Irish and Flemish agencies become non-significant in most subsamples. Comparing service delivery agencies with a board, the share of Flemish and Irish agencies with full autonomy increases to 33 per cent of Flemish and 67 per cent of Irish agencies. However, the dominant pattern is that Norwegian agencies have significantly higher levels of autonomy in relation to promotion, whereas Irish and Flemish agencies show no significant differences ($N > (I = F)$, see Table 8.2)

Compared to salary and promotion, autonomy in respect of evaluation of personnel seems to be again more widespread, with all Norwegian agencies and the vast majority of Irish and Flemish agencies having some autonomy. Full autonomy is granted to 69 per cent of the Irish agencies but to only 20 per cent of the Flemish agencies. Again, Mann-Whitney

Table 8.2 Agency autonomy in Norway, Ireland and Flanders. Rankings of states, based on Mann-Whitney or X^2 tests

	HRM aut. re: salary	HRM aut. re: promotion	HRM Aut. re: evaluation	FM aut. re: loan taking	FM aut. re: tariff setting	FM aut. re: budget shifts between years	Pol. Aut. re: choice of policy instruments
Total sample *All agencies*	$N > (I = F)$	$N > (I > F)$	$N > (I > F)$	$N < (I = F)$	$N = I = F$	$N > (I = F)$	$N = I = F$
Size (FTEs) *Agencies with 200 employees or more*	$N > (I < F)$	$N > (I = F)$	$N > (I > F)$	$N < (I = F)$	$N = I = F$	$N > (I = F)$	$N = I = F$
Primary task *Agencies with service delivery task*	$N > (I < F)$	$N > (I = F)$	$N > (I > F)$	$N < (I = F)$	$N = I = F$	$N > (I = F)$	$N = I = F$
Source of income *Agencies with only governmental funding*	$N > (I < F)$	$N > (I = F)$	$N > (I > F)$	$N < (I = F)$	$N = I = F$	$N > (I = F)$	$N = I = F$

Agency age *Agencies created 1990 or later*	N > (I = F)	N > (I > F)	N > (I > F)	N < (I = F)	N = I = F	N > (I = F)	N = I = F
Governance structure *Agencies with a governing board*	N > (I < F)	N > (I > F)	N > (I > F)	N < (I = F)	N = I = F	N > (I < F)	N = I = F
Subsample *Service delivery agencies with a governing board*	N > (I <= F) (N > F)	N > (I = F)	N > (I > F)	N < (I = F)	N = I = F	N > (I = F) (N = F)	N = I = F
Dominant pattern	N > (F > I)	N > (I = F)	N > (I > F)	N < (I = F)	N = I = F	N > (I = F)	N = I = F

tests reveal significant differences between the three states, and in a more pronounced way when compared with promotion (N > I > F; see Table 8.2). In the subsamples, these significant differences between the three states remain. Service delivery agencies with a board all have full autonomy in Norway, compared to 82 per cent in Ireland and only 33 per cent in Flanders.

Overall, but particularly in Ireland (and to a lesser extent in Flanders), HRM autonomy is more frequently granted on 'softer' issues such as evaluation, compared to HRM autonomy on issues having financial consequences, like promotion and salary. Norwegian agencies clearly seem to enjoy both a higher level, and more encompassing forms, of HRM autonomy compared to Irish and Flemish agencies. The vast majority of Norwegian agencies are able not only to take individual decisions about salaries, promotions and evaluations, but also to set general rules about these issues themselves. About 70 per cent of the Norwegian agencies have both operational and strategic autonomy on all three issues.

The autonomy levels of Irish and Flemish agencies are closer to one another, with Flemish agencies ranking mostly higher than Irish agencies in relation to salary, and the other way around with respect to autonomy in respect of evaluation. In Ireland, issues with long-term financial implications such as salary are much more strictly controlled than 'softer' issues. Moreover, agencies usually have both operational and strategic autonomy for a specific HRM issue or else they have no autonomy in relation to that issue at all. In other words, if Irish agencies are granted autonomy on (for example) promotion, they can usually set general principles and take individual decisions.

In Flanders, agencies are more homogenous in terms of HRM autonomy, particularly when compared with Irish agencies, where a considerable variety exists. About 30 per cent have no HRM autonomy at all, which is similar to Ireland. However, about 40 per cent of the Flemish agencies may take individual decisions on two or three HRM issues, but only within the general rules set by government. In Flanders, the dominance of agencies with a lack of strategic HRM autonomy, but with operational autonomy, is obvious. Only very few agencies combine decision-making power on general principles and individual decisions, ranging from 7 per cent with respect to salary, to 20 per cent with respect to evaluation.

8.2.2   Financial management autonomy

To what extent do agencies with similar features in the three states show similar or dissimilar levels or patterns of financial management autonomy? As noted in Chapter 2, we use three different measures as an insight into financial management autonomy in agencies in the three states: (a) taking loans, (b) shifting budgets between years and (c) setting tariffs/prices.

Table 8.1 shows clearly that all three states adopt a very careful position in relation to taking loans. The majority of agencies cannot take loans on the capital market at all, and only a few can do this without prior approval or without limits set by the superior bodies: less than 3 per cent of agencies in all states report maximal autonomy in this regard. In Norway, the autonomy to take loans is most restricted; and almost all agencies report that they lack this autonomy completely. However, the situation in Ireland and Flanders is comparable: more than one-third of the Irish and Flemish agencies report that they are able to take loans within limits set, or after approval, by the parent department or other superior bodies.

Clearly, Irish and Flemish agencies' autonomy ranks significantly higher than in Norway (N < I = F). In all subsamples this general pattern holds, with Irish and Flemish agencies ranking significantly higher than Norwegian agencies (N < I = F; see Table 8.2). In the subsample of service delivery agencies with a board, more agencies within this subsample have some report that they autonomy, compared to the total sample. Ninety-four per cent of such Norwegian agencies cannot take out loans, but about half of such Irish and Flemish agencies are able to do so, although mostly within set limits.

We now turn to the autonomy of agencies to set tariffs for their services and products – another important dimension of autonomy. From Table 8.1 showing the distribution for the total sample of agencies, we see that there are great similarities between agencies in the three different states with regard to how many report having some level of autonomy in this respect. In all three states about 60 per cent of the agencies report that they have either partial or full autonomy in setting tariffs. The larger portion report being able to set tariffs within limits set by an oversight authority. Although Norway and Ireland see more of their agencies having full autonomy than Flanders, we find no significant differences in non-parametric tests between the three states with respect to tariff-setting autonomy (N = I = F). This similar pattern holds for all subsamples of agencies with similar features (Table 8.2). Even when comparing service delivery agencies with a board, no significant differences emerge between the states. However, in that subsample an even larger share of the agencies in the three states report having some level of autonomy in setting tariffs.

Being able to shift budgets between years represents an important tool for financial flexibility. Table 8.1 reveals a striking difference between Norway and the two other states, which proves to be significant in X^2 tests (N > I = F). In contrast with autonomy in respect of taking out loans, 71 per cent of Norwegian agencies are able to shift budgets between years, while this is the case for only one third of the Irish and Flemish agencies. Again, this Norway's distinctive position holds when we take a closer look at agencies with similar features (see Table 8.2). However, agencies with a board rank similarly in Norway and Flanders, and significantly higher than Irish agencies with a board. Indeed, if we focus on our subsample of service delivery agencies with a board, such agencies are comparable between Norway and Flanders in having more autonomy than Irish agencies. For Flemish agencies we find a substantial increase in this subsample of agencies that can shift budgets between years, from 33 per cent in the total sample to 59 per cent in this subsample.

The analysis of financial management autonomy in the three states gives a rather mixed picture. Overall, Irish and Flemish agencies exhibit largely similar levels of financial management autonomy, but taking into account this particular aspect of autonomy, we find that Norwegian agencies have lower or substantial higher levels of financial management autonomy.

8.2.3 Policy autonomy

As described in Chapters 2 and 4, the level of policy autonomy is measured by the extent to which an agency can take decisions about the policy instruments it employs. The first thing we notice from Table 8.1 is that policy autonomy appears to be quite substantial in all three states. Almost all Norwegian agencies locate themselves at either the next highest level of policy autonomy or the highest; this is also the case for 88 per cent of the Irish agencies and more than 80 per cent of the Flemish agencies. But as it is most common for the Norwegian and Flemish agencies to make most of the decisions regarding policy instruments *in accordance with conditions or restrictions from parent department – or after having consulted parent department,* half of the Irish agencies report that they make most decisions on policy instruments themselves, *with the superior bodies being only slightly involved.* However, Mann-Whitney tests on the total samples show that there are no significant differences with respect to the level of policy autonomy that the agencies have in the three states ($N = (I = F)$). In contradiction with findings for HRM and financial management autonomy, agencies in the three states do not seem to differ significantly to the extent that they can decide themselves on the policy instruments that they will use.

This quasi-similar approach in allocating policy autonomy to agencies is confirmed when we look at subsamples of agencies with similar size, task and presence of a governing board (see Table 8.2). The corresponding finding in our subsample of agencies with service delivery tasks and a board diverges somewhat from the general pattern found for our total sample. First, no agencies report having no policy autonomy. Second, we find a substantial decrease in the share of Irish agencies having the highest level of policy autonomy: from 52 per cent in the total sample, to 33 per cent in the subsample. Third, and most importantly, the allocation of policy autonomy to service delivery agencies with a board follows an even more similar pattern across the three states than for the total sample of agencies.

8.3 Agency control

Do agencies in the three states or agencies with similar features (like similar governance structures and tasks) in the states show similar or dissimilar levels and patterns of control? As outlined in Chapter 2, we distinguish between three elements of control of agencies. First of all we look closely at the accountability of the CEO and the character this takes across agencies in Norway, Ireland and Flanders in terms of accountability for results and for legality. Next we focus on control of agencies through the use of rewards or sanctions of different kinds: those of a financial kind related to individuals (wages/bonuses) or to the organization as a whole (increased budget allocation), or rewards and sanctions in terms of increased or decreased autonomy levels for the organization vis-à-vis the parent department. Lastly, we analyse the extent of result control to which an agency is subjected. The extent of result control is measured by the extent to which an agency CEO is accountable for results and whether or not this result accountability goes hand in hand with the promise (or threat) of potential performance-based rewards or sanctions.

Table 8.3 shows the different kinds and levels of control and the corresponding shares of the agencies in the three states. As in the previous analysis, the core focus is the extent of similarities or differences between the states.

Table 8.3   Extent of agency control in Norway, Ireland and Flanders (percentages)

Kind of control	Level of control	Norway	Ireland	Flanders
Upwards CEO accountability for results	No	17	3	40
	Yes	83	97	60
	N	*101*	*64*	*45*
Upwards CEO accountability for legality	No	16	3	33
	Yes	84	97	67
	N	*101*	*65*	*45*
Upwards CEO Accountability overall	Not accountable for either results nor for legality (none of both)	10	2	24
	Accountable for either results OR legality (not both)	13	3	24
	Accountable for both results and legality	77	95	51
	N	*101*	*61*	*45*
Rewards or sanctions – wages	No rewards and sanctions concerning re: wages	96	95	62
	Either rewards or sanctions re: wages	4	2	24
	Both rewards and sanctions re: wages	0	3	13
	N	*103*	*66*	*45*

Table 8.3   (Continued)

Kind of control	Level of control	Norway	Ireland	Flanders
Rewards or sanctions related to financial resources for the agency	No rewards and sanctions re: resources	73	88	89
	Either rewards or sanctions re: resources	16	8	7
	Both rewards and sanctions re: resources	12	5	4
	N	*103*	*66*	*45*
Rewards and sanctions related to autonomy/ discretion	No rewards and sanctions re: discretion	76	80	84
	Either rewards or sanctions re: discretion	19	11	16
	Both rewards and sanctions re: discretion	5	9	0
	N	*103*	*66*	*45*
Rewards or sanctions of any kind	No rewards or sanctions of any kind	58	68	49
	Either rewards or sanctions of at least one kind	26	18	33
	Both rewards and sanctions of at least one kind	16	14	18
	N	*103*	*66*	*45*
Result control	No result control (no CEO accountability for results)	17	3	40
	CEO accountability for results	47	66	16
	CEO accountability for results AND rewards or/and sanctions of at least one kind	37	31	44
	N	*101*	*64*	*45*

8.3.1   CEO accountability

Table 8.3 shows the accountability of the CEO in agencies in Norway, Ireland and Flanders for the total sample. Let us compare accountability for the total sample of agencies and look for similarities or dissimilarities between the states. Virtually all agencies in Ireland, and to a lesser extent in Norway, report the CEO to be accountable, while only 75 per cent of the Flemish agencies report the same.

So, most agency CEOs are held accountable, but for what? Is this account-ability oriented towards legality and compliance to regulations, or rather focused on results, as is advocated by NPM? In Ireland, virtually all agencies report that the CEO is accountable for results; and a same share states that the CEO is accountable on legality. In Ireland 95 per cent of the agencies have a CEO who is both accountable for results and legality. About 77 per cent of the Norwegian agency CEOs are accountable for both results and legality. Far fewer agencies in Flanders report having CEO accountability related to results (60 per cent) and legality (67 per cent). Only half of the Flemish agencies report their CEO to be accountable for both results and legality. The differences between the states are reflected in statistically significant differences in X^2 tests and Mann-Whitney tests for the total sample: The CEO is significantly more accountable for results, legality, as well as for both results and legality in Irish and, to a lesser extent, in Norwegian agencies, compared to Flemish agencies $(I > (N > F))$.

However, when comparing subsamples with similar single features, these differences are still present between two or all three states but they are no longer statistically significant. No significant differences between any of the three states are noticeable for large-sized agencies. In all other subsamples, Irish agencies rank significantly higher than Flemish agencies, but not necessarily higher than Norwegian agencies $[(I > (N = F))$ or $((I = N) > F)]$. When we look at our subsample of service delivery agencies with a board, we can clearly see an increase in Flemish agencies where the CEO is accountable for either results (73 per cent), or legality (78 per cent), when compared with the total sample. No similar increase is found for the other two states.

Overall, we get a quite mixed picture. The dominant pattern for CEO accountability on results, legality and overall accountability would be that for all variables Irish agencies rank significantly higher than Flemish, but not higher than Norwegian, agencies $(I > F$ and $I = N)$.

8.3.2 Rewards and sanctions for performance

Our second element of control in agencies is the existence of rewards for 'good' performance and goal accomplishment or sanctions in the case of 'bad' or unsatisfactory performance. The threat of sanctions in cases of 'bad' performance and the promise of rewards in cases of 'good' performance are considered within NPM doctrines to be strong incentives, which stimulate agencies to direct their efforts to pursue the goals they have been set. The existence of both sanctions and rewards for goal attainment is therefore considered to reflect a rather mature arrangement of result control by government, which goes further than simply setting measurable goals and monitoring or evaluating them.

Clearly, incentives in the form of sanctions and rewards are not that common for the vast majority of agencies we studied. Table 8.3 shows that about 68 per cent of the Irish agencies and 58 per cent of Norwegian agencies lack such incentives, although earlier we observed that in these two states result accountability for agency CEOs is widespread. In Flanders, rewards and sanctions seem to be stressed somewhat more as a control mechanism, as over half of all agencies are confronted with the existence of either rewards or sanctions. In all three states about 15 per cent of agencies face both sanctions and rewards of a specific kind. Although the differences between Flanders and the other two states seem to be substantial, non-parametric tests show only less than a borderline statistical significant difference between Flanders and Ireland when Mann-Whitney tests are performed for the total sample (F = N = I, but F > = I) (see Table 8.4). Although the difference between Flanders and the other states in the subsamples is also quite consistent, no other significant differences between the states are to be found. For agencies with a governing board, there is a borderline statistical significant difference between Flemish agencies and lower-ranked Irish agencies. With respect to the subsample of service delivery agencies with a board, the share of agencies confronted with either sanctions or rewards in whatever form increases for Flanders to more than 60 per cent, and for Norway to more than 50 per cent, whereas for Ireland the share decreases to less than 30 per cent. Comparing these subsamples, Flemish agencies rank significantly higher than Irish agencies when performing Mann-Whitney tests (F > I) (see Table 8.4).

What kind of rewards and sanctions are used in the three states? Rewards or sanctions with respect to wages of individuals are much more common for Flemish agencies (about 48 per cent) than in Norway and Ireland, where they are almost non-existent. The difference is statistically significant (F > N = I) and holds for all subsamples studied. In the case of the subsample of service delivery agencies with a board, Flemish agencies rank significantly higher with respect to rewards and sanctions through wages. About 55 per cent are subject to these kinds of sanctions, whereas no agencies in Norway and Ireland are.

Incidents of rewards or sanctions through the adjustment of the agency's financial resources are quite uncommon in all three states, although 27 per cent of Norwegian agencies face these kinds of sanctions and rewards. The difference between Flanders and Ireland is significant in the total sample, but turns out to be non-significant in most of the subsamples. In all three states, service delivery agencies with a board are more often faced with these kind of rewards and sanctions (about 40 per cent in Norway, 30 per cent in Flanders and 24 per cent in Ireland), though with no clear significant differences emerging in non-parametric tests.

Rewards or sanctions by changing the autonomy or discretion at both agency and individual level seem to be used for about one fifth of all agencies in Ireland and Flanders, and for one quarter of all agencies in Norway. However, non-parametric tests on the total sample and the subsamples do not result in significant differences between the states (see Table 8.4). Interestingly, in Flanders service delivery agencies with a board are much less confronted with these kinds of rewards and sanctions when compared to the total sample (about 6 per cent).

Table 8.4 Agency control in Norway, Ireland and Flanders. Rankings of states, based on Mann-Whitney or X^2 tests.

	Upwards CEO account-ability on results	Upwards CEO account-ability on legality	Upwards CEO account-ability overall	Sanctions and rewards overall	Sanctions and rewards concerning: Wages	Sanctions and rewards concern-ing: org. finances	Sanctions and rewards re: discretion	Result control
Total sample *All agencies*	I > (N > F)	I > (N > F)	I > (N > F)	N=I=F F>=I (.066)	F > N=I	N > (I=F)	N=I=F	N=I=F
Size (FTE's) *Agencies with 200 employees or more*	I=N=F	I=N=F	I=N=F	N=I=F	F > N=I	N=I=F (N > I .038)	N=I=F	N=I=F
Primary task *Agencies with service delivery task*	I > (N=F)	(I=N) > F	(I=N) > F	N=I=F	F > N=I	I=N=F (N > = F .066)	N=I=F	N=I=F
Source of income *Agencies with only governmental funding*	(I=N) > F	(I=N) > F	(I=N) > F	N=I=F	F > N=I	N=I=F	N=I=F	(N=I) > F

Table 8.4 (Continued)

Agency age *Agencies established after 1990*	(I=N)>F	(I=N)>F	(I=N)>F	N=I=F	F>N=I	N=I=F	N=I N>F	I=N N>F
Governance structure *Agencies with a governing board*	I>(N=F)	I>(N=F)	I>(N=F)	N=I=F F>=I (.058)	F>N=I	N=I=F (N>I .033)	N=I=F	N=I=F
Sub sample *Service delivery agencies with a governing board*	I>(N=F) I>F I>=N (.048 borderline sign.)	I=N=F I>=F (.048 borderline sign)	I>(N=F) I>F I>N (.040)	N=I=F F>I (.027)	F>(N=I)	N=I=F	N=I=F	N=I=F
Dominant pattern	I=(N>=F) I>F	(I=N)>F	(I=N)>F	N=I=F (F>=I)	F>(N=I)	N=I=F	N=I=F	N=I=F

Finally, it is interesting to note that states differ to the extent that they stress negative sanctions or positive rewards. For both Flanders and Norway it is in general more common to be rewarded for good performance, rather than being sanctioned for unsatisfactory goal achievement. The use of sanctions is most prevalent among the Irish agencies, where close to 40 per cent of the agencies report that this is the case. Being sanctioned is thus a good deal more 'normal' for the Irish agencies than having rewards linked to good performance.

8.3.3 Result control

Linking the data on CEO result accountability with the data on rewards and sanctions gives us a more complete picture of what result control on agencies in a country encompasses. Table 8.3 shows that the result control which 65 per cent of Irish agencies are subjected to entails the CEO being accountable for good or bad performance without any incentives for better performance being present. Less than one third of the Irish agencies face rewards or sanctions as a consequence of their accountability in relation to results. In Norway we see a somewhat similar situation, with less than half of the agencies' CEOs being accountable for results without rewards or sanctions. In Flanders, however, a dual picture emerges with, on the one hand, 40 per cent of the agencies not being subjected to result control at all and, on the other hand, about half of the agencies being confronted with both result accountability and performance-based incentives. In Flanders, result control is less practised overall, but where applied, it comes in its full form with result accountability being reinforced by the threat of potential rewards or sanctions. This is quite different from Norway and Ireland, where result accountability remains more frequently without consequences. This difference becomes even sharper when comparing service delivery agencies with a board between the three states. Whereas 23 per cent of the Irish agencies and 39 per cent of the Norwegian agencies face both result accountability and rewards or sanctions, 61 per cent of the Flemish agencies are confronted with this harder form of result control.

These differences are not translated into statistically significant outcomes in the Mann-Whitney tests we performed for the total sample, or for the subsamples. Only in the case of agencies fully funded by government and those established in 1990 or later do both Norwegian and Irish agencies rank significantly higher than Flemish agencies. The dominant pattern is that in all three states the result control towards agencies is not significantly different. However, as noted above, the nature of result control is to some extent different with result accountability of agency CEOs being less prevalent, but where it does exist it is more strongly related to performance-related incentives in Flanders then in Ireland and Norway.

Additional information stemming from state-specific studies and analyses leads us to conclude that:

1) The level of result control in Ireland is certainly not developed in a way that is comparable to Norway or Flanders. The underlying systems of CEO accountability for results, such as formulation of objectives and performance indicators, monitoring and evaluation are rather weakly developed in Ireland.
2) Overall result control seems to be developed more consistently in Norwegian agencies than in the other two states.

In the following sections we check the extent to which this assessment of result control (based on two criteria) aligns with a more complete picture of result control for each state, which we build using state-specific data. This extra data was not included in the joint database used for the analyses in this book because of divergence in the way survey questions were asked. We describe some additional aspects for each state which are part of the result control cycle, and which entail the setting of objectives and result norms by minister or parent department in negotiation with the agency, the reporting of results towards these objectives by the agency, the evaluation of these results by the minister or parent department, and the consequences for over-performance and under-performance in terms of rewards and sanctions. Table 8.5 presents some additional information on result control systems in the three states.

8.3.4   Result control in Norwegian agencies

Lægreid et al. (2006a) reach clear conclusions (see Table 8.5) in analysing the extent of result control in Norwegian agencies, and find that the general ideas of result control have been widely implemented in Norwegian central government. In the majority of agencies, elements of the specification of objectives, formulation of performance indicators, performance reporting and performance steering can be observed. They also find that the goal formulation process is, to a great extent, a cooperative effort between the agency and the parent department, and that, as perceived by the agencies at least, it is more a bottom-up than a top-down process. This setting of objectives and targets is carried out through the letter of allocation, which is issued by the parent department. The agencies make an effort to formulate performance indicators, but with a rather loose coupling to objectives. Performance indicators are used in the steering relationship, at least to some extent. Performance reporting is done through regular documents and formal steering meetings, and there is an increased formalization of the information system.

What are the consequences of this performance reporting for the agencies? Only a minority report that this performance information is used for future

Table 8.5 Result control systems in Norway, Ireland and Flanders. Additional information

Elements of result control	Norway (Laegreid et al. 2006)	Ireland (McGauran and Humphreys 2004; McGauran et al. 2005)	Flanders (Verschuere and Verhoest 2003; Verhoest et al. 2004b)
Objective setting	20% set their goals alone, 45% formulate goals in cooperation with the parent ministry, 27%: parent ministry set the goals in cooperation with the agency.	86% have a document outlining objectives, but 20% do this in an agency-internal document, not directed to government.	41% set their objectives alone; 45% set objectives in negotiation with the minister or the parent department.
Prevalence of performance indicators	For 91% of agencies performance indicators measure outputs, for 50% 'to a large extent'. For 80% of agencies performance indicators measure quality with one quarter assessing to a large extent.	In 65% non-financial targets were outlined, but only for a half of the agencies this was done in a document directed towards government or known to the public.	For 68% of the agencies indicators measure outputs. For 40% of the agencies quality is measured. Only 10% of the agencies do not use performance indicators.
Standard document for objectives & indicators	Letter of allocation for all agencies	No formal document in which objectives and indicators are set	Performance management contract in 14% of the agencies

Table 8.5   (Continued)

Elements of result control	Norway (Laegreid et al. 2006)	Ireland (McGauran and Humphreys 2004; McGauran et al. 2005)	Flanders (Verschuere and Verhoest 2003; Verhoest et al. 2004b)
Performance evaluation and steering	38% agencies performance indicators are used to a large extent in the steering relations between the agency and the parent ministry, 43% to some extent.	Pro memoric	For about half of all agencies, the minister or parent departments are involved in evaluating their performance About 40% does the performance evaluation solely internally.
Performance reporting	Almost all agencies report to the parent ministry through annual reports, and quarterly reports are also common.	61% of all agencies reports on non-financial targets; 43% agencies does this in documents directed to government or to the public.	12% of the agencies do not measure and report their results.
Formal steering meetings	Formal meetings as part of a steering dialogue between the parent ministry and state agencies, at least once a year.	No formal steering meetings	No formal steering meetings

Performance auditing	Pro memorie	One third of all Irish agencies: Auditing focuses on organizational results	One fifth of all agencies: Performance auditing by external actors Another fifth: performance auditing is done internally.
Rewards for good performance	40%: rewarding good performance Mostly with increase resource allocation	15%: rewards for achieving their objectives and non-financial targets.	About 40% of the agencies report that they face rewards.
Sanctions for bad performance	When it comes to using sanctions in case of bad performance, 24% report that this happens to some extent and 9% to a large extent.	24% of the agencies is sanctioned for non-achievement of the set objectives, whereas 18% are sanctioned for not meeting their non-financial targets.	About 30–40% of the agencies report that they face sanctions.
Rewards and sanctions concerning re: wages	Only for 10% of the agencies	Increased or decreased wages are virtually absent as form of rewards or sanctions.	One third of all agencies report rewards concerning wages; 10% report such sanctions

resource allocation. In cases where it is used in this manner, normally more than 10 per cent of the total budget of the organization is linked to this type of allocation. The weakness seems to be with sanctions and rewards. Overall, the majority of agencies are not rewarded to any great extent for good results or punished for poor results. Pay-for-performance systems are only introduced for a small minority of the agencies. Thus, in Norway there is narrower product-oriented performance measurement and broader process-oriented version, which is more dialogue-oriented and more trust-based (see also Lægreid et al. 2008; cf. De Bruijn, 2002).

8.3.5 Result control in Irish agencies

With respect to Irish agencies, where CEO accountability on results was reported to be almost omnipresent, McGauran and Humphreys (2004) sketched a rather sobering picture of result control (see Table 8.5). Case studies in McGauran et al. (2005), and by the OECD (2008), further attenuate this picture of quite weakly developed systems of result control. The OECD (2008) stated that the cascade of targets seems to follow a consistent approach, with officials reporting well-articulated contributions on how to achieve clear sector objectives. But this cascade is essentially just a paper process, since the procedure for target setting is loosely defined, with usually no formal dialogues between departments and agencies. In general, most agencies do not appear to have a well-developed cycle incorporating the setting, meeting and monitoring of non-financial targets (McGauran et al. 2005). A great variability in the extent to which agencies have put performance measures in place was noted. Even the targets specifically to be achieved by the CEO in order to hold him or her accountable proved to be absent in half of the case studies done by McGauran et al. (2005). The OECD (2008) observed a discrepancy between the constant and well-developed financial reporting by agencies to their line department and to the Department of Finance, and the more customary and less developed reporting on policy targets. The analyses showed that reporting and dialogue on performance targets tends to take place with boards or internally within agencies, but much less within the relationship with parent departments. Performance reporting is mainly considered as being a formal process with little importance in the relationship between agencies, parent departments and the Department of Finance. Sanctions, just like rewards, were underdeveloped and usually implemented for financial 'failure' rather than policy failure, reflecting again the existence of more comprehensive measurement of financial rather than policy issues (McGauran et al. 2005).

8.3.6 Result control in Flemish agencies

Verschuere and Verhoest (2003; see also Verhoest et al. 2004b) assessed that several aspects of result control are present in the majority of the Flemish agencies (see Table 8.5), but observed that in most organizations of all types, this result steering is only a *partial* phenomenon. This means that most organizations have an incomplete result control system. Moreover, there are indications that some of the aspects (for example, using indicators or measuring results) are generally used internally in the organization rather than being part of the steering relationship between the organization and its superior bodies.

8.3.7   The comparison of result control revisited

Based on this additional information and more in-depth description of the result control systems in the three states, Norwegian agencies seem comparatively to have the most developed and internally coherent result control cycle. Most elements are present for the majority of agencies and sub-systems of goal formulation, monitoring and evaluation are more strongly integrated, with one major exception: the scarcity of rewards and sanctions. Flanders and Ireland both show a more dispersed picture. Therefore, in the remainder of the analysis, we will use a corrected dominant pattern for result control, which ranks Norway higher than the other two states: $N > (I = F)$.

8.4   Internal management

The topic addressed in this section relates to the question of whether agencies in the three states use management techniques to similar or dissimilar extents (RQ2). We focus on six particular management techniques.

At the first level of analysis, the total sample of agencies is used for answering the question: *To what extent do agencies in the three states show similar or dissimilar use of management techniques?* Figure 8.1 shows the extent to which agencies use management techniques, per state and per particular management technique.

Two selected performance management techniques – multi-year planning and public reporting – are widespread. Nearly all Norwegian agencies in the total sample declare that they use multi-year planning, suggesting that they set their goals over several years. This is also the case for most Flemish and Irish agencies in the total sample. Almost all agencies in all three states report applying the practice of public reporting by means of, for example, annual reports or a website. Quality management techniques are used to a lesser extent. In all three states, 60–70 per cent of the agencies declare that they use of customer surveys. To the contrary, more than 60 per cent of agencies in Norway, Flanders and Ireland report that they do *not* apply quality management systems or procedures such as CAF in their organization. Remarkably, we can also observe from Figure 8.1 that most Norwegian and Flemish agencies claim that they are able to allocate resources internally in the organization and have developed cost-calculation systems, while in Ireland most agencies declare that they do *not* apply these financial management techniques.

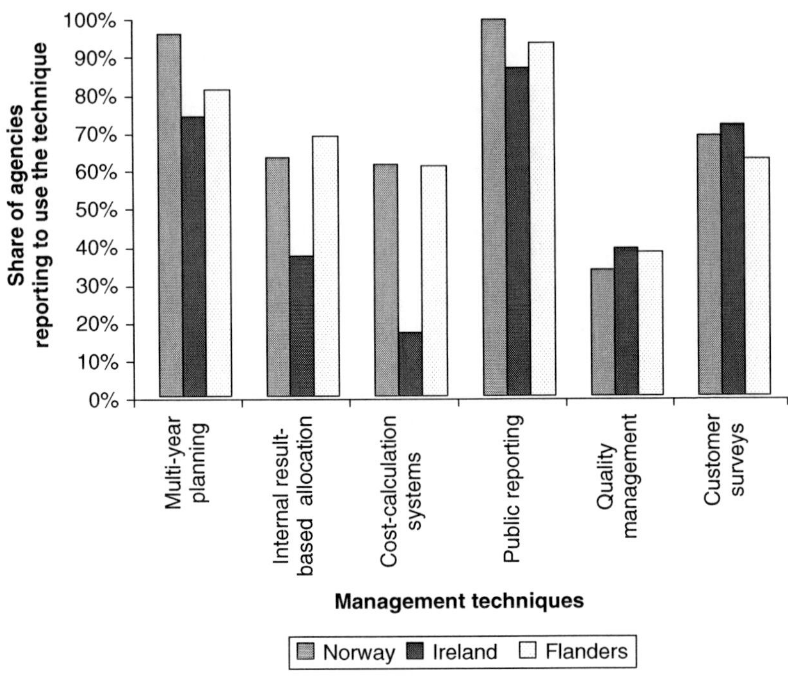

Figure 8.1   The use of internal management techniques in Norway, Ireland and Flanders (percentages)

This raises some interesting points about the extent to which the use of modern management techniques differs significantly between states. In addressing this issue, we use the Pearson X^2-test, which looks for statistically significant differences in the use of management techniques by agencies in the three different states. Table 8.6 shows the results of the X^2 analyses.

Looking at the total sample of agencies, we can conclude that Norwegian agencies tend to use more managerial tools and techniques compared to Irish agencies; particularly planning over years, internal allocation of resources, cost-calculation systems and public reporting on results. Concerning multi-year planning and public reporting, Norwegian agencies tend to use these more than Flemish agencies. However, Table 8.6 shows that these differences do not always hold when comparing subsamples.

In analysing the dominant patterns across total sample and subsamples, with regard to the managerial tools linked to organizational *quality management* (the use of quality management systems and customer surveys), we observed no differences between states. Most Norwegian, Irish and Flemish agencies do survey their customers. Next to that, only a minority of the

Table 8.6 The use of management techniques in Norway, Ireland and Flanders. Rankings of states, based on X^2 tests

	Multi-year planning	Internal result-based allocation	Cost-calculation systems	Public Reporting	Quality management systems	Customer surveys
Total sample *All agencies*	N > (I = F)	(N = F) > I	(N = F) > I	N > (I = F)	N = I = F	N = I = F
Size (FTE's) *Agencies with 200 employees or more*	N = I = F	(N = F) > I	(N = F) > I	N = I = F	N = I = F	N = I = F
Primary task *Agencies with service delivery task*	N = I = F	N = I = F	(N = F) > I	N = I = F	(I = F) > N	N = I = F
Source of income *Agencies with only governmental funding*	N > (I = F)	F > N > I	(N = F) > I	N = I = F	N = I = F	N = I = F

Table 8.6 (Continued)

	Multi-year planning	Internal result-based allocation	Cost-calculation systems	Public Reporting	Quality management systems	Customer surveys
Agency age *Agencies est. After 1990*	N > F > I	(N = F) > I	(N = F) > I	N = I = F	N = I = F	N = I = F
Governance structure *Agencies with a governing board*	N = I = F	(N = F) > I	(N = F) > I	N = I = F	N = I = F	N = I = F
Sub sample *Service delivery agencies with a governing board*	(N = F) > I	N = I = F	(N = F) > I	N = I = F	(I = F) > N	N = I = F
Dominant pattern	N > (I = F)	(N = F) > I	(N = F) > I	N = I = F	N = I = F	N = I = F

agencies in the three states use quality management systems. Concerning managerial tools that are linked to *financial management* (internal allocation of resources based on results and development of cost-calculation systems), we found that Irish agencies use these tools to a lesser extent than their Norwegian and Flemish counterparts. Managerial tools that can be linked to organizational *performance management* (multi-year planning and the public reporting on organizational results) are more frequently used by Norwegian agencies compared to Irish and Flemish agencies. However these significant differences do not hold when comparing subsamples in relation to their use of public reporting.

We also analysed the extent to which agency features interact with state-level pressures for dissimilarities when analysing the use of management techniques by agencies belonging to different states. The question is to what extent state differences in the use of management techniques decrease when comparing agencies with similar organizational features, such as size, task, age, governance structure and financial resources. We found that agencies of the similar (large) size, irrespective of the state they belong to, tend to use managerial tools to a similar extent. Only in relation to tools for financial management do the state differences observed for the total sample remain. Concerning public reporting, the differences in practice by large agencies in different states are less pronounced compared to the total sample. The task of the agency also seems to have an effect. Looking at agencies with the same kind of task – service delivery – no state differences in the use of multi-year planning and allocation of resources in the organization can be found (contrary to what we found for the total sample). In addition, differences in the use of public reporting on results seem to be less pronounced in the sample of service delivery agencies, compared to the total sample. Furthermore, when isolating organizations of the same age (agencies which have been recently established) we found fewer differences between agencies in different states in using managerial tools, compared to the total sample. To conclude, it appears that large agencies, agencies performing service delivery tasks, or recently established agencies, tend to use modern management techniques more often and to the same extent, irrespective of the state they belong to.

8.5   Similarities and dissimilarities between states

At the beginning of this chapter we asked three basic descriptive questions:

1) To what extent do the autonomy, control and internal management of agencies in the three states correspond with the NPM ideal-type?

2) Do we find similarities between agencies with respect to autonomy, control and internal management in the three states?
3) If we find similarities, are these consistent with NPM ideal-type prescriptions?

8.5.1   Variations across states

The main conclusions emerging from the comparison of agency autonomy, control and management across the three states are threefold. First, there are substantial and significant differences between at least two of the three states with regard to managerial autonomy, CEO accountability of agencies and, to a much lesser extent, rewards and sanctions in relation to wages. Also, with regard to the use of management techniques in relation to performance and financial management, there are significant differences between at least two of the three states. These differences hold in most cases, even at the level of comparable subgroups of agencies with similar features, like service delivery agencies or agencies with a board. Only in a few aspects do Norwegian, Irish and Flemish agencies not rank significantly different when considering the dominant pattern that arises from comparing the total samples with subsamples. These aspects are the autonomy to set tariffs, the level of policy autonomy, the level of result control, the level of sanctions and rewards in relation to resources and discretion. Also, the use of two quality management techniques agencies in the three states do not significantly differ.

Second, for most kinds of autonomy and control, these differences and similarities between the three states largely hold when we compared subgroups of agencies with similar features which we expected to be more receptive or influenced by NPM ideal-type images of agencies. In such subgroups, such as large-sized agencies, state-sponsored agencies, service delivery agencies, agencies with a governing board and agencies created in 1990 or later, the degree of similarity between all three states was, taken *in toto*, not substantially higher than in the total sample. Large-sized agencies seem to display greater similarities in levels of HRM autonomy for promotion and evaluation in two states, and more similarities with respect to CEO accountability. Agencies created in 1990 or later, agencies with a board and state-funded agencies show similar autonomy levels with regard to CEO accountability, at least in two states, compared to agencies in the total sample. However, the overall conclusion is that when comparing subsamples of similar agencies, state differences do not disappear. This could suggest that agency-level factors such as size, age, task and governance structure do not have a strong direct effect on levels of autonomy and control, independently of state-level factors. This is tested in more depth in Chapter 13, where we also include the influence of agency-level factors on autonomy and control. Nevertheless, we should be careful in our conclusions here as we compared only some of the similar subsamples in this chapter (for example, agencies of a large size only, or agencies created in 1990 or later). We, therefore, cannot fully assess the direct influence that agency-level characteristics like size, age, task and governance structure may have on agency autonomy, control and management.

However, when considering the use of management techniques in subgroups of similar agencies, the state differences seem to attenuate clearly in the case of large-sized agencies, agencies created in 1990 or later and those agencies with a service delivery task. These findings suggest that agency size, task and age are agency-level factors that may have potentially strong explanatory power as regards the extent to which agencies use internal management techniques, irrespective of the state to which these agencies belong. We return to this in Chapter 13. Most agency-level factors do not seem influential enough to bring about uniformity between agencies in the three different states. They may bring some convergence compared to the total sample, but their potential harmonizing influence does not seem strong enough to overrule state-level factors. Hence, the persistence of significant state differences across subgroups of agencies with similar features suggests that international pressures and doctrines have not (yet) brought full convergence across the three states among groups of similar agencies. Hence, state-specific factors still seem to influence the autonomy and control of agencies to a considerable degree.

Third, we can define, at least to some extent, a state-specific picture of agencies. Overall, agencies in Norway differ from those in the two other states in that they generally have high levels of managerial autonomy, particularly in relation to HRM autonomy and budget shifts between years. Autonomy to take out loans is almost absent. Levels of policy autonomy are substantial, just as in the two other states. When it comes to control, a vast majority of the agencies report CEO accountability for results, and most sub-systems for result control seem to be quite well developed. However, about 60 per cent of the Norwegian agencies do not face the threat of rewards and sanctions. When applied, rewarding is more common than sanctioning, and they affect mostly the financial resources or the discretion of agencies. Sanctions and rewards in relation to CEO wages are applied to a very low degree. Moreover, the Norwegian agencies mainly use management techniques to a moderate or great extent. They use three management techniques significantly more than in Ireland, and one management technique significantly more than in Flanders. Lægreid et al. (2007: 405) also conclude, on the basis of an analysis of 18 modern management techniques, that the use of such tools is widespread within state agencies in Norway.

Irish agencies show a much more mixed pattern of HRM autonomy with low levels of autonomy in relation to salaries and high levels vis-à-vis evaluation. Financial management autonomy is at a more moderate level, with autonomy aspects applying only to half, or even less than half, of the agencies. As in Norway and Flanders, policy autonomy is substantial with about half of Irish agencies reporting to have very high levels of policy autonomy. The OECD review of the Irish public service assesses this mixed pattern of autonomy as follows:

> Ireland seems to be in an ambiguous position when compared with other OECD countries that have carried out extensive agencification. Agencies have a high degree of policy independence, but little managerial capacity. Ireland has sought to avoid mission creep and the implementation of fragmented and divisive policies by keeping a tight managerial control over agencies, although the autonomy of boards has led to challenges in this area. (OECD 2008: 309; see also McGauran et al. 2005)

CEO accountability, both on results and on legality, applies to almost all agencies, and is significantly more evident in Ireland than in Flanders and, in the case of result accountability, than in Norway. However, this result accountability of CEOs is not very meaningful, because subsystems of norm setting, monitoring and sanctions are rather weakly developed and coupled. Only one-third of the agencies experience rewards and sanctions. When applied, sanctions are dominant, but CEO wages are generally not affected by such incentives. As such, the level of result control is rather modest. The use of management techniques is at a rather low to moderate level, except for multi-year planning, public reporting and customer surveys, and generally lower than in Norway and Flanders for most management techniques.

Flanders has a contrasting pattern of HRM autonomy, with a considerable number of agencies having operational autonomy on softer HRM issues, and a considerable number without any HRM autonomy. One third of all agencies have some autonomy to take loans or to shift budgets between years, as in Ireland. Overall, levels of managerial autonomy for Flemish agencies are low to moderate. As in the other states, perceived policy autonomy is reported to be quite substantial, but with only one third of all agencies reporting quasi-full autonomy on that aspect. Another typical aspect is that the level of CEO accountability on results or on legality is lower than in Ireland and Norway, with 25 per cent of CEOs not being accountable and only 50 per cent being accountable on both legality and results. On the other hand, the threat of rewards and sanctions is present for half of the agencies, particularly in relation to wages, with an emphasis on positive incentives. Therefore, result control is very dualistic in Flanders with, on the one hand, 40 per cent of the agencies not being subjected to result control at all and, on the other hand, about half of agencies being confronted with both result accountability and performance-based incentives. However, the moderate level of managerial autonomy and result control goes together with a quite extensive use of management techniques which, with the exception of one management technique, is similar to Norway.

Overall, the analysis in this chapter points to the following major state differences and similarities. When considering HRM autonomy and financial management autonomy together, Norwegian agencies surpass Irish and Flemish agencies in relation to the level of most aspects of autonomy. Considering all aspects of managerial autonomy, Irish and Flemish agencies seem to have roughly equivalent levels of autonomy. Taking into account differences on particular aspects, the dominant pattern for managerial autonomy is thus overall $N > (I = F)$. Regarding policy autonomy, however, the dominant patterns show no significant differences between the three states $(N = I = F)$, although Ireland ranks higher than Flanders in the total sample and in one of the subsamples.

When it comes to CEO accountability, the dominant overall pattern is that Ireland and Norway ranks higher than Flanders $(I = N > F)$, but when considering rewards and sanctions, there are similarities. However, Flanders ranks significantly higher than Ireland, making the dominant pattern for rewards and sanctions $I = N$, $N = F$, with $I < F$. Particularly in the case of rewards and sanctions concerning wages, Flemish agencies rank significantly higher than Irish and Norwegian agencies $(F > (I = N))$. Given these differences, result control in all three states can be labelled as being moderately developed and do not rank significantly different for the level of result control $(N = I = F)$. However, from additional information (see Table 8.5), it is clear that this result control is quite different in nature in the three states, with Norway having more agencies with substantial result control systems in place and with Flanders having a stronger system of rewards and sanctions for those agencies with result accountability for their CEO. The additional information has led us to correct the rankings, and we therefore rank Norway higher than the other two states $(N > (I = F))$. Overall, the use of management techniques within agencies is more developed in Norway, followed by Flanders, and then Ireland $(N > (F > I))$.

8.5.2 NPM ideal-type agencies and practice

States differ to the extent in which their agencies reveal the features as advocated by the NPM ideal-type agency model. Overall, when considering autonomy, result control and internal management in combination, Norwegian agencies match NPM characteristics most, combining high levels of managerial autonomy (except for loans), a rather high level of result control and a quite extensive use of management techniques. Gamma correlations show that managerial autonomy, in particular, HRM autonomy, and result control variables are more often and more strongly correlated in Norway, when compared with Ireland and Flanders (Roness et al. 2008). However, other features of these agencies in Norway seem to contradict the NPM model to some extent, such as substantial levels of policy autonomy, the inability to take loans, the prevalence of CEO accountability in relation to legality, and moderate levels of sanctions and rewards. Therefore, Norway cannot be considered as an orthodox NPM-follower, implementing the full NPM catalogue. Rather, it seems to be a rather selective implementer, choosing and implementing some elements from the NPM toolbox. We discuss this in more detail in Chapter 9.

Flanders and Ireland shift positions depending on what is most emphasized: in the case of rewards and sanctions and the use of management techniques, Flemish agencies fit more the NPM ideal-type agency model, but for CEO accountability on results Irish agencies are closer to NPM.

A final observation is in support of the claim that the NPM ideal-type agency (combining structural disaggregation, result control and managerial autonomy) does not seem to be so widespread in OECD states (Pollitt et al. 2004). Such agencies are quite rare in the states under review, in particular Flanders and Ireland, since they lack at least substantial level of managerial autonomy or specific elements of result control. Moreover, the substantial level of policy autonomy of agencies in all three states is quite the opposite of what we would expect based on NPM lines.

How can we explain these state differences in the autonomy, control and management of agencies, given that all three states are small parliamentarian European states, which are all known as rather slow implementers of international NPM doctrines? This issue is tackled in Chapter 9.

9

Explaining Similarities and Dissimilarities in Agency Autonomy, Control and Internal Management Between States

9.1 Introduction

The previous chapter shows that the dominant pattern for managerial autonomy, result control and use of management techniques is that Norwegian agencies rank higher than the other two states, and that they are closer to the NPM ideal-type model of agencies. Flemish agencies report using more management techniques than Irish agencies, but with regard to managerial autonomy and result control, agencies in these two states are quite similar, demonstrating low to moderate levels. In this chapter we discuss the third research question:

*RQ 3:   How can we explain similar/dissimilar levels and patterns
of autonomy, control and use of management techniques
between the three states by referring to aspects of their
politico-administrative regimes (state-level characteristics)?*

In Chapter 7 we formulated hypotheses on the importance of environmental pressures, politico-administrative culture, structural and functional elements of polity, and actor constellations and deliberate actions on agency autonomy, control and internal management (see Table 7.1). In the change management approach, hypotheses focused on the influence of environmental or state-level characteristics on the extent to which a state would adopt more radical NPM-type agency reforms. Such reforms would result in agencies which report relatively higher levels of managerial autonomy, result control and use of management techniques. The principal agent delegation approach focused on the managerial and policy autonomy of agencies, and led to somewhat contrasting expectations. We analyse the extent to which explanations fit more closely with the change management approach or to the principal-agent delegation approach. Moreover, the extent to which states adopt NPM ideal-type agency features with or without institutional adaptation to the institutional regime will be discussed.

We focus mainly on the statistically significant differences found between Norwegian agencies and the agencies from the other two states, which were more similar. The discussion is centred primarily around those agency features where we found significant dissimilarities between the three states: managerial autonomy, result control and the use of internal management techniques. These features are mainly related to NPM doctrine concerning ideal-type agencies. The aspect of policy autonomy, on which agencies in the three states do not differ significantly, will not be tackled in depth. However, if we consider the 'overall autonomy' of agencies, that is, combining the overall discretion agencies have in terms of policy and management, Norwegian agencies again score more strongly than Irish and Flemish agencies. Therefore, in some instances we also refer to this concept of 'overall autonomy'.

Table 9.1 presents the extent of empirical support for the different hypotheses and the related expectations with respect to state rankings for the different aspects under consideration.

For reasons of readability, we tackle the different state-level characteristics and their hypotheses developed in Chapter 7, but in reverse order. We start by discussing the explanatory power of the deliberate actions taken in the form of reform programmes in the three states, then move to the actor constellations, elements of polity, politico-administrative culture, before ending with a discussion of the relevance of environmental characteristics to explain the autonomy, control and internal management of agencies in the three states. How can we explain Norway's position compared to Flanders and Ireland, when looking at the different characteristics listed in Chapter 7, and based on the information on the three states regarding these characteristics presented in Chapters 5 and 6?

9.2   Deliberate actions of politico-administrative actors

A first element which could account for the different levels of managerial autonomy, result control and use of management techniques, which are reported by agencies in the three states, are the deliberate actions taken by political and administrative leaders in the form of reform programmes and initiatives. We question to what extent announced reform initiatives have indeed been put into effect via reform actions and clear reform results. In this way, actual and perceived managerial autonomy, result control and internal management should be, to a considerable extent, brought about by the general reforms and government-wide agency reform programmes which have been launched by these politico-administrative actors. In the following paragraphs we analyse the extent to which such reform initiatives could account for the reported state differences. We first discuss deliberate

Table 9.1 Hypotheses on comparing states based on the change management approach and the principal-agent delegation approach. Extent of support marked in grey

Hypotheses based on change management approach	Hypotheses concerning managerial autonomy result control, and management techniques	Hypotheses based principal agent delegation approach	Hypotheses concerning autonomy (management/ policy)
Environmental pressures			
Hc1. Time and high intensity of EU-adhesion fosters agency-reforms along NPM lines	(F & I) > N		
Hc2. High intensity of economic and budgetary-fiscal crises since 1980s fosters agency-reforms along NPM lines	(F > I) > N	Hp1. Economic and budgetary-fiscal crises causes risk-averse politicians to reduce (management) autonomy of agencies	N > (I > F) in case of managerial autonomy and 'overall autonomy'
Hc3. Relatively low level of trust in government fosters agency-reforms along NPM lines	(F > N) > I		
Politico-administrative culture			
Hc4. Legal tradition in common law, public interest model, low values re. power distance and uncertainty avoidance and high values re. masculinity foster agency-reforms along NPM lines	I > N > F Less strict regulated Less uniform		

Table 9.1 (Continued)

Hypotheses based on change management approach	Hypotheses concerning managerial autonomy result control, and management techniques	Hypotheses based principal agent delegation approach	Hypotheses concerning autonomy (management/policy)
Polity			
Hc5. A relatively limited involvement of private sector in economic life, in public service delivery and policy implementation fosters agency-reforms along NPM lines	N > (F > I)		
Hc6. A strong centralization of service delivery and policy implementation fosters agency-reforms along NPM lines (at central level) compared to states where local governmental levels are strongly involved in service delivery and policy implementation	I > (F > N)		
Hc7. A more majoritarian cabinet structure (in the period 1980–2004) fosters agency-reforms along NPM lines	N = (I = F) But Norwegian cabinets did not take a majoritarian stance at all	Hp2. Higher policy conflict in more consensualist-type cabinet structures lead to more autonomous agencies	F > (N & I)

Hc8. Longer cabinet lifespan (in the period 1980–2004) fosters agency-reforms along NPM lines	F > (N & I)	Hp3. Higher policy uncertainty, as visible in shorter cabinet lifespans, lead to more autonomous agencies	(N & I) > F in case of managerial autonomy and 'overall autonomy'
Hc9. More dominance of right-wing political parties in cabinet (in the period 1980–2004) fosters agency-reforms along NPM lines	I > (F > N)		
		Hp4. The presence of more *ex post* parliamentary controls on the actions of the executive in general and of agencies in particular allows for more autonomous agencies	(N & F) > I in case of managerial autonomy and 'overall autonomy'
Hc10. Less corporatist state tradition and less involvement of strongly organized interest groups in policy formulation and implementation fosters agency reforms along NPM lines	I > (F & N)	Hp5. More involvement of strongly organized interest groups in policy formulation and implementation (corporatist tradition) leads to more autonomous agencies	(N & F) > I in case of managerial autonomy and 'overall autonomy'
		Hp6. The presence of stronger 'fire alarms' and extra-parliamentary controls (ombudsman, FOI, judicial review) allows for more autonomous agencies	(N & F) > I in case of managerial autonomy and 'overall autonomy'

Table 9.1 (Continued)

Hypotheses based on change management approach	Hypotheses concerning managerial autonomy result control, and management techniques	Hypotheses based principal agent delegation approach	Hypotheses concerning autonomy (management/policy)
Actor constellations			
Hc11. Politico-administrative relations (between ministers and senior civil servants) which are relatively adversarial and distrusting, with limited involvement of senior civil servants in policy making, fosters agency-reforms along NPM lines	F > (I & N)	Hp7. Politico-administrative relations (between ministers and senior civil servants) which are relatively cooperative and trusting, with high involvement of senior civil servants in policy making, combined with low ministerial capacity to control agencies' actions, lead to more autonomous agencies	**(N & I) > F** in case of managerial autonomy and 'overall autonomy'
		Hp8. A weak position of the parent department with limited capacity to control agencies leads to more autonomous agencies	**N > (F > I)** in case of managerial autonomy and 'overall autonomy'

Hc12. Stronger position of PM and central departments versus line ministers and line departments fosters agency-reforms along NPM lines	(I > F) > N	Hp9. Weaker position of PM and central departments, with less capacity to control line ministers and line entities leads to more autonomous agencies	N > (F > I) in case of managerial autonomy and 'overall autonomy'
Deliberate action – reform programmes			
Hc13. General and government-wide agency-specific reform programmes (see Chapter 6) explain the actual levels of agency autonomy, result control and use of management techniques (talk about reform, reform actions and reform results are aligned)	In case of Norway. Much less in case of Flanders and Ireland		

Legend:

Deep grey tint: hypothesis is strongly supported; hypothesis is supported by ranking of two states vis-à-vis one state.

Medium grey tint: hypothesis is partially supported; hypothesis is supported by ranking of two states vis-à-vis each other (these two states are in bold), but with observations for one state not in line with hypothesis.

Light grey tint: hypothesis which was apparently partially supported by empirical material, but where additional empirical material make this support more questionable.

No tint: hypothesis is not supported; empirical state rankings differ fundamentally from the expected ranking.

Bold: expected country ranking that is supported by empirical findings.

actions and reform programmes in Norway, then Ireland and subsequently Flanders.

9.2.1   Deliberate actions and reform programmes in Norway

As shown, in Norway the vast majority of agencies have very high and uniform levels of HRM autonomy, compared to Ireland and Flanders. Agencies also have the autonomy to shift budgets between years to some extent. Both kinds of extended managerial autonomy may surprise observers, since the agencies under review in Norway are civil service organizations without their own legal identity. As a form of internal devolution, the civil service organizations in Norway are subject to ministerial control and directions. They are regulated through the state budget and accompanying financial regulations, the state collective wage agreement, the state pension scheme, the Freedom of Information Act and administrative law. That may explain the high level of uniformity, but not the high level of managerial autonomy and overall autonomy.

The reason for the high levels of managerial autonomy in Norwegian agencies relates to the comprehensive budget reforms from the mid-1980s onwards. These reforms affected both financial management and HRM autonomy, by granting greater flexibility between running costs and personnel costs, as well as a loosening of the government personnel statute. The subsequent abolition of the general personnel statute and of the limits on numbers in the civil service has clear consequences, as we have seen. Even if state-wide pay scales, collective agreements and central negotiations between the Ministry of Government Administration and the civil service unions still constitute a key element in wage determination, there has been a considerable degree of decentralization and greater flexibility through local negotiations and individual placement on extended scales. Other aspects of personnel policy, like recruitment and training remain quite decentralized (Roness 2001b). Hence, most agencies have considerable leeway in designing salary, promotion and evaluation schemes themselves, as well as applying them to individual staff members. There is a substantial degree of uniformity between agencies in terms of high levels of autonomy, because of the abolition of the general personnel statute. This contrasts with Flanders, where uniformity between agencies concerning HRM autonomy is due to a strict general personnel statute.

The budget reforms granted all Norwegian civil service organizations some freedom to shift resources between different budgets and between years. However, the accompanying emphasis on self-generated income does not lead to relatively higher levels of autonomy with regard to setting tariffs, for this is quite similar across the three states. The budget reforms have led to a greater discretion in the use of budgets, but taking out loans for investments is still prohibited. Civil service organizations in Norway do not have individual legal identities and thus cannot act for themselves in capital markets. However, by allowing them some latitude to shift budgets between years, agencies can lend or save on their own budget, taking a multi-year perspective.

In the vast majority of cases, result control of Norwegian agencies by their parent departments is reported to be quite well developed. This is primarily due to the introduction in the early 1990s of a formalized performance-assessment system MBOR, as a main tool for regulating relations between ministries and subordinate bodies (Lægreid et al. 2006a). The price for increased devolution was that the agencies were required to pay closer attention to the use of documents reporting on activity, goal achievement and resource use, formal control procedures and dialogues, and performance management techniques. However, the use of MBOR as a result control model does not necessarily include the threat of sanctions and rewards, as shown in Chapter 8. Moreover, despite the introduction of the pay-for-performance system for top managers in 1991, rewards or sanctions affecting wages were reported to be present in only a minority of agencies, high-lighting the difficult and uneven implementation of this system (Lægreid 2001). The introduction of MBOR within the administrative system was at first mandatory for all line units and centrally defined by the Ministry of Finance with a formalized approach. However, because of resistance and slow implementation, more room for sectoral and organizational differences was later permitted and emphasis was placed more on the progress of general results than on an expansive set of output indicators. There has been a long period of adaptation and adjustment, which has resulted in variations between agencies (Lægreid et al. 2006a: 266–7). This explains the development of the Norwegian MBOR system in a broad process-oriented, dialogue-oriented and trust-based way, with goals often being formulated jointly by the ministry and the agency, with an emphasis on mutual learning. Under the MBOR system, the majority of agencies report that they consult their parent department or minister when taking decisions regarding policy instruments.

In a similar vein, it was observed that management techniques are widely used in Norwegian agencies – more so than agencies in Flanders and Ireland. The extended use of specific management techniques like multi-year planning and public reporting in the form of an annual activity report, is due to the governmental financial regulatory framework, to which all agencies in our sample are subjected. Both management techniques are a compulsory part of the MBOR system for agencies. However, other management techniques are not enforced by governmental regulations, but the decision of agencies to use these techniques is at least indirectly stimulated by the compulsory nature of the MBOR system like the use of customer surveys, the development of cost-calculation systems and the allocation of financial resources to subunits on the basis of results (Lægreid et al. 2007). These techniques help to increase customer-orientedness, cost-awareness and efficient behaviour within the organization and, in turn, supports the performance goals set out in MBOR documents.

The Norwegian reform programmes made clear reference to the more managerial aspects of NPM, and resulted in a relatively high level of perceived managerial autonomy and result control. With regard to these reforms, Norwegian agencies experience a considerable consistency between reform talk, actions and results.

9.2.2   Deliberate actions and reform programmes in Ireland

Can we explain the relative low to moderate levels of managerial autonomy, result control and use of management techniques in Irish agencies by referring to deliberate actions in the form of reform programmes of politico-administrative actors? Since the mid-1980s, and in particular since 1994, under the umbrella of the 'Strategic Management Initiative', the Irish government has been quite active in initiating administrative reform initiatives (cf. Chapter 6). To what extent is the observed pattern of autonomy, control and management techniques in Irish state agencies the outcome of these reform initiatives?

Irish agencies show a very divergent pattern of HRM autonomy, with very low levels of autonomy with regard to salaries and rather high levels in respect of evaluation. Unlike Norway and Flanders, a common personnel statute for the civil service and its agencies was never developed, which means that certain softer elements like personnel development and evaluation are not strictly regulated. For such issues, the level of HRM autonomy is mostly decided ad hoc in the process of enacting the founding legislation for the agency. As outlined in Chapter 6, this enactment is not directed by a general law or framework (McGauran et al. 2005), and creates a substantial variety among agencies. On such softer aspects, the Department of Finance has an advisory role only. Despite the intentions of various reform initiatives to devolve the more significant HRM aspects to line entities, agencies still exercise very little discretion over the number of their employees, their grades and pay levels (OECD 2008: 305). These issues are principally decided by the Department of Finance with strong input from unions. Strict controls are exercised by the Department of Finance (next to the parent departments), even at the level of operational decisions concerning individual staff members. The Department of Finance has no explicit communicated guidelines to guide its decisions, other than the aim to control or reduce overall public staff numbers. When it comes to decisions with financial implications, many agencies have to negotiate each time with their parent department and the Department of Finance for decisions concerning individual personnel (for example, appointments, salary level of individuals) (McGauran et al. 2005; OECD 2008).

Despite reform plans since 1994, the introduction of multi-annual budgets and more flexible administrative budgets in 1991 and 1998, as well as the adoption of a new financial management system in 1999, budget flexibilities are only allowed to a minor share of the agencies. Unlike Norway, Irish agencies do not enjoy flexibility in allocating funds between different types of spending, and most importantly, between personnel and other expenses. The financial management autonomy of agencies is determined by constraints laid down in their establishing legislation, as well as by general regulations on financial management to which most of them must comply, such as regulations on grants-in-aid. These general regulations still emphasize the annual nature of the budget allocation process and prohibit shifting of budgets between subheads of the grant-in-aid and over years without *ex ante* approval. In case studies (McGauran et al. 2005), these restrictions were found to discourage cost-efficient behaviour within agencies. As Boyle and Humphreys (2001: 59) assert, 'financial management systems traditionally have been over-centralized, short-term in orientation and more concerned with the control of inputs than the efficient and effective delivery of outputs'. Thus, the announced reforms, aimed at devolving managerial flexibilities, did not really materialize in a convincing way in increased HR and financial management autonomy for most of the agencies.

Almost all CEOs in the surveyed agencies are accountable for results. However, as was made clear, the underlying systems of norm setting, performance monitoring and sanctions are quite weakly developed. The emphasis on performance and targets goes back to the 1994 Strategic Management Initiative, and the Public Management Act of 1997 in which strategy statements with targets and performance reporting was required from each line entity. Under the SMI process and the *Code of Practice for the Governance of State Bodies* parent departments are responsible for checking if strategy, targets and adequate monitoring and reporting systems are being devised by the agencies. However, the extent to which these reforms are rolled out to agencies and the extent to which parent departments monitor this process varies considerably, as shown by the lack of strategy documents or performance indicators in a substantial number of cases. Case studies show that the drive for strategy and target formulation often comes from the agency itself or its governing board, rather than because of pressure by the parent departments (McGauran et al. 2005). This is also reflected in the evidence that agencies have high level of policy autonomy. Also, the observed lack of rewards and sanctions linked to wages is surprising since, during the 1990s, the Irish government introduced a performance-related pay system for all senior managers, in the form of a potential annual bonus of up to 25 per cent of basic salary (OECD 2008). However, evaluations in 2002 and 2004 pointed at the problematic implementation across the civil service and the quasi-absence of performance-related pay (PRP). As the OECD (2008: 108) found, 'agency boards theoretically have the opportunity to award good performance but they rarely do so'.

Irish agencies use management techniques to a low or moderate extent, except for multi-year planning, public reporting and customer surveys. Multi-year planning and public reporting, which are stimulated through the SMI reform and the Code of Practice for the Governance of State Bodies, are used in most of the agencies. The requirement for a three-year corporate plan is included in the enacting laws of newly created agencies, but not fully rolled out to pre-existing agencies. The relatively well-developed use of quality management instruments, in particular customer surveys, may be related to the increased emphasis on customer-orientation, embedded in the 'Delivering Better Government' and subsequent 'Quality Customer Service' initiatives. Both reforms urged line departments to develop action plans and instruments for increased customer consultation and feedback, and required them to roll out these initiatives to the agencies under their remit. This rolling out was considered to be problematic in an assessment done in the early 2000s (Boyle and Humphreys 2001). Modern techniques linked to result-oriented financial management are substantially less developed than in Norway and Flanders, which relates both to the fairly centralized financial management and input-oriented practices, and to the underdevelopment of performance measurement systems.

As assessed by several observers (Hardiman and MacCarthaigh 2008; OECD 2008), Irish reform initiatives as described commonly display some elements of NPM thinking, but overall reforms have been guided by an ad hoc approach to improving administrative efficiency. The main targets of these initiatives are the core administration (the civil service line departments), rather than the complex organizational periphery of the Irish state administration. Furthermore, these reforms bear resemblance only to the managerial aspects of NPM, rather than to the radical aspects of slimming down the governmental apparatus by outsourcing or corporatization. Finally, individual reform initiatives are pursued under the SMI umbrella, but in an incremental and loosely coupled way. The 2008 OECD Review, although quite optimistic about the progress made, asserted that efforts have been primarily focused on putting processes in place and found a coherent reform package to be lacking (OECD 2008: 24). Other observers are more critical, and refer to an 'implementation deficit' (Boyle and Humphreys 2001). In its *Evaluation of the Strategic Management Initiative* (SMI), the PA Consulting Group (2002) identified 'the challenge of implementation' as the key theme to emerge from its analysis. According to Hardiman and MacCarthaigh (2008: 7), the Irish government is still largely a 'classic' Whitehall-type state administration that retains core features of classic bureaucratic design.

In sum, the story of Irish reform programmes (at least with respect to autonomy and control of agencies) is one of inconsistency between reform talk on the one hand, and reform actions and results on the other. This is related to the absence of an explicit adherence to a model of NPM-based reform (as in the case of Norway), as well as an overall lack of implementation capacity which has inhibited the roll-out of reforms within agencies.

9.2.3   Deliberate actions and reform programmes in Flanders

To what extent do reform initiatives taken by politico-administrative leaders account for the comparatively low to moderate level of agencies' managerial autonomy and result control, as well as the rather well-developed use of management techniques, which was observed in Flemish agencies?

Although the Flemish government issued a new general personnel statute for Flemish civil servants in order to introduce many instruments for modern HRM policies, agencies reported that they are very restricted in their HRM autonomy, with such autonomy being mainly related to operational decisions around promotion and evaluation. This paradox is to be explained as follows: Since the 1954 law stipulated that the staff number and legal statute of public law agencies was to be determined by the government, most public law agencies were required to adopt a similar personnel statute in line with this general personnel statute. Almost no organization-specific exceptions were allowed by the Minister of Civil Service and the Minister of Finance. However, the new personnel statute was very extensive and detailed in the procedures and regulations it imposed. By simply transposing this strict procedural statute to most agencies, the central departments and their ministers meant to force public law agencies to adopt the same modern HRM practice as the core administration, to enhance uniformity between departments and agencies in order to build similar cultures, as well as to foster mobility in an internal labour market. This strict approach was also necessary in order to convince the labour unions to accept this modernization of HRM policies and to take away their fear of civil service systems fragmenting within the Flemish administrative apparatus. This left most agencies with operational autonomy on only some issues. Only a few public law agencies in Flanders were exempted from this regulatory framework and were allowed full strategic and operational autonomy.

Despite several reform measures regarding financial management, Flemish agencies have low to moderate levels of financial management autonomy. This is mainly because most reforms undertaken in this period aimed to introduce modern financial management practices in agencies through strict regulations, while budgetary-fiscal pressure encouraged strict controls. Formally, all public law agencies were subjected to financial management rules set out in the 1954 law, with budget shifts within and between years and loan taking being subject to prior approval from the Minister of Finances. Moreover, all financial decisions were subject to a general veto right by the 'Commissaires de Gouvernement'. Budget and accounting systems and rules were to be set by government. However, in reality, the initiatives were less restrictive than anticipated, as the government failed to set budget and accounting schemes, and some agencies did not apply the 1954 regulations strictly. Budget shifts within and between years and loan taking were carried out without prior approval and systems were opaque, greatly frustrating the Court of Audit and Parliament. Because of pressure from the latter, as well as the need for drastic budget savings, the Minister of Finance and the Department of General Affairs launched several initiatives to curb this informal financial management autonomy of agencies on several fronts. Several centralizing measures with regard to cash management and other aspects restricted the autonomy of agencies to take loans, to hold too much cash and to invest money in stock markets.

From 1998 onwards, public law agencies were required to apply a common and uniform accounting and reporting scheme in order to improve the budgetary transparency of agencies and the consolidation of their budgets with that of the departments. All these general initiatives increased input control by government and brought the state substantial budgetary gains. Nevertheless, during that period some agencies were granted exemptions from financial and budgetary regulations on an ad hoc basis because of their task or because they negotiated a performance contract with the government. This explains the limited number of agencies with greater financial management autonomy for loan taking and shifting budgets. Also, forced by severe budgetary constraints, the government stimulated agencies to find additional sources of income, allowing them more discretion in setting tariffs. As part of the 'Beter Bestuurlijk Beleid' reform a new financial management regulatory framework was introduced, which provided greater budget flexibility for operational costs. But as of 2009, this framework had not been implemented because of the lack of interest on the part of several key actors.

The multitude of initiatives piloted by the Flemish government to enhance result based control, did have some impact on Flemish agencies, albeit limited, as described in Chapter 8. Most of the initiatives launched were aimed at the departments, rather than agencies. As a large share of the agencies set and evaluate performance targets themselves, these targets are mainly developed for reasons of internal control or external reputation. Although performance agreements became a government-wide objective after 1995, by 2003 only ten public law agencies had negotiated performance agreements with their minister. The first generation of these agreements was propagated mainly by the Minister of Finance in order to enforce hard budgetary constraints on agencies, which in return were allowed some budget flexibility during the year. CEO accountability was linked to individual performance objectives and financial rewards from 1998 onwards. This was part of a more general aspiration on the part of the Flemish government during the 1990s to increase its direct influence on the CEOs of the agencies.

The use of management techniques was quite extensive in Flemish agencies, but to what extent do official reform programmes help to explain this? Public reporting through annual activity reports is obligatory for all agencies. As in Ireland, since the mid-1990s, core departments and their ministers have had to prepare strategic multi-year plans. This planning initiative was never officially rolled out to the state agencies though it became regarded as good practice. Hence, a large majority of public law agencies developed similar strategic plans. Financial management tools such as cost-calculation systems or internal result-based resource allocation are used by a majority of 60 per cent of agencies, as in Norway. However, neither of these tools were part of an official reform programme. The use of cost-calculation systems was encouraged by the increasing reliance of public agencies on non-budgetary sources of income, as stimulated by the Department of Finance. Additionally, the general introduction of accrual based accounting in 1997 and experiments with performance budgeting, efficiency analysis and performance contracting facilitated the development of cost-calculation systems and the internal result-based allocation of resources. However, there was no general policy to allocate budgets to public law agencies based on outputs and results. Agencies seem to have developed and introduced these tools, not because of coercive pressure, but for reasons of internal functionality or external legitimacy (Verhoest 2002; Verhoest et al. 2007). Several network conferences and sectoral projects stimulated an increasing awareness and emphasis on quality management systems, but there were no general regulations. Although reform programmes envisaged an overall shift towards modern management and result control, this was mainly pursued by centrally imposed regulations, which restricted the managerial autonomy of the Flemish agencies. Moreover, the general introduction of result control through performance contracts did not materialize. As in Ireland, Flanders has seen considerable inconsistency between announced reform programmes, actual reform actions and effective reform results.

9.2.4 Comparing deliberate actions and reform programmes in the three states

To what extent can the deliberate actions taken by political and administrative leaders in their reform programmes and initiatives explain differences in the perceived level of managerial autonomy, result control and management techniques in the three states? From a change management approach we expected that reform talk and consequential reform actions would explain reform results (Pollitt 2001), as formulated in Hc13. However, we found such consistency between reform talk, and reform actions and results, mainly in Norway, but to a much lesser extent in the other two states. Reform actions in Flanders turned out to be much more centralizing then the announced reform initiatives suggested. In Ireland, announced reform initiatives were not well rolled out to, or implemented in, agencies for several reasons. Therefore, Hc13 is only partially supported by the case of Norway. Of course, the (lack of) consistency between reform talk, reform actions and reform results, relates also to the nature and the relative position of the actors involved. We turn now to these actor constellations.

9.3   Actor constellations

As defined in Chapter 7, actor constellations deal with the intentions, interests, discourses and the 'will and skill' of the relevant political, administrative and socio-economic actors (Wollmann 2003b) with regard to public sector reforms in general, and agency reforms in particular. In this part we focus on the relative power positions and the intentions of the major politico-administrative actors involved in agency policy and reforms in the three states. First, we take a broad scope, encompassing Parliament, cabinet, central departments, line departments, agencies and interest groups. We then analyse the extent to which hypotheses with regard to actor constellations, as developed in Chapter 7, are supported by our empirical data.

9.3.1   Actor constellations in Norway

By making reference to different Norwegian reform programmes we can quite easily explain the perceived high level of managerial autonomy and result control, as well as the prevalence of several management techniques in at least an indirect way. But who drove these Norwegian reforms concerning agency policy? Who took action? Who were the major actors and what were their roles?

First, we should remember that the Norwegian agencies studied here represent a form of internal devolution. There is a long history of using this form in agencies without their own legal identity, grounded in informal norms concerning administrative organization related to professionalism, with the objective of relieving the departments from routine operational decisions. However, in Norway, even if governmental proposals to create agencies that require additional funding or new or amended laws have to be approved by the Storting, the Parliament usually does not interfere (Roness 1995). Only specific cases, related to sensitive sectors, get much attention in Parliament. As the introduction of the MBOR system within the civil service was achieved through changing financial regulations, Parliament was not involved in this reform. In addition, the legislators did not play a central role in the preparation of the comprehensive reform programmes in the mid-1980s, nor were the programmes handled separately in the Storting (Roness 2001a).

In contrast, Parliament (together with the civil service unions) was quite active in relation to administrative reforms that involved external structural devolution, converting civil service organizations into state-owned companies. In the 1990s, when it came to specific changes in the form of affiliation, such as that for the national telephone company, the Post Office and the Norwegian State Railways, there were extensive deliberations in the standing committees and parliamentary debates. Moreover, politically salient sectoral reforms such as those in the health care sector could only be passed after substantial parliamentary discussion (Christensen 2007: 25).

The reforms since 1985 occurred under minority governments, either single-party Labour governments or centre- or Conservative-centre minority coalitions. In the context of Labour losing electoral power, the party gradually changed stance from an anti-NPM stance in the 1990s towards a more pro-NPM one, which enabled a broad NPM coalition. However, most cabinets have been reluctant to expend extensive resources on administrative reforms, and it has not been considered a main area of priority. A study conducted in 2000/2001 showed that cabinet members of a centre government were quite reluctant to accept more extreme market-oriented parts of NPM and structural devolution, but did not perceive similar problems of control loss in relation to the managerial aspects like MBOR and increased autonomy for regular state agencies. Top civil servants also share this attitude, although they are less critical of the more extreme elements of NPM (Christensen 2007: 30). More extreme aspects of NPM are mainly advocated by Conservative and right-wing political parties and managers of state-owned companies.

The political and administrative leadership in the Ministry of Government Administration and the Ministry of Finance did play a central role in the preparation of the reform programmes. However, this leadership was not based on a centralized and hierarchical dominance of line entities. The programmes which were formulated were primarily advisory in nature and not binding directives. The MBOR programme was initially more centralized and uniformly imposed, but that changed later on. Hence, the central administrative policy departments did not have the means to ensure an authoritative follow-up through instructions, directives, order and hierarchical authority. Their role was reduced to providing assistance, stimulation and motivation, as specific responsibility for following up reform programmes was transferred to the individual line departments and agencies. Knowledge relating to administrative reform was largely concentrated in specialized units based in the individual departments (Lægreid and Roness 1999).

It may seem surprising that in such a polycentric and administratively dominated reform setting, with relatively little active involvement by politicians, reform programmes can be developed and implemented, which are more far-reaching in certain ways and in their outcome than in Ireland and Flanders. There are several possible explanations for this development (cf. Lægreid et al. 2003, forthcoming). Perhaps most important is that, in accordance with the established political-administrative structure in Norway, the concrete reform measures can be interpreted as a political cooperation process where, with a starting point in established relationships based on trust, an approach is made to effect those solutions that are administratively and politically reasonable, and in the light of opposing views and demands (cf. March and Olsen 1989). The administrative policy reform style is scarcely distinguishable from the decision-making processes that have characterized Norwegian politics in the post-war period, and which have been seen as peaceful coexistence and revolution in slow motion based on common interests rather than a situation of clear winners and losers (cf. Olsen et al. 1982). Under such conditions, successful reform will be a matter of keeping the reform process alive long enough so that the many small measures can be aggregated into a more comprehensive adjustment of the state apparatus. So, consensus-building, trust and incrementalism are crucial.

Another element was that individual organizations were allowed substantial leeway in introducing centrally issued reform programmes, allowing for sectoral or organizational deviations and particularities, making those reforms legitimate and more acceptable. For example, there seems to be a lot of leeway for different agencies to apply their own variants of MBOR, which can deviate widely from the ideal model of performance management. This could have facilitated the implementation and enhanced compatibility with existing administrative culture and procedures (Lægreid et al. 2006a: 267).

9.3.2   Actor constellations in Ireland

Which actors were active in the Irish agencification policy and administrative reforms? According to Hardiman and MacCarthaigh (2008: 4; cf. Boyle and Humphreys 2001: 63; OECD 1999), public sector reform in Ireland was mainly initiated and undertaken by senior civil servants themselves. The Oireachtas, the Irish Parliament, was no explicit driver in reform initiatives, nor were the generally weak Oireachtas committees firmly engaged in scrutinizing progress with regard to modernization (Boyle and Humphreys 2001: 63; Boyle 2004: 18). This even holds for the All-Party Oireachtas Committee on the SMI, which was established in 1998. Cabinet holds agenda setting powers and dominates the legislative initiative; However, this does not fully explain the rather weak parliamentary leadership. The conventional left-right division is only present in a limited degree in the party political landscape, since both of the largest parties, Fianna Fáil and Fine Gael, present themselves as centre-right catch-all parties and their party programmes are quite alike. Moreover, they have historically tended to alternate in cabinet. This stimulates or even forces cross-party consensus on administrative reform programmes. Likewise, inclusive policy stances and the avoidance of overt ideological partisanship is strengthened by the trend towards coalition government. As Hardiman and MacCarthaigh (2008: 4) put it: 'This may help to explain why no government has taken up a strong stance that could risk bringing it into confrontation with the public administration, but has preferred to allow these issues to be dealt with through negotiation', making it 'more difficult to implement deliberate "sweeping change"-type programmes of agencification'.

The same holds largely true for the commitment of cabinet, ministers and the Taoiseach to public sector reform. Continuing cross-party support has facilitated a consistent longer-term approach to modernization (Boyle and Humphreys 2001: 63). Despite their support, politicians from different parties show little proactive engagement or instigation in change, themselves. Therefore, according to Boyle and Humphreys (2001: 63; cf. Hardiman and MacCarthaigh 2008: 7) 'political direction can very much be characterized as "support" rather than "initiation" or leadership', which 'limits the scope of change, as fundamental questions about the role of the state cannot be addressed other than in a political context'. Moreover, it limits the prioritization and urgency given to implementation of the modernization programme.

The SMI/DBG programme was an initiative that came mainly from within the civil service itself, housed within the Department of Finance and driven by the senior civil servants in the Department of the Taoiseach, under the broad remit of a 'modernization agenda'. The reform strategy was meant to be participatory, involving consultation with, and involvement of, management across the civil service. Networks of senior managers from different levels across the civil service were organized and supported by the Department of Finance. Responsibility for directing and leading the SMI process was shared between a Coordinating Group and an Implementation Group, which were primarily dominated by senior civil servants, mainly secretaries-general from departments. This participatory approach to the SMI/DBG programme was influenced by previous reform initiatives, such as those of the mid-1980s, which were seen to have failed, partly because they were perceived as having been centrally devised and centrally imposed (Embleton 1999).

The overall participatory approach does not mean that the centre (the Departments of the Taoiseach and of Finance) in administrative reforms has been merely to facilitate bottom-up changes in administrative reforms. For example, the performance management and development system (PMDS) was instigated and designed centrally, allowing little local flexibility in the implementation of performance management systems (Murray 2001; Boyle 2004). In other fields the centre was rather weak in prioritizing and pushing for changes in such issues as strategic HRM, and devolution of resource management (Boyle 2004: 38; O'Riordan 2004). In an evaluation of SMI progress of 2002, a consultant recommended the strengthening, widening and deepening of the range of central support for civil service modernization provided by the Departments of Finance, the Taoiseach and the Implementation Group of Secretaries General (Boyle 2004).

The Department of Finance, in particular, was blamed for not balancing its 'controlling' and 'promoting' roles well, with regard to public service provision (Boyle 2004). Control was seen to be overemphasized, both in terms of detailed control of the reforms itself, and of resource (human and financial) management in general. Tensions were reported between, for example, controlling the public service pay bill on the one hand, and management and development functions aimed at enhancing the efficiency and effectiveness of the public service on the other (Boyle 2004: 19, 35). According to the OECD review of the Irish public service, one possible explanation for the general reluctance to relax input controls is that the very high budget deficits in the 1980s left a cultural and systematic legacy, which continuously stressed controlling inputs and overspending. This helps to explain the Department of Finance's lack of enthusiasm for increasing flexibility (OECD 2008: 173; Hardiman and MacCarthaigh 2008). In a similar vein, it was suggested that, in line with the economic slowdown around 2003, there was a reassertion within the Department of Finance of the 'traditional' control ethos and consequent diminution in trust (Boyle 2004).

The reluctance of the Department of Finance to devolve managerial decisions to the line departments may also stem from concerns about the capacity of line departments to manage new responsibilities (Hardiman and MacCarthaigh 2008). Various guidelines such as the *Public Financial Procedures* and the *Code of Practice for the Governance of State Bodies* place responsibility for controlling and monitoring agencies in relation to their financial and non-financial performance very clearly with the parent departments. However, line departments and their senior civil servants were considered to be key actors in promoting and introducing reforms within their agencies (Murray 2001). Moreover, although the reform programmes did not target agencies as such, the idea was that through a process of 'osmosis' reforms would spread to the organizational periphery of the Irish state administration (OECD 2008). However, case studies showed that in many instances departments do not seem to encourage or stimulate the agencies to adopt reforms. Departments failed to reorient their control and monitoring towards objectives and results, although several tools were put at their disposal to set up a performance-oriented accountability system. And such countervailing instruments such as the Management Information Framework and PMDS were insufficiently implemented in order to allow for greater delegation of centralized input control (OECD 2008). Most line departments, although comparatively large, lack the capacity to monitor and control agencies. In general, they do not perceive their role in terms of strategic direction or monitoring of agencies' actions, but as supporting and enabling the agency to perform its statutory function by helping them to obtain the necessary resources (McGauran et al. 2005).

Many departments still associate the effort to improve the performance of agencies with imposing fiscal discipline, as earlier performance initiatives were implemented with the aim of strengthening budget discipline. Hence, when dealing with agencies, departments still focus very much on input and process controls. Sanctions towards agencies are reported as being implemented mostly because of financial 'failure'. In many instances where parent departments have the power to decide on financial or human resources for agencies, the responsibility is often shifted to the Department of Finance in order to avoid blame (McGauran et al. 2005). In general, while the Department of Finance is blamed for excessive central control of managerial freedoms, most parent departments are reluctant to proactively change accountability systems, and the dialogue with agencies towards a performance focus, although the instruments to do so are increasingly available, at least formally (OECD 2008).

For those agencies which experienced changes in their internal and external accountability mechanisms, reform seemed to come mainly from an internal drive to strengthen their legitimacy, as shown in case studies (McGauran et al. 2005). However, this proactive stance should not be overestimated, as many agencies do not steer internally on results (OECD 2008: 297). Non-commercial agencies, although numerous, do not form a strongly organized power group, unlike commercial agencies. Most non-commercial agencies were established quite recently and the Irish government, unlike Norway, never adopted an explicit vision on the role and position of agencies, nor a blueprint for their autonomy or control. In contrast, the agencification wave in Ireland has not grown out of a 'delegation of authority environment' (OECD 2008: 297). Many agencies were created in the context of economic expansion to execute new governmental tasks or services, for which line departments lacked capacity. Moreover, many Irish agencies are quite small in size, which inhibit the development of internal management support services for personnel or financial management. Hence, many small agencies depend on their parent department for such issues as recruitment or for accounting. As agencies are small and very diversified, centrally initiated reform programmes tended to overlook implementation in agencies. Traditionally, managing a large number of bodies at arm's length was not a core feature of the Irish Public Service culture. This may explain why the Irish government has taken little risk with delegating managerial autonomy to agencies (OECD 2008: 297). In addition, when establishing new agencies for new tasks, no provisions were made for extended control and monitoring capacities in the line departments.

Although Ireland scores relatively low on comparative indices of corporatism, social partners do play an important role in administrative modernization initiatives. Since 1987 subsequent three-year national agreements between the government and the social partners were concluded, and these partnership agreements have often been regarded as having contributed significantly to Ireland's social and economic development (National Competitiveness Council 1999; Boyle and Humphreys 2001). With the introduction of the fourth national agreement, *Partnership 2000* (1996), each government department/office had to establish a partnership committee comprised of senior management, union representatives, and staff. The partnership initiative was intended to foster joint ownership of the modernization agenda, through the development of jointly agreed action plans. The introduction of these partnership committees and the inclusion of the social partners in the high-level Coordinating Group represented an important attempt in changing what has been a traditional adversarial approach to industrial relations in the public service (Boyle and Humphreys 2001). Labour unions are powerful in the public sector, with coverage in the public sector estimated at about 80 per cent. As the inclusion of labour unions in decision-making processes on reforms have strengthened the legitimacy of the reforms, it was said to have scaled down the likelihood of more radical reforms, in particular, in the absence of a driving political commitment (Hardiman and MacCarthaigh 2008: 4–9).

9.3.3   Actor constellations in Flanders

Which actors were dominant in taking deliberate actions in Flanders concerning agency policies? What form did the Flemish actor constellations take? First, it should be remembered that prior to federalization Belgium already had a considerable tradition of agencification, with a large expansion of bodies following the Second World War, until the end of the 1970s. However, no clear blueprint or explicit motives existed to guide this agencification. The 1954 Law was a pragmatic law intended to bring some consistency in control and accountability arrangements into the 'organizational chaos' which then existed, but it did not provide any formal criteria to establish agencies or delineate a clear task division between them and departments. Nor did any later Belgian governments do so. Moreover, the 1954 Law became weakened through practice, with many regulations being ignored by the agencies, and with the *ex ante* control mechanisms proving to be largely ineffective. When federalization began, the Flemish government inherited this legacy of ad hoc agencification as well as strict, but ineffective, control arrangements. This legacy was combined with the dynamics of a young emerging state, in which political and administrative leaders acted deliberately to create a new administrative apparatus as they envisioned it. This incentive for 'tabula rasa' reforms that would differentiate the Flemish administration from the federal administrative tradition became more explicit in the 1990s. However, this did not materialize into drastic NPM-like agency reforms, but rather in centralizing measures.

The Flemish Parliament, dominated by majority governments, was largely absent in the formulation of the administrative reforms undertaken by the Flemish government. However, it did play an important role in pressing for reforms concerning public law agencies, since Parliament perceived a fragmentation of the state apparatus which resulted in agencies being largely out of control. Four parliamentary resolutions in the period 1997–2004 demanded a critical evaluation of the Flemish public sector and the diversity of agencies. These resolutions requested clear criteria for agency creation, a clearer division of tasks between departments and agencies and more emphasis on performance-based control. The parliamentary resolutions were instigated by several very critical reports from the Court of Audit from 1996 onwards. These reports, including an in-depth evaluation of performance contracts in 2001, suggested a general move to more result control. However, the Court of Audit, followed by the Parliament, simultaneously stressed the need for more effective *ex ante* control by the 'Commissaires du Gouvernement' and for maintaining strict controls on inputs. Better and extended mechanisms for accountability and transparency were at the core of their demands. These parliamentary demands were initially met with caution and suspicion by the agencies themselves and their responsible line ministers.

The multi-party cabinet was the main political actor in relation to initiatives for agency creation and reform programmes. Before the 1990s, the cabinet generally followed the federal 'ad hoc' policy of agencification. In the 1990s, cabinets were dominated by the Christian-Democratic and Socialist parties in coalition. However, while these two political parties did not influence the content of the reforms to any great degree, some of their individual ministers did. More specifically, the reforms were mainly driven by the ministers of Finance and of Civil Service, supported by their political secretariats. In the early 1990s, the power of both ministers and central departments was formally enhanced by the installation of a matrix structure, giving them great control over managerial matters. Ministers, their central departments, as well as the senior officials of the line departments, were initially quite sceptical of agencies and their capacity to manage. Moreover, they were worried by the rapid expansion of agency staff and the grants allocated to them, particularly at times where the Maastricht criteria placed a huge budgetary pressure on the Flemish government. Most of the reforms that affected agencies directly were, therefore, issued from the top down and without much involvement from the agencies themselves.

These reforms had several objectives, such as imposing modern management techniques in the case of the strict personnel statutes, or to enhance financial and budgetary control of agencies. The draft framework law which was developed by the Minister of Finance in 1994 and which was meant to substitute the 1954 Law, was an exponent of this centralistic and cautionary approach. This law never reached Parliament because both agencies and their responsible line ministers feared a further centralization of power in the Finance ministry. Only at the end of the 1990s, when budgetary hardship ended, did trust between the ministers of Finance and Civil Service and the agencies increase.

Another tension existed between the senior managers of the line departments and the senior managers of the agencies. The latter did not accept control or monitoring from the line departments, and saw both departments and agencies as being controlled directly by the responsible ministers and their political secretariats. Ministers and their political secretariats favoured direct influence over these agencies, since it enabled them to bypass senior managers with whom they perceive to have loyalty problems. Division of tasks between departments and agencies was very unclear in terms of policy design and implementation, leading to very competitive relationships. Moreover, on most policy domains on which agencies were active, no expertise existed within the line departments. Therefore, the senior managers of the departments advocated a stricter division between policy design and policy implementation, and a clear role for line departments in controlling and monitoring the agencies.

In the 1990s, the agencies organized themselves into a lobby network to oppose these control attempts from the departments. This network, called MOVI, became a very powerful actor in the Flemish administrative landscape, and was able to convince line ministers to block several central initiatives. Many of the larger agencies took a proactive attitude towards the use of management techniques and performance indicators, in order to differentiate themselves from the line departments and to enhance their legitimacy with ministers and Parliament (Verhoest et al. 2007). This combined strategy of lobbying and legitimizing behaviour was successful.

This period also saw growing scepticism about the exact role of public law agencies' governing boards. Although it was not an official policy, the Flemish government adopted measures to strengthen the position of the agencies' CEO vis-à-vis the governing boards, which in turn strengthened the power of ministers over CEOs (Verhoest 2002). Government also became more reluctant to establish new public law agencies with their own governing board. In this manner, they made the agencies more responsive to the governments' political wishes.

This conflicting and mutually distrusting actor constellation made all-encompassing reforms very difficult. Initiatives to introduce results control by performance contracting were only implemented partially, because of agencies' fear that such contracts would lead to more control and accountability, without clear gains in autonomy. Line ministers were sceptical that such long-term performance contracts would decrease their direct influence on their otherwise flexible interaction with agencies. At different levels, centralizing tendencies were noticeable: Parliament towards agencies; horizontal ministers and their departments towards agencies; ministers towards CEOs, to the detriment of governing boards and interest groups. This centralization tendency was part of the emancipation of the young Flemish state.

Although during the 1990s the most important actors had moved closer towards an NPM-inspired vision of agencification, the reforms implemented before 2003 do not express a univocal doctrine. The political and administrative leaders in these reforms were theoretically and rhetorically in favour of more managerial autonomy on condition of commensurate result control, but mutual distrust inhibited them to link both in practice (Verhoest 2002).

Also, the 'Beter Bestuurlijk Beleid' reforms, implemented in 2006, which were clearly aligned with NPM doctrine on agencification, were implemented in this environment of distrust, leading to structural reforms which further enhanced the power of agencies and individual line ministers to the detriment of line departments (Spanhove and Verhoest 2008). Although performance contracts were introduced more generally, the envisioned increase in managerial autonomy for agencies did not materialize, at least not until the beginning of 2009.

9.3.4 Comparing actor constellations in the three states

The two contrasting sets of hypotheses concerning actor constellations formulated in Chapter 7 referred to (a) the nature of relations between ministers and senior civil servants and the ministerial capacity to control agencies' actions; (b) the relative power position of the parent department and its capacity to control agencies; and (c) the relative position of the prime minister, horizontal ministers and central departments, and their capacity to control line departments and agencies. All three factors may help us to explain why Norwegian agencies have developed with relatively more managerial autonomy, result control and management techniques, when compared with Flanders and Ireland. At a first glance on Table 9.1, all hypotheses based on the principal agent delegation approach (Hp7–9) are quite strongly supported in the relative rankings of the three (or at least two) states. In sum, specific actor constellations seem to matter in explaining the extent of managerial autonomy in a specific combination: one could hypothesize that the combination of (a) relatively cooperative and trusting relationships between ministers and top civil servants, with (b) relatively low ministerial and parent departmental capacity to control agencies under their remit and (c) a relatively weak position of central departments and prime minister, could provide a fruitful context for more autonomous agencies, at least in terms of managerial autonomy. However, there is more to say about this.

The Norwegian preference for agencies with high managerial autonomy, as well as considerable hands-off result control, may indeed be due to the trusting and cooperative relations between ministers and senior civil servants, combined with a relatively limited ministerial capacity to micromanage agencies' actions. The existence of mutual trust seemed to reduce the need for detailed controls. However, the mutual trusting relationship between Irish ministers and senior civil servants, which fosters the consensual nature of the administrative reforms, does not seem to affect the managerial autonomy and control of agencies directly, since parent departments, in most cases, deal with the subordinated agencies. In contrast, the distrust in the Flemish context, brought about by political appointments and unclear divisions of labour between politico-administrative actors, stimulates direct control by the large political secretariats of individual ministers over the agencies.

The relative position and capacity of parent departments seems to play a role, but in a more nuanced way than expected (Hp8). Control of the Norwegian agencies is traditionally considered to be one of the core tasks of the departments, rather than of the minister. These parent departments are small, so they do not have the capacity for detailed control of agencies. However, their limited resources are partially used to develop hands-off, result-oriented control relationships, which enable them to guide and monitor the relatively autonomous agencies at a strategic level. In that way, departments became active users of the MBOR system. The large Irish parent departments do use considerable resources to control the mainly small agencies under their remit, but in a detailed and input-oriented way. They did not take up their expected roles as change agents to enhance performance-oriented control. They steer on inputs, not on content, as reflected in the high level of policy autonomy of Irish agencies. As the main wave of agencification only happened quite recently in Ireland, parent departments are relatively inexperienced in controlling a wide range of agencies. Moreover, there is no overall (explicit or implicit) blue-print about labour division between departments and agencies in Ireland. In the Flemish context, the relatively large line departments traditionally do not play any substantial role in controlling agencies and, as such, did not affect the level of autonomy of agencies. With regard to result control, performance contracts were mainly negotiated between the agency and the political secretariat of the involved minister, with line departments only being involved marginally. In this process, agencies frequently take the lead, as reflected in their rather high level of policy autonomy.

The comparatively weaker role of central departments and the prime minister in Norway could account for the greater managerial autonomy of Norwegian agencies, since these horizontal actors have less capacity and power to control line entities, including agencies. In contrast, Irish and Flemish central departments and their respective ministers (such as the PM and minister of Finance) have much more power to impose regulations and controls on other public sector organizations. Hence, hypothesis Hp9 achieves quite strong support (see Table 9.1). However, the contrasting hypothesis (Hc12), that strong central actors can enforce more radical agency-related reforms, is not supported by our findings. In both Ireland and Flanders the central departments and their ministers used their dominant position and their extended capacities mainly to strongly regulate and control resource management in line entities, and were less inclined to impose or facilitate far-reaching NPM reforms with respect to agencies. In both states the emphasis of the Department of Finance on micro-control made their role as promoter of change less legitimate. In Norway the rather weak central departments made the most of their limited resources by relaxing input controls and, instead, concentrating it on the role of facilitator and broker for NPM-inspired administrative reforms in the line departments and agencies. In that way, hypothesis Hc12 could be reformulated: *the strength of the position of PM and central departments may not influence the degree to which agency reforms are radical as such. But the reforms are influenced by the way in which central departments use their resources and their position, as well as the extent to which there is a high degree of compatibility between the way they control line entities and the changes they promote.*

9.4 Structural and functional elements of polity

With regard to the expectations based on polity characteristics, we find quite strong support for Hc5, which expected that states with relatively little involvement from the private sector in service delivery and policy implementation would experience more radical reforms with respect to agencies' autonomy and control. This factor could explain Norway's position, where public sector employment is substantial and an advanced social democratic welfare model has been developed, compared to Ireland, which adheres to a more liberal welfare regime and where public expenditure accounts for only one-third of GDP. The Norwegian state provides more comprehensive services by its own public organizations, making NPM-like reforms aimed at strengthening managerial autonomy, result control and internal management of public sector organizations more useful and beneficial, compared to Ireland. Indeed, whereas in Ireland only one-third of all agencies are involved in direct service delivery, in Norway, the equivalent figure is about 50 per cent. Flanders, with substantial public expenditure, as well as large-scale funding of markets and non-profit institutions to provide public services, was expected to hold a middle-position, which is more or less confirmed. However, the fact that Ireland is a liberal market economy (Hall and Soskice 2001) with heavy reliance on trade, exports, and especially non-manufactured service-sector internationally tradable activities, did not cause the Irish government 'to be (comparatively more) attuned to market-based disciplines in the state sector, and to be (more) at the forefront of NPM experiments' in practice (Hardiman and MacCarthaigh 2008: 4).

On the other hand, the strong centralist state structure and comparatively small involvement of local government in providing public services in Ireland did not lead to sweeping NPM-like changes or substantially higher levels of overall autonomy and result control. Hypothesis Hc6, which expected a positive influence of large centralization of service delivery and policy implementation at central level on the extent to which NPM-like agency reforms are radical (Pollitt and Bouckaert 2004) is not supported by our evidence. It is hard to draw straightforward conclusions from this, since one could assume that strong decentralization in Norway leaves the central level with not much more comprehensive service delivery than in Ireland, where many services are delivered by private actors.

What seems to matter more here is that Norway has a long and widely accepted tradition of hiving off policy implementation to agencies, albeit with intensive links to their parent departments. So, public service delivery has been either devolved to state agencies or decentralized to the local authorities. The Irish state traditionally did not have an explicit strategy for agencification or separating policy implementation from design. Agencification mainly occurred as a response to limited departmental capacity to take on new tasks in an era of economic prosperity. Similarly, in Flanders (and Belgium), agencification was never a clearly formulated strategy, but happened in a tradition of ad hoc devolution. This long and explicit agencification tradition in Norway, together with the tradition of comprehensive service delivery by the public sector clearly helps to explain why the idea of expanding autonomy of agencies, controlled through results, was easily accepted across the political and administrative spectrum. Moreover, the fact that the Norwegian agencies studied here do not have their own legal identity and are legally more akin to Next Steps-agencies in the United Kingdom, together with the fact that Norwegian parent departments have traditionally clearly defined roles in controlling agencies helps to reduce the fear of uncontrollability, a fear that clearly paralysed reforms in Flanders.

The kind of cabinet structure as a polity factor seems to be weak with respect to its explanatory potential. Thus hypothesis Hc7 which expected similarities in consensual cabinet structure to result in similarities in connection with agency autonomy, result control and management techniques is only weakly supported by our findings, since only some aspects of agency autonomy and control (policy autonomy, autonomy regarding tariff setting, and rewards and sanctions) proved to be similar between the three states. All governments in the three states sought and received cross-party consensus regarding autonomy and result control reforms. However, despite its highly consensual cabinet structure, Norwegian governments were able to implement more drastic agency reforms that were more in line with the NPM ideology, compared to the other two states. This signals the need to acknowledge that consensual, as well as majoritarian, cabinet structures may embark upon significant reforms, under certain circumstances (cf. Pollitt and Bouckaert 2004).

Hypothesis Hp2, emphasizing that higher policy conflict in coalition governments would lead to the creation of more autonomous agencies, was not supported. This can be quite easily explained: in Ireland or Flanders, individual ministers or individual coalition partners cannot take independent decisions on agency creation or autonomy. They need at least the support of the entire cabinet, and hence, from the other coalition partners. In addition, in all three states, much of the decisions concerning agency creation and changes in autonomy have to be voted in Parliament. The idea that coalition partners safeguard their policies in autonomous agencies to protect them from interference from other coalition partners in matters of high policy conflict, fails to take into account the institutional requirements of Norwegian, Irish and Flemish coalition governments with regard to decisions of agency creation. In that way, hypothesis Hp2 was formulated in a quite blunt manner. This calls for a refinement in structural choice theory in the case of parliamentary European systems (see below).

Does the stability or the partisan composition of cabinets play any potential role in explaining the state differences in terms of agency autonomy, result control and internal management? Relatively more cabinet stability, as visible in Flanders during the period 1980–2004, does not lead in a straightforward way to agencies which are more NPM-like (except for rewards and sanctions with respect to individual wages). So, Hc8 does not get much support. The case of Norway vis-à-vis Flanders seems to fit the predictions of the competing hypothesis Hp3, stating that relatively less cabinet stability, and hence higher policy uncertainty, does lead to more autonomous agencies. However, since the changes in managerial autonomy took place mainly after 1980, when cabinet instability in Norway was much higher than in Flanders, we should not consider this as a support for hypothesis Hp3.

The relatively more frequent dominance of right-wing political parties within cabinet in Ireland since 1980 did not bring about more radical agency reforms. Hypothesis Hc9 is not supported, for in all three states a cross-party consensus was found for the reforms. Moreover, in Norway, the Labour Party took a more pro-NPM position, which strongly enhanced the reforms. Hence, there is no evidence that in relation to reform of agency autonomy and control, there are intense partisan conflicts among political parties, nor that the partisan composition of cabinets plays a major role (cf. Lonti 2005). Indeed, in some countries which took on more extreme forms of NPM, reforms were launched by social-democratic governments, for example, New Zealand (Pollitt and Bouckaert 2004). However, for Norway the story becomes much more conflictual when considering more extreme NPM reforms like corporatization and regulation, which are strongly advocated by right-wing parties, but opposed by the more left-wing parties.

Based on structural choice ideas, we expected that Parliament would more easily allow the creation of highly autonomous agencies in states where *ex post* parliamentary controls on the actions of cabinet and agencies were relatively more strongly developed (Hp4). This hypothesis is at least partially supported, in that it explains quite well the relative levels of managerial autonomy in Norwegian agencies when compared with Irish agencies. According to that line of reasoning, the relaxation of budgetary and HRM rules, which gave Norwegian agencies more managerial autonomy, would have been relatively acceptable for the Norwegian Storting because it holds sufficient instruments to control the behaviour of these increasingly autonomous agencies *ex post*. Indeed, these reforms were hardly discussed in the Storting, but *ex post* controls became more rigorous from the 1990s onwards.

In Ireland, the relatively weak *ex post* controls held by the *Oireachtas* combine low managerial autonomy for state agencies, which supports the hypothesis. Again, the position of Flanders is less easily explained. Until 2003 parliamentary activism did not lead to substantial relaxation in the autonomy of all agencies. On the contrary, in order to reduce the perceived lack of controllability and accountability of agencies, Parliament pressed for both stronger *ex ante* and *ex post* result controls. After 2003, however, Parliament agreed with a major reform by which more autonomous agencies would be created in exchange for an increase of formal *ex post* parliamentary control instruments, but at the time of writing no substantial increase in terms of managerial autonomy of Flemish agencies had been observed.

The degree of corporatism, understood as the involvement of strongly organized interest groups in public decision-making and policy implementation, was also expected to influence the autonomy of agencies. The strong Norwegian corporatist tradition has potentially led to the creation of agencies exhibiting high levels of both managerial and policy autonomy. This partly supports hypothesis Hp5, regarding the position of Norway vis-à-vis Ireland. This hypothesis is based on the idea that corporatist groups will favour agencies which are shielded from political influence, since this reduces policy uncertainty that subsequent enacting coalitions may substantially change the initial beneficial set-up of agencies. Moreover, it supports the idea that a majority in Parliament will more easily allow the creation of highly autonomous agencies because of the strong extra-parliamentary check on agencies' actions provided by the involvement of corporatist groups in their governance. Indeed, the involvement of traditional corporatist groups (mainly employer and employee organizations) in agency boards is quite substantial in Norway and Flanders, but less so in Ireland, where other stakeholders and independent experts are more dominant. But there are some counter-indications.

First, the position of Flanders does not correlate with its fairly strong corporatist tradition. Second, 70 per cent of the Irish agencies have a board, allowing for stakeholder involvement, compared to only half of all agencies in Norway and Flanders. Moreover, also in Ireland, despite its tradition of plural interests, the social partnership agreements gave the social partners and the civil service unions a central position in economic and social policy, as well as in administrative reforms. Moreover, the hypothesis (Hc10) that less involvement of strongly organized interest groups would lead to more radical reforms was not supported, as Norway did involve social partners and civil service unions quite extensively in their reforms. However, Norwegian civil service unions accepted increases in agency autonomy more easily, even in the field of HRM, than in Flanders and Ireland.

Similarly, the existence of relatively strong extra-parliamentary checks, such as the ability of citizens to appeal to an Ombudsman or administrative courts against agencies' decisions, or the ability to publicly access information on agencies' decisions (Freedom of Information), may potentially help to explain why agencies are allowed more managerial autonomy in Norway than in Ireland (Hp9). In Norway, more managerial flexibility and policy autonomy for agencies seems to be balanced with well-developed mechanisms for accountability to Parliament available to interest groups and to the wider public. Such accountability mechanisms are relatively less well-developed in Ireland, which may help to explain the reluctance of politicians to grant more leeway to agency heads, at least with respect to managerial issues.

9.5   Politico-administrative culture and legal tradition

Can differences in politico-administrative culture and legal tradition help us to explain state differences with respect to managerial autonomy, result control and internal management (Hc4)? We believe it can, at least in some measure in the cases of Norway and Flanders. However, the relatively lower level of managerial autonomy and use of management techniques in Ireland is very hard to explain. It seems as if the way Ireland deals with public management reforms is not fully consistent with the cultural values Hofstede (2001) assigns to it.

In the case of Flemish agencies, with a *Rechtsstaat* legal tradition, high uncertainty avoidance and power distance, we expected relatively low levels of autonomy, in particular for autonomy aspects with financial repercussions. This is indeed the case. Managerial autonomy of agencies was traditionally restricted by uniform and detailed regulations, which were reinforced during the 1990s. The cultural emphasis on administrative rules, detailed planning, elaborate procedures and firm hierarchy also does not provide fertile ground for the development of effective result control systems, as shown by the Flemish case. The preference of ministers to have direct political control over their agencies matches this picture. The relatively higher prevalence of rewards and sanctions with regard to individual wages could be explained by moderate masculinity levels within the Flemish cultural profile. However, private-sector style management techniques within agencies do seem to flourish well in this cultural setting. It has been proved elsewhere research that Flemish agencies, in order to protect and enlarge their position against competing principals (Parliament, ministers and line departments) in a strongly distrusting and hierarchical setting, use these management techniques as a legitimacy-enhancing tool (Verhoest et al. 2007). In several agencies, these techniques are also used in internal principal-agent relations to strengthen the position of the CEO in controlling lower levels of management (Verhoest 2002).

Norwegian agencies seem to fit the cultural profile of Norway quite well. Lower degrees of uncertainty avoidance and power distance facilitate the relatively large degree of managerial autonomy and the Norwegian form of result control. Parent departments and agencies seem to be able to develop a quasi-contractual relationship, based on frequent interaction and common goals. This reflects a more egalitarian attitude. Also, the virtual absence of individual financial sanctions and rewards for personnel seem to reflect the lower degree of masculinity.

Irish agencies were expected to be in the pole position of those agencies with the highest levels of managerial autonomy, result control and management techniques, because of a public interest tradition, combined with a more entrepreneurial and pragmatic administrative culture, low uncertainty avoidance, low power distance and high masculinity scores. However, the practice of Irish agencies is much less convincing than in Norway on all dimensions. Indeed, in line with the absence of an administrative law tradition, HRM autonomy is not strictly and uniformly regulated, but it is mainly determined on a case-by-case approach by the Ministry of Finance. Also, the trust between ministers and senior civil servants may reflect the low degree of power distance in Irish culture. But most Irish change actors do not exhibit strong risk-taking behaviour when it comes to public sector reforms. Both the Department of Finance and line departments emphasize detailed input controls, and reforms are very incremental and dispersed. Politico-administrative actors are quite similar to their Norwegian colleagues in that consent among many actors is first sought on the content of reforms, which contradicts the low degree of uncertainty avoidance and high masculinity values. The latter are also not translated in firm measures to install performance-related financial rewards and sanctions.

Thus, whereas the agency reforms in Norway and Flanders are consistent with the cultural profile in these states, agency reforms in Ireland do not match its cultural profile. Overall, we find rather mixed and only partial support for the expected influence of administrative culture and legal tradition on state differences in autonomy, result control and internal management of agencies (Hp4). This is in line with other empirical studies (Schedler and Proeller 2007). When explaining coordination patterns in four countries since 1980, Beuselinck et al. (2007) found that empirical links are, at most, indirect. Cultural values comprise only one element of the larger 'habitats' in which reforms are initiated and implemented. The causal chain from cultural influences to specific design and outcome of administrative reforms is very long with many intermediating variables.

9.6 Environmental pressures

We now consider the relevance of environmental pressures. The ranking of the three states seem to match, at least partly, the expectations formulated by two different hypotheses (Hp1 and Hc3).

According to Norwegian observers, Norwegian admission to the European Economic Area (EEA) in 1994 provided the impetus to adopt more NPM-like administrative policies (Lægreid et al. forthcoming). But, apparently, the timing of this admission and the indirect link to EU matters (hypothesis Hc1) contradicts the pole position of Norway in terms of managerial autonomy, result control and management techniques, compared to Ireland and Flanders which are long since full members. One reason could be that, in contrast with the developed hypothesis in Chapter 7, the isomorphic pressure from EU membership is mainly felt in terms of policy content rather than in terms of similar administrative structures. Moreover, when urging for similar structures, like in the case of independent regulatory agencies, this pressure from the EU is indirect and limited to certain policy areas (in particular, economic policy areas) or to specific situations, like new member states which are involved in a twinning process (Goetz 2000; Knill 2001).

The assertion of many comparative public reform students (for example, Pollitt and Bouckaert 2004) that states facing economic or fiscal crises embark on more radical NPM changes, leading to agencies with high managerial autonomy, high result control and high use of management techniques (our hypothesis Hc2), did not find any empirical support in our study. On the contrary, the lower level of managerial autonomy in Ireland and Flanders could be due to the prevalence of economic crises and budgetary-fiscal stress that both states experienced, as formulated by hypothesis Hp1. According to this hypothesis, such crises induce politicians to restrict the managerial autonomy of agencies in order to reduce the risk of uncontrollable budget deficits. This factor explains at least some developments from the 1980s until late 1990s, the period in which, for example, Flanders introduced some restrictive financial management measures to reinforce budgetary orthodoxy within its expanding agencies. During this time, Flemish politicians were socialized at the federal level during the major economic crisis of the 1980s. According to some observers (OECD 2008), one possible explanation for the general reluctance to relax input controls and increase flexibility in Ireland is that the very high budget deficits in the 1980s left a cultural and systematic legacy, which led to the continuously stressed practice of controlling inputs and overspending during the 1990s.

The influence of that legacy was clear in the behaviour of the Department of Finance and the line departments. So, economic and fiscal crises may inhibit drastic reforms in terms of more managerial autonomy and result control even when the crises themselves are over. Although Lægreid et al. (forthcoming) state that the absence, in Norway, of national fiscal pressure and the accumulation of a huge governmental petroleum fund may reduce the external pressure for devolution, Norwegian agencies do display a comparatively high level of managerial autonomy, which was brought about by the modernization programmes from the mid-1980s onwards. In line with Hp1, this evolution in Norway could take place because of the large budgetary surpluses brought about by the exploitation of petroleum, which relaxed the need for detailed input controls. The absence of a major budgetary or economic crisis could, nevertheless, explain the relative lack of enthusiasm among Norwegian political and administrative leaders for extreme market-oriented NPM reforms, which was noticeable after 2000. In sum, we find strong support for Hp1 at least when considering reforms affecting agencies' autonomy and control.

The state ranking seems to at least partially match the predictions of hypothesis Hc3. The continuing high level of public confidence in the Irish civil service (Van de Walle et al. 2008) since the 1980s could signal a lack of pressure in the mind of key Irish actors to drastically reform state administration and agencies. Flanders tells a somewhat more mixed story. On the one hand, the lack of drastic reforms in Flanders concerning managerial autonomy and result control contradicts the reform pressure arising from a low level of public trust. On the other hand, agencies in Flanders do use quite a lot of 'modern' private-sector-type management techniques, which could be seen as a response to low public trust and as a means to increase legitimacy. The modernization efforts in Norway could be explained by the strong pressure that may have arisen from the sharp decline in public confidence in the Norwegian civil service since the 1980s, as evidenced in Chapter 5. However, this finding is not supported by any reference in Norwegian public administration literature.

9.7   Explaining differences and similarities by state-level characteristics

From this chapter it is clear that the three states under review adopt NPM ideal-type agency features and widely adapt them to suit their politico-administrative regime and environment. Based on our analysis, the following characteristics of that regime and their effects, may help to explain state differences, either with a positive or a negative influence on reported managerial autonomy, result control and use of internal management techniques:

– with respect to other environmental pressures

  • a legacy of budgetary-economic crises (–);
  • (to a lesser extent) a low or declining level of public trust in public administration (+);

– with respect to culture

  • a strong administrative law tradition (–);
  • a strong *Rechtsstaat* tradition (–);
  • a high level of power distance and uncertainty avoidance (–);
  • a high degree of compatibility between culture and the way in which reforms are decided and implemented (+);

 – with respect to structural and functional aspects of polity

 - a strong involvement of state administration in service delivery (+);
 - a strong tradition of agencification for policy implementation; explicit doctrines on the roles and positions of agencies and their parent departments; and tradition of departmental agencies within concept of an integrated state apparatus (+);
 - a high degree of political partisan consensus on reforms (+);
 - a lack of strong *ex post* controls by Parliament (−);
 - a lack of strong extra-parliamentary controls (−);

 – with respect to actor constellations

 - a high degree of distrust between ministers and senior civil servants, and also large ministerial capacity to control (−);
 - a limited capacity within central departments and parent departments for micro-control (+);
 - a high degree of distrust between central departments and agencies (−);
 - a high degree of distrust and unclear role division between parent departments and agencies (−);
 - a lack of consensus among central departments, line departments and agencies about reforms (−);
 - a high degree of compatibility between the way central departments control line entities and the reforms they promote (+);
 - a strong need for agencies to increase their legitimacy within a highly distrusting environment, which positively influences the use of management techniques (+);

 – with respect to deliberate actions

 - a considerable degree of consistency between reform talk on the one hand and reform actions and results on the other (+).

The list of state-level characteristics with potential explanatory power is long. However, some characteristics seem to matter more than others. First and foremost, the legacy of budgetary-economic crisis seems to explain to a great extent the very cautious and reluctant attitude of central departments and their ministers towards the relaxation of input controls in Ireland and in Flanders. Second, cultural aspects matter: a strong administrative law tradition; a strong adherence to the *Rechtsstaat* model; combined with high levels of power distance and uncertainty avoidance seem to strengthen the orientation of politico-administrative actors towards strict controls and extensive regulations to the detriment of managerial freedom and result control.

Norway also showed a high degree of compatibility between its culture and the way in which reforms are decided and implemented: the political and administrative decision-makers sought large-scale consensus on administrative reforms. Moreover, the facilitating implementation strategy, which allowed for local discretion and tailor-made approaches, took into account the egalitarian, polycentric nature of the Norwegian state apparatus. A polity factor that appears to matter very strongly, is the combination of heavy state involvement in policy implementation, but combined with a strong tradition of hiving off implementation to agencies, with a clear and explicit vision on the role and position of such agencies within a broader concept of an integrated administrative apparatus. Norway provides an distinct example of this, whereas such traditions and explicit visions were lacking in both Ireland and Flanders. Neither cabinet structure nor cabinet turbulence seems to matter much, but consensus across partisan lines seems to matter in all three states. Flanders shows very clearly that a high degree of distrust within (politico-) administrative actor constellations, together with unclear divisions of roles between agencies and departments, provides a setting in which positive attitudes towards managerial freedom and result-based control are very hard to spread, and in which consensus among administrative actors on reforms is absent. The limited capacity of Norwegian central departments and line departments for micro-control, and the strong match between their hands-off control and the reform content and approach they promoted, increases mutual trust between departments and agencies. The high degree of consistency of the announced reforms and the actual reform actions has a similar trust-enhancing effect in Norway, whereas in Ireland and Flanders reform talk was not consistent with reform actions and the results agencies perceived.

In this chapter we have sought explanations for state differences in respect of agencies' autonomy, control and internal management, based on expectations developed from two approaches, the change management approach and the principal-agent delegation approach. To what extent do these explanations fit more to one of these approaches? Most of the hypotheses based on the change management approach were not (strongly) supported, except for the hypotheses referring to politico-administrative culture and the relations between state and private sector. The convergence between reform talk, actions and results has, as expected, a strong influence on perceived autonomy, control and internal management. The principal-agent delegation approach, based on the structural choice theory of Moe (1990) and others, finds quite strong evidence, as described in Chapter 9. However, interestingly enough, evidence is much weaker for hypotheses that were strongly based on the notions of policy conflict and policy uncertainty. These notions are the core in recent developed variants of structural choice theories (cf. Horn 1995; Huber and Shipan 2002; Elgie 2006; Yesilkagit and Christensen forthcoming). The other hypotheses within that framework, which were more strongly supported, were based more on simple principal-agent elements. Ideas with respect to policy conflict within coalition governments as a driver for agencification do not take into account the fact that agency creation and changes are in most states a matter of decision for the whole cabinet and mostly involve the parliamentary majority. In that respect, there is a further need for more refined theory building within this framework, adjusted to the institutional requirements of European parliamentary consensual regimes. In addition, we have to keep in mind that this approach is focused mainly on the formal creation of agencies, and has less to say about the actual, perceived functioning of agencies, the main focus in this book.

Part IV
Comparing Agencies

10
Theories on Similarities and Dissimilarities Across Agencies

10.1 Introduction

In this chapter we formulate hypotheses on variations in autonomy, control and internal management among agencies, based on three perspectives: (1) a structural-instrumental perspective (emphasizing formal organizational structure and rational choice of actors), (2) a cultural-institutional perspective (emphasizing organizational culture and organizational path dependency) and (3) a task-specific perspective (emphasizing the characteristics of organizational tasks). The environmental perspective (emphasizing institutional environments, isomorphism and myths) is considered mainly in Part III and functions here as a null hypothesis.

Agency characteristics may affect the way autonomy and control and internal management of agencies are regarded from above, in other words, whether and how the superior bodies (principals) are willing and able to make an impact on the agencies. They may also affect the way autonomy and control and internal management are regarded from below, that is, whether and how the agencies (agents) are willing and able to resist pressure from above and act on their own. From a cultural-institutional perspective, the importance of agency characteristics are primarily seen from below, emphasizing actions based on a logic of appropriateness by the agencies. From a structural-instrumental perspective and a task-specific perspective, the importance of agency characteristics are seen from above as well as from below; in both instances emphasizing actions based on a logic of consequentiality by principals as well as by agents.

As noted in Chapter 2, our starting point for the concept of autonomy is the level of decision-making competencies of the agencies. Thus, autonomy is about discretion, or the extent to which the agency can make decisions about matters it considers important. Control focuses on the constraints that the superior bodies can develop to effect the actual use of these decision-making competencies in order to influence the decisions made. In discussing this relationship between autonomy and control, in most instances, our hypotheses will imply variations in opposite directions. To simplify the presentation of the hypotheses we focus on autonomy, where expectations of more autonomy in *some* agencies also mean that these agencies are expected to be subjected to less control than the others. However, based on principal-agent theory and internationally proclaimed NPM doctrines, some forms of autonomy may be combined with some forms of control (Roness et al. 2008). Thus, in agencies particularly affected by these doctrines we may have high autonomy and high control. In these instances we also include expectations on variations of control in the hypotheses.

The use of internal management techniques may be seen from above or from below (cf. Lægreid et al. 2007). In some instances, certain types of techniques can be initiated by superior bodies as a way to carry out control activities within agencies. In those cases, management techniques will be an expression of regulation inside government. In other instances, the use of management techniques may be initiated by the agency itself, based on a logic of consequentiality or a logic of appropriateness. Here, management techniques will be an expression of a wilful or an appropriate choice for the shopping basket. Whether the use of management techniques is seen from above or from below, agency characteristics may be important. In this chapter we formulate specific hypotheses on the impact of structure, culture and tasks, taking the agencies as the point of departure, but also add some comments on what we will expect regarding management techniques as an expression of regulation inside government. Moreover, the extent of autonomy and control may also be important for internal management. Thus, we also formulate hypotheses on how the extent of autonomy and control will affect the use of management techniques.

10.2 Structure matters

As noted in Chapter 3, this structural-instrumental perspective focuses on the way formal organizational structure is designed in an instrumental-rational way, as well as on how this structure affects rational behaviour within the organization. The formal structure of an organization consists of positions and rules for who shall or can do what, and which defines the way various tasks should be executed (cf. Christensen et al. 2007). Organizations are composed of a set of positions and subordinated units, and can themselves fall under other larger units. In addition, organizational units can be divided up and coordinated in different ways. In this perspective, decisions are made based on a logic of consequentiality (March and Olsen 1989; March 1994): organizations and their formal structure are thus considered as tools or instruments for achieving certain goals by (fully or bounded) rational actors. The importance of the formal organizational structure is related to its impact on rational calculation and social control (cf. Dahl and Lindblom 1953).

The basic idea in this perspective is that aspects of formal organizational structure (for example, the forms and extent of hierarchy, specialization and coordination) affect they way autonomy and control and internal management are regarded by superior bodies and by the agencies themselves. For example, Gulick (1937) argues that the way formal authority is distributed among hierarchical levels is important for autonomy in practice. If a system is characterized by independent agencies, this distribution is biased against the political executive, and we will thus generally expect to find a rather high level of autonomy in the agencies. As the formal instruments of steering are diluted, the distance between administrative levels increases, and political signals are generally weaker in independent bodies (Egeberg 2003). It makes a difference whether central government is an integrated system under ministerial responsibility or a disintegrated system of autonomous or semi-autonomous organizations, whether it is centralized or decentralized, and whether it is specialized according to the principle of geography and/or other principles (Christensen and Lægreid 2006).

The principal-agent model is often presented (or at least empirically tested) as a top-down political model, generally taking the political principal as the point of departure, and emphasizing the motives of that political principal who seeks to control the behaviour of the bureaucratic agent (Waterman et al. 2004: 94). Even though some of these scholars (for example, Pollack 2002; Krause 2003; Waterman et al. 2004) recommend that the behaviour of the agent(s) also should be included in the analysis, the agent(s) are generally modelled as passive, although they may have motives of their own (for example, a wish to shirk). Thus, in most cases of principal-agent models and other rational choice ideas, it is taken for granted that agency behaviour follows from formal structure, or at least that it is constrained by formal organizational structure. If the formal autonomy and control of agencies are designed and changed in different ways, the way the agency heads perceive and use autonomy will differ correspondingly. Likewise, if the formal structure is similar across agencies, their perceptions and behaviour will also be similar.

10.2.1   Implications for autonomy and control

As information on structural characteristics of agencies across states is limited, we are unable to explore the importance of hierarchy, specialization and coordination fully. However, the impact of some structural characteristics may be explored.

First, the term *type of agency* refers to the internal organization of the agencies. Based on Gulick's (1937) principles of specialization, we will differentiate between agencies organized on the principle of purpose, process or clientele at the national level without any regional or local branches, and those that have a territorial component. We assume that agencies with a territorial component will be more embedded in regional or local networks, which in turn will tend to increase their autonomy and reduce the extent of control by their parent department and other superior bodies. Thus, we may formulate the following hypothesis on the importance of type of agency:

HA1:   *Agencies organized according to geography in combination with another principle will have more autonomy than agencies without a territorial component.*

Second, the term *governance structure* refers to the existence and composition of a governing board. Thus, some agencies have collegial structures attached to their leadership, while others do not. Such governing boards may have governmental representatives, representatives from interest groups, representatives from political parties and independent experts. As noted by Egeberg (2003: 123), executive boards at the top of agencies seem to balance and reconcile several interests and concerns simultaneously. They are arenas not only for political steering and control from above, but also for the articulation of affected group interests and expert appraisals. This means that the existence of a governing board blurs political signals on their way down through the hierarchy, thus allowing the agency more autonomy (Egeberg 1994). Likewise, Christensen (2001: 121–2) and Christensen and Yesilkagit (2006: 208) discuss the importance of the existence of a board in agencies, concluding that inserting a board into the hierarchy will increase the autonomy of agencies. Thus, seen from below we will expect that:

HA2:   *Agencies with a governing board will have more autonomy than agencies without a governing board.*

The same applies when viewed from above, assuming that the government may exercise control through the appointment of board members, implying less need for control of agencies with a board. Alternatively, seen from above, there may also be less need for control of agencies without a board, since they are structurally closer to the government. From this point we would expect that agencies without a board will have more autonomy than agencies with a governing board.

The *composition* of the governing board, that is, whether it consists solely of government representatives or is combined with representatives of interest groups or other stakeholders, may also matter. Seen from below, agencies with boards having representatives of interest groups will be more able to have autonomy and resist control than agencies with boards composed solely of government representatives. Alternatively, seen from above, there is less need for control of agencies with boards composed solely of government representatives, since the government may exercise control through their representatives. However, as identified in Chapter 6, only a handful of agencies have a board consisting solely of government representatives, making it impossible to test hypotheses derived from the composition of the governing board.

Third, *agency size* may be regarded as an indicator of structural capacity (cf. Egeberg 2003: 120). In the study of organizations, size has been treated either as a dimension of organizational structure (along with formalization and centralization) or as a contextual variable (Scott 2003: 263–4). Most studies on the relationship between organizational size and structure have used the number of participants (for example, employees) as an indicator of size. One advantage of this measure is that it reflects the capacity of organizations for performing its tasks (Verschuere 2006). According to Scott (2003: 264), this is particularly relevant when the dependent variables are methods for control and coordination of people. Likewise, size may refer to the agencies' capacity to forge more autonomy or to resist control efforts from superior bodies (Carpenter 2001). A large size may imply more resources for agencies to build their own expertise and power as well as to pursue their own objectives. From a principal-agent perspective, it may aggravate the problem of information asymmetry and goal incongruence, and make it harder for the principal to monitor the behaviour of the agent. Thus, assuming that size is a relevant aspect of structure, we will expect that:

HA3:   *Large agencies will have more autonomy than small agencies.*

Summing up, we have formulated specific hypothesis based on the importance of type of agency, existence of a governing board and size for agency autonomy. All three variables reflect central aspects of formal organizational structure. However, owing to the substantial variety of organizational forms across states (cf. Chapter 6) we were not able to check the importance of the legal status of agencies.

10.2.2   Implications for management techniques

With regard to the importance of structure for the use of management techniques, this depends to some extent on whether they are seen from above as an expression of regulation inside government or from below as a wilful choice for the shopping basket. Taking the agencies as the point of departure, we will expect mostly the same pattern for the use of management techniques as for autonomy, in other words those structural characteristics that will imply high autonomy will also imply high use of management techniques.

For *type of agency*, assuming that the use of management techniques is a wilful choice of agencies, we will expect that:

HA1T: *Agencies organized according to geography in combination with
         another principle will use management techniques to a greater
         extent than agencies without a territorial component.*

Agencies with a territorial component may be presumed to have more opportunities and capacity to choose freely to use managerial techniques, because of their physical distance from the centre of government. The opportunities to choose freely that are the result of the agencies' embeddedness in local or regional networks increase the chance that agencies will apply management techniques, if they consider the use of these techniques as beneficial for their goal and mission attainment, from which they expect a larger legitimacy.

However, assuming that the use of management techniques is an expression of regulation inside government, we will expect that agencies with a territorial component will use management techniques to a lesser extent than agencies without a territorial component. This is particularly the case if the agency wants to avoid oversight and regulation from above, as it will try to resist the use of those management techniques that come with this regulation. The fact that the agency is embedded in regional or local networks, and hence is physically distanced from the centre of government, will increase the chances of this resistance to using management techniques is more successful.

For *governance structure*, seeing management techniques from below as a wilful choice of agencies, we will expect that:

HA2T: *Agencies with a governing board will use management techniques to a greater extent than agencies without a board.*

As with agency type (having a territorial component or not), this is primarily due to the ability of agencies with a governing board to choose on their own whether they use managerial techniques or not, without interference from above. Having a governing board serves as an intermediate level in the hierarchical line between the centre of government and the agency, which may blur oversight signals from the government. Hence, if the agency considers the use of management techniques as beneficial for the organization (for goal attainment or efficiency, from which legitimacy may stem), it will use them accordingly.

The same applies when the use of management techniques is seen from above as an expression of regulation inside government, assuming that there may be less need for control of agencies without a board, since they are structurally closer to the government. On the other hand, assuming that the government may exercise control through the appointment of board members, we would expect less need for control of agencies with a board, also through the use of management techniques.

Finally, taking *agency size* as an indicator of structural capacity and regarding management tools as instruments for goal attainment, large agencies will have a better capacity to choose on their own. We expect that large agencies have greater internal capacities to develop and work with innovative management techniques, since working with such techniques requires a certain level of capacity and expertise within the agency. Thus, seeing management techniques from below as a wilful choice we will expect that:

HA3T: *Large agencies will use management techniques to a greater extent than small agencies.*

On the other hand, viewing management techniques as an expression of regulation inside government, and based on the ability of large agencies to resist pressure from above, we will expect that large agencies will use management techniques to a lesser extent than small agencies.

10.3 Culture matters

As noted in Chapter 3, the cultural-institutional perspective focuses on how organizational culture affects behaviour within the organization. Organizational culture has to do with the informal norms and values that are important for the activities of organizations. Like other public sector organizations, agencies can have a distinct organizational culture. The agencies are not primarily instruments for obtaining goals, but may be value-bearing institutions with their own identities and opinions about what is seen as appropriate behaviour.

The basic idea in this perspective is that aspects of organizational culture affect whether and how autonomy and control and internal management are regarded as appropriate. Norms, values and identities are developed gradually, and are internalized in organizational members through processes of socialization. Members will gain experience of an institutional culture by learning what is appropriate. This also implies a form of path dependency, where patterns of behaviour that are seen as appropriate over time become reinforced and quite resistant to change. Major changes are primarily possible, or probable, when an organization is created or exposed to a crucial external shock: a critical juncture.

The organizational culture also represents 'filters' producing different outcomes in different agencies. Internal forces contributing to the organization's robustness and stability will be more important than signals and pressures from superior bodies, and the fate of reform initiatives from above will depend on whether and how they are compatible with established norms and values in the agencies (Yesilkagit 2004b).

Thus, the main types of explanatory factors from a cultural-institutional perspective are connected to the constraints inherent in established traditions and cultures, as they have developed over time. Compared to structure, it is more difficult to uncover cultural characteristics of organizations. Owing to the lack of relevant data for one of the states, we are unable to explore the importance of organizational culture of the agencies in a more straightforward way. Nevertheless, we use two measures that, we argue, may be related to culture.

10.3.1   Implications for autonomy and control

The first measure, *agency age* – referring to the year in which the agency was set up for the first time as some form of autonomous body – is clearly linked to organizational culture. Normally, the development of a distinct culture and tradition within an organization takes some time. Thus, the older the organization is, the more it will tend to have developed a strong institutionalized identity, and the potential for the socialization of its members into a common culture becomes higher (cf. Krause 2003 refers to agency stability). Old organizations will, therefore, be more able to resist pressure from outside actors. Based on these assumptions, we will expect that:

HA4:   *Old agencies will have more autonomy than young agencies.*

Based on the timing of agencification and major public sector reforms in the three states (cf. Chapter 6), we have distinguished between agencies established before 1990 and agencies established in 1990 or later. First, in all three states, many agencies were created after 1990, partly in accordance with the international agencification trend. Second, in all three states, some pre-existing agencies changed their formal relationship with their parent department in the 1990s and 2000s. As noted by Yesilkagit (2004b), organizational culture together with formal autonomy can create expectations in agencies about its future actual autonomy. Thus, even if the organizational culture of old agencies may change to match their new formal autonomy, we still assume that pre-existing agencies will be influenced to a large extent by the culture they acquired during their formative period and its gradual development over many years.

The second measure, *agency size*, was previously seen as an indicator of structure, but may also be seen as an indicator of culture. The argument is that small agencies may generally have a more homogeneous culture and a more distinct identity than large agencies, and are therefore more able to modify signals coming from the parent department and other superior bodies. Thus, assuming the primacy of homogeneous identity, we formulate the following hypothesis:

HA5:   *Small agencies will have more autonomy than large agencies.*

This means that size is expected to affect autonomy and control in opposite directions, depending on whether we take size as an indicator of structure or of culture.

10.3.2   Implications for management techniques

With regard to the importance of culture in the use of management techniques, this will be much the same whether they are seen as an expression of regulation inside government or following appropriate choices for their shopping basket. In both instances, techniques that are incompatible with established norms and values will be rejected by organizations that have a strong or distinct identity, while those that are compatible will be adopted. Assuming that older agencies and smaller agencies have had a better chance to develop a distinct organizational identity and set of values, we may thus expect older and smaller agencies to use fewer management techniques, where those techniques are incompatible with their strong distinct organizational culture. From these ideas we formulate two hypotheses:

HA4T: *Old agencies will use management techniques to a lesser extent than young agencies.*

HA5T: *Small agencies will use management techniques to a lesser extent than large agencies.*

The fact that some management techniques may be 'newer', or 'more modern', than others can affect the readiness of agencies, whether old or young, to adapt these management techniques. Assuming that there are technique-specific features such as 'newness' or 'adaptiveness', this mediates the effect of the age of the agency on the use of the particular technique. It may, for example, be the case that techniques such as public reporting and planning over years are regarded by agencies to be easier to apply, or more appropriate (because they are more common in the public sector), than cost-calculation and quality management systems. Assuming that many of the management techniques are quite unfamiliar and that agency size is an indicator of culture, we will expect older agencies to use management techniques to a lesser extent. In addition, assuming that small agencies may generally have a stronger and more homogeneous culture than large agencies, we can claim that this makes them more resistant to techniques that are regarded as incompatible with established norms and values. Here, too, it will depend on the particular management technique in question as to whether it will be seen as appropriate or not by the agency. But if we contend that for many agencies in a public sector context many management techniques are still relatively unfamiliar, we will expect that smaller agencies (with a stronger organizational identity) will use management techniques to a lesser extent, whether they are able to choose to use them or not.

10.4 Task matters

As noted in Chapter 3, the task-specific perspective emphasizes the role of the technical environments of an organization. The technical environments are to a large extent determined by the type of tasks that the organization performs. These tasks may vary according to their measurability (Wilson 1989), as well as their political salience (Pollitt et al. 2004).

The basic idea in this perspective is that task characteristics affect how autonomy, control and internal management are regarded by superior bodies and by the agencies themselves. Seen from above, the extent of measurability is important for whether, and how, the principal is willing to grant the agent autonomy and in being able to control the agent. Likewise, the extent of political salience is important for whether, and how, the principal is willing to grant the agent autonomy and being interested in controlling the agent. Seen from below, the extent of measurability and political salience is important for whether, and how, the agent is interested in gaining autonomy and resisting control from above. In all instances, superior bodies and agencies are primarily seen as acting according to a logic of consequentiality.

Recent studies of public sector agencies reveal that there are significant variations in their behaviour depending on their primary tasks (Pollitt et al. 2004). In the academic literature as well as in the more prescriptive reform literature, several categorizations of state organizations (according to type of task) have been launched (cf. Roness 2007). As with the previous characteristics, we experienced problems in collecting full information on organizational tasks across states, forcing us to work with rather crude variables. Compared to culture, and particularly structure, the elusiveness of the concept 'task' made it more difficult to find encompassing indicators, implying that our assumptions and expectations on tasks are to some extent vulnerable for discussion, like our assumptions and expectations on culture. The four measures we are using are, nevertheless, strongly rooted in the existing literature on public sector agencies, and can be related to relevant characteristics of organizational tasks.

10.4.1   Implications for autonomy and control

First, the importance of the type of activity an agency engages in has been emphasized by several authors (Wilson 1989; Krause 2003; Bouckaert and Peters 2004; Pollitt 2004, 2005a). As noted in Chapter 6, we differentiate between four types of primary tasks as our starting point:

1) policy formulation,
2) regulation, scrutiny and inspection,
3) other ways of exercising public authority (for example granting subsidies),
4) service delivery.

The interest in autonomy seen from the agencies, and the interest in control seen from above, may vary according to activity, and also depends on the kind of autonomy and control at stake.

The question is to what extent theorists will expect agencies with different tasks to have different levels of autonomy and control. Rational choice based theories (transaction costs theory, agency theory and public choice theory) seem to emphasize specific task characteristics in this respect (Ter Bogt 1998; Bouckaert and Verhoest 1999): tasks can be put at a distance more effectively, 1) if their results are easily measurable (Williamson 1981: 561–3; Wilson 1989), 2) if there is a high potential for a clear definition of objectives by the principal (Jensen and Meckling 1976; Wilson 1989), 3) if the activities are homogenous in kind (Wilson 1989; Ter Bogt 1998), and 4) if the level of asset specific investments is relatively low (Williamson 1985; Van Thiel 2001). These task features refer to the extent to which the principal can relatively easily monitor the results of the agency, and create effective incentive structures for risk-sharing, thereby reducing the problems of information asymmetry, goal incongruence and opportunistic behaviour (Jensen and Meckling 1976; Williamson 1985; Wilson 1989). Moreover, these features, namely those based on transaction costs theory, help to decide on the most efficient organizational forms (in terms of minimizing transaction costs), like hierarchy, market or in-between forms (Williamson 1985).

Of the categories of tasks listed above, service delivery tasks exhibit relatively more of these features than the other tasks, which are harder to measure and more diverse (policy formulation, regulation, scrutiny and inspection, and other ways of exercising public authority, like granting subsidies). Rational choice theorists will thus expect agencies with service delivery tasks to have relatively more autonomy than agencies involved in policy advice, regulation and exercising other forms of public authority (Verschuere 2005). More specifically, these agencies will have more *managerial autonomy*, since this is the kind of discretion that allows agencies to freely choose their inputs, while being tied to specific objectives with regard to outputs. Such service delivery agencies would have most interest in managerial autonomy, because they interact most frequently with the citizens and private organizations as users, and high quality, efficient processes and product innovation is most valued by their stakeholders. Moreover, these agencies may be active in competitive markets, and in order to guarantee a level playing field, the operations of such agencies will be shielded from political interference. However, in accordance with NPM doctrines, a high degree of managerial autonomy is combined with a high degree of result control. Thus, based on these arguments, we formulate the following hypothesis:

HA6:   *Agencies with service delivery as a primary task will have more managerial autonomy and be subjected to more result control than agencies with other types of primary tasks.*

The extent of regulatory tasks may also be important. This is based on functional theories and principal-agent theory, in particular, emphasizing the notion of credible commitment and time consistency for regulatory decisions. Thus, the agencies' shape and degree of autonomy and control can be influenced by the rational choice of the political principals who delegate powers and functions to agencies. In this mainly functional logic, principals are willing to pay the costs of delegation, if they expect benefits to outweigh those costs (Thatcher and Stone Sweet 2002). Consequently, they will grant an agency some discretion to achieve the benefits of delegation, while trying to minimize the risk of agency loss. According to this approach, the main explanatory factors of agency discretion and autonomy are elements such as policy complexity, credible commitment (Pollack 2002) and policy conflict and uncertainty (Moe 1990). For regulatory tasks in particular, governments want to ensure that regulatory decisions are taken independently in order to increase the trust of market actors in the sustainability and objectivity of regulatory policies (Horn 1995). Therefore, regulatory agencies are given considerable leeway to take regulatory decisions in individual cases, shielded off from political pressure. This implies that a regulatory agency must have a considerable level of policy autonomy and, preferably, a high level of managerial autonomy. Thus, assuming that these considerations on credible commitment and time consistency are particularly relevant for regulatory agencies, we have a partly overlapping and partly contrasting hypothesis on the importance of the primary task:

HA7:   *Agencies with regulation as a primary task will have more autonomy (and particularly policy autonomy) than agencies with other types of primary tasks.*

This hypothesis is also in line with recent international doctrines on regulation and regulatory agencies (cf. OECD 2002b; Christensen and Lægreid 2006). As indicated in Chapter 3, the importance of political salience has also been examined, being particularly relevant for the autonomy and control of agencies (Krause 2003; Pollitt et al. 2004). Hood and Dunsire (1981: 76–94) include it as an important aspect, but they are aware of the problems in using this type of blanket term. They assert that public sector organizations will tend to be highly salient if they are of a relatively large size in terms of personnel and budget, and/or have a face-to-face relationship with a relatively large proportion of the public. Pollitt (2005a: 128) relates this concept of political saliency more directly to certain policy issues, but adds that this is a tricky variable since political saliency may surge upwards or die back quickly (for example, prisons and food safety). Nevertheless, he asserts that there are some issues which may be regarded as quite politically salient on a fairly continuous basis (for example, health care, education and race relations).

Based partly on Pollitt et al. (2004) and Pollitt (2004, 2005a, 2005b), we take what we call *policy area* as one possible indicator of political salience. Using a simplified version of the United Nation Classification of Functions of Government (COFOG) we distinguish between three groups of agencies (cf. Chapter 6): 1) agencies in the welfare and social policy area, 2) agencies in the economic policy area and 3) agencies in other policy areas. Here we assume that agencies in the welfare and social policy area will be most politically salient because they affect relatively more citizens (cf. Pollitt 2005a: 128). In the area of welfare and social policy, the proportion of citizens with which agencies are involved in a face-to-face relationship is relatively larger (for example, paying welfare benefits and implementing health care programmes) than in economic or other policy areas, where policy actions are more directed to specific professional target groups. Thus, based on these arguments on political salience, we expect that:

HA8:   *Agencies within the welfare and social policy area will have less autonomy than agencies in other policy areas.*

Next to that, many agencies in the economic policy area are subject to competition or to be active on a contested, liberalized market, as induced by international/ supranational organizations (in this case, mainly the EU). In these instances, considerations of credible commitment will be particularly relevant (Elgie and McMenamin 2005). Assuming this to be the case, we may formulate a supplementary hypothesis on the importance of policy area:

HA9:   *Agencies within the economic policy area will have more autonomy than agencies in other policy areas.*

Our third indicator of task is the *size of the budget*. This may also be related to political salience. Thus, large budget tasks or agencies can be assumed to be more salient than small budget tasks or agencies, and their functioning will be more prone to critical scrutiny by media and Parliament (Hood and Dunsire 1981; Pollitt et al. 2004). A big budget reduces the chances of a quiet life for an agency. This means that every time public expenditure savings have to be made, agencies with a big budget will be scrutinized for potential reductions in spending (Pollitt 2005a: 129).

Moreover, large budgets generally refer either to service delivery agencies with very large staff or to heavy investments, which may take on substantial long-term financial liabilities, potentially endangering the financial stability of government in the future. Heyman (1988) shows rather convincingly that autonomy which allows for long-term financial liabilities is most severely restricted, particularly under pressure from departments with financial and budgetary responsibility. Large budgets may also refer to agencies that are involved in receiving or transferring payments, benefits and subsidies to citizens or specific target groups (taxing or transfer agencies as defined by Dunleavy 1991). Such agencies are crucial in the implementation of policies, making it important for political principals and other superior bodies to control them. Thus, based on these arguments we formulate the following hypothesis on the importance of budget size:

HA10:   *Agencies with a large budget will have less autonomy than agencies with a small budget.*

It would also be relevant to check the importance of the relative and absolute size of what Dunleavy (1991) calls an agency's core budget, in other words, those expenditures which are spent directly on its own operations. Thus, he asserts that having a high core budget is more crucial for top bureaucrats than having a high total budget (including contracts and transfers). However, it is very difficult to delimit the core budget with the available data.

Our final indicator of task is *source of income*. Pollitt (2005a) also adds some comments on the importance of where the money comes from. Based on Gains (1999), he suggests that if an agency is unable to generate any income itself, and it has a big budget, a superior department (the parent department as well as the Department of Finance) is likely to control the agency to a large extent. On the other hand, if an agency can earn all it needs to survive, it does not need a superior financing department and may try to avoid control. If there is a balance, however, both parties may have some need for each other (cf. Gains 1999; Pollitt 2005a). Nevertheless, we expect a positive relationship between source of income and chances for autonomy, where having a large part of money generated independently will imply high interest in, and chances of, autonomy for the agencies. Agencies which mainly depend on sales of their services to users need flexibility in order to be maximally responsive to the users' needs and wishes. Next to that, one could assert on functional grounds that financial independence should align with managerial autonomy, in the sense that an organization which raises its own resources must have the flexibility to use them (Verhoest et al. 2004a). Alternatively, it may also be the case that agencies which are only partially funded by government budget are less receptive to the wishes and demands from the government (and the other way around: 'Who pays the piper, calls the tune'). Moreover, the extent to which agencies draw their resources from the general government budget affects the level of political salience, media and parliamentary scrutiny. Overall, on the importance of source of income we will expect that:

HA11:   *Agencies with a large proportion of own income will have more autonomy than agencies with small proportion of own incomes.*

Based on a task-specific perspective, we have formulated six hypotheses on agency autonomy and control. Some of them are partly contrasting or only partly supplementary, reflecting different independent variables or ideas on why they are important.

10.4.2   Implications for management techniques

As with structure, the importance of task on the use of management techniques depends to some extent on whether they are seen from above as an expression of regulation inside government or from below as a wilful choice for the shopping basket. Here, too, taking the agencies as the point of departure, we will expect much the same pattern for the use of management techniques as for autonomy, that is, those task characteristics that will imply high autonomy will also imply high use of management techniques. When the use of management techniques is seen as a wilful choice for the shopping basket, the choices made by agencies are based on their value for the agency in fulfilling the task. This may vary according to the task in question.

For type of primary task, assuming that management techniques are a wilful choice of agencies, we will expect that:

HA6T: *Agencies with service delivery as a primary task will use management techniques to a greater extent than agencies with other types of primary tasks.*

This is primarily due to the interest of service delivery agencies in choosing management techniques on their own. Seen from this angle, it may be advantageous for these agencies to apply more management techniques in order to optimize their production and service delivery processes. This may result in higher levels of user satisfaction, and in the end, increased trust and legitimacy with the main stakeholders. However, assuming that management techniques are seen as an expression of regulation inside government, we will expect that service delivery agencies will use management techniques to a lesser extent than other agencies. This is primarily due to the reduced interest of control from above. If management techniques are instruments for governmental control, then these will not be applied that often in cases where control is regarded as unnecessary, or of low interest (for example, when stakeholders deliberately want to free agencies from control, because innovation, efficiency and effectiveness in service delivery is valued).

Based on the considerations of credible commitment and time consistency outlined above, and assuming that management techniques are a wilful choice of agencies, we will expect that:

HA7T: *Agencies with regulation as a primary task will use management techniques to a greater extent than agencies with other types of primary tasks.*

As with the case of service delivery agencies, this is primarily due to the interest of regulatory agencies to choose management techniques on their own. For regulatory agencies, it is particularly important to 'prove' their independence, impartiality and objectivity to government and the general public (for example, via annual reports, or quality management systems for guaranteeing independence in agencies' judgements). On the other hand, assuming that management techniques are seen as control from above, we would expect that regulatory agencies will use management techniques to a lesser extent than other agencies. The argument here is that superior bodies have an interest in independent and objective regulators, hence management techniques as control instruments that may be a threat for the regulatory agencies' independence should be avoided. For primary task and management techniques, then, seen from below we have partly contrasting hypotheses on service delivery and regulation, and in both instances the hypotheses are in contrast to what we will expect when management techniques are seen from above as an expression of regulation inside government.

A second task-related feature of the agency is the policy area in which it is active. In a politically salient area like welfare and social policy, where a lot of public money circulates and where a large number of citizens are influenced by the policies, we may expect that agencies will try to increase their legitimacy as much as possible. The political salience of the area urges them to constantly prove their efficiency and effectiveness. This is even strengthened by the fact that in the area of welfare and social policy, many agencies face increasing competition from other players in the area (for example, private care providers), which may directly or indirectly pose a threat to their legitimacy. Hence, considering the use of management techniques as wilful choice for the shopping basket, we may expect the agencies in the field of welfare to actively engage in the use of management techniques. By actively using these techniques, they hope to improve efficiency and effectiveness of their service delivery and, as a result, to increase their legitimacy. Thus, our hypothesis is:

HA8T: *Agencies within the welfare and social policy area will use*
         management techniques to a greater extent than agencies in
         other policy areas.

Seeing management techniques from above as an expression of regulation inside government we will also expect agencies within the welfare state and social policy area to use these techniques to a greater extent than agencies in other policy areas, owing to the interest of superior bodies of controlling agencies in politically salient areas.

Concerning agencies that are players in the economic policy area, we will assume these agencies to be subject to competition, or to be active in a competitive liberalized market. Here, too, it may be advantageous for agencies to use management techniques, in order to guard their position in a competitive environment. This is supposed to increase their efficiency and effectiveness, from which a better 'market position' and greater legitimacy may stem. Thus, we will expect that:

HA9T: *Agencies within the economic policy area will use management techniques to a greater extent than agencies in other policy areas.*

Two final indicators for the task of the agency are the size of its budget, and its sources of income. With regard to budget size, and seeing management techniques as a wilful choice for the shopping basket, our hypothesis is:

HA10T: *Agencies with a large budget will use management techniques to a greater extent than agencies with a small budget.*

Two reasons can be given to underpin this hypothesis. First, as is the case with organizational size, large budgets may also lead to greater capacity for using management techniques. Second, agencies with large budgets may experience greater pressure from the environment, for reasons of political salience. Large budgets for organizations are indicators of high political salience. In this situation, the use of modern management techniques may provide proof of efficiency and effectiveness, which may increase the organization's legitimacy. Taken together, organizations with the will to prove legitimacy may use management techniques in order to increase the (perception of) efficiency and effectiveness of the organization, in the eyes of the main stakeholders (users, government). Not surprisingly, agencies with a large budget may have more opportunities or competences to apply modern management techniques. When considering management techniques as devices for control from above, governments will enhance the use of management techniques in order to enhance control over these salient agencies.

We will also expect a positive relationship between source of income and opportunities to use management techniques. Agencies that generate a large proportion of their income on their own may have a greater interest in using management techniques. Agencies which are mainly depending on sales of their services to users need to know and monitor the efficiency and quality of their products and services, in order to optimize their outputs and sales. It may also be that using management techniques in itself feeds the perception of being an efficient and effective organization. Thus, seeing management techniques as a wilful choice for the shopping basket, we will expect that:

HA11T;   *Agencies with a large proportion of own income will use management techniques to a greater extent than agencies with a small proportion of own income.*

However, like most other aspects of task, we will expect a different pattern if the use of management techniques is seen as an expression of regulation inside government.

10.5 Autonomy and control matters

The extent to which agencies are autonomous, and the extent (and the way) to which to which they are controlled, may also have an effect on their use of management techniques. To a large degree, the effect of autonomy and control on the use of management techniques opens the discussion on using management techniques as a combination of regulation inside government and wilful choice for the shopping basket on the part of the autonomous agency. Verhoest et al. (2007) develops an NPM-inspired model for innovative public agencies. In essence, this model assumes that agencies are put under pressure to behave innovatively or to adopt modern management techniques by controlling these agencies on their results. In other words, *ex post* result control via performance standards and contracts 'makes' managers manage and innovate. Hence, we may expect that agencies which are controlled to a large extent *ex post* for their results may be forced, or induced, to use management techniques which it is assumed are beneficial for their overall performance. As such, there is an element of rationality on behalf of the agencies' superior bodies, who 'force' agencies to behave in a managerial way by putting stress on performance control. Moreover, we may expect that in a context of 'letting' managers manage and innovate (for example, when agencies and their management have a high level of discretion), the chances of agencies using management techniques will be higher. Hence, having autonomy or decision-making competences in managerial affairs may be a facilitator, enabler or inducement for using management techniques. According to the latter line of reasoning, there is a rational argument, as seen from the agency: having managerial decision-making competences creates opportunities for agencies to apply modern management tools, which in turn can be a source of legitimacy or trust in the eyes of the superior bodies or the general public. Moreover, by applying modern management techniques, agencies hope to increase their overall performance in response to the demands of result control. In sum, we formulate the following hypotheses:

HA12T: *Agencies with high levels of managerial autonomy will use management techniques to a greater extent than other agencies.*

HA13T: *Agencies subject to high levels of result control will use management techniques to a greater extent than other agencies.*

Thus, we are here primarily interested in the importance of certain forms of agency autonomy and control for the use of management techniques.

10.6 Summary

Drawing on ideas from organization theory and institutional theory, we have formulated a broad set of hypotheses on the importance of agency characteristics for autonomy, control and internal management of agencies. Some of the hypotheses are contrasting; if one of them gets support the other does not. Mostly, however, the hypotheses are supplementary; several of them may get support at the same time. The extent to which the hypotheses are supported is examined in the following chapters. In Chapter 11 we focus on the importance of agency characteristics for various aspects of autonomy and control, while in Chapter 12 the dependent variables are the use of management techniques. A more comprehensive discussion of the relevance of the theoretical perspectives and independent variables is then carried out in Chapter 13, where we also control for the importance of state-level characteristics.

Most hypotheses are formulated quite generally, where certain structural, cultural and task features are expected to make an (equal) impact on all forms of autonomy and control, and on the use of all management techniques. Based on the empirical findings in Chapter 11, we also discuss whether and how agency characteristics are particularly relevant for some forms of autonomy and control. Likewise, based on the empirical findings in Chapter 12 we may uncover whether some agency characteristics and some forms of autonomy and control are particularly relevant for the use of certain management techniques. Thus, while the overall design of this part on comparing agencies is deductive, we also make room for some inductive elements.

11
Comparing Autonomy and Control of Agencies

11.1 Introduction

In Chapter 8 we presented the extent of perceived agency autonomy and control for all agencies and for agencies within each of the three states. We emphasized comparisons across states, and examined whether the similarities and dissimilarities were upheld for agencies with certain features. In this chapter we check whether, and to what extent, agency characteristics make a difference for their autonomy and control. Thus, we aim to answer the fourth research question:

RQ 4:   What agency-level factors influence the degree and pattern of autonomy and control of agencies?

The analysis is based on the discussion of the importance of structural, cultural and task features for agency autonomy and control in Chapter 10. As noted, in most instances the hypotheses being formulated imply variations in opposite directions for autonomy and control. The hypotheses are summarized in Table 11.1, together with the main arguments why these agency characteristics will make an impact on agency autonomy (and control).

We examine autonomy and control in separate sections, and their main manifestations in sub-sections. In each section we start by presenting a table summarizing the results of the bivariate analyses (using gamma as correlation coefficient) as well as the multivariate analyses (using estimates from logistic regression) for the variables involved. These tables provide the main basis for discussing the extent to which the hypotheses get some support or not. For some of the strongest or most interesting relationships we also include some more detailed information on the extent of autonomy for different groups of agencies.

While the discussion of the hypotheses in this chapter only are based on analysis of agency-level characteristics, in Chapter 13 we check whether

Table 11.1 Overview of hypotheses on comparing autonomy (and control) of state agencies. Main arguments and expectations

Agency characteristics	Effect on autonomy (and control)
HA1 Type of agency	Agencies with a territorial component will have more autonomy, owing to their local and regional embeddedness.
HA2 Governing board	Agencies with a governance board will have more autonomy, as signals from above may be blurred through the existence of an extra element in the hierarchy.
HA3 Agency size	Large agencies will have more autonomy, as they may have larger capacity for doing the job.
HA4 Agency age	Old agencies will have more autonomy, owing to path-dependency and the development of a distinct culture.
HA5 Agency size	Small agencies will have more autonomy, owing to the development of a distinct identity and ability to modify signal from above.
HA6 Primary task: service delivery	Agencies with service delivery as a primary task will have more managerial autonomy. Delivering products and services is a task that makes it more interesting for agencies to have autonomy. These tasks may be more tangible and measurable, reducing the problem of giving the agencies autonomy.
HA7 Primary task: regulation	Agencies with regulation as a primary task will have more autonomy, owing to considerations of credible commitment.
HA8 Policy area: welfare and social policy	Agencies within the welfare and social policy area will have less autonomy, since these areas are more politically salient.
HA9 Policy area: economic	Agencies within the economic policy area will have more autonomy, owing to considerations about credible commitment.
HA10 Size of budget	Agencies with a large budget will have less autonomy, since having a large budget makes an agency more politically salient.
HA11 Source of income	Agencies with a large amount of own income will have more autonomy, because they have an interest in being free to use it, and because they are less prone to such effects as 'the one who pays the piper, calls the tune'.

the effects of these factors are upheld when state-level characteristics are included in the analysis.

11.2   Agency autonomy

As noted in Chapter 2, we define autonomy as the extent to which the agency can decide, of itself, about matters it considers important. We distinguish between three main types of autonomy: human resource management (HRM) autonomy, financial management autonomy and policy autonomy. HRM autonomy and financial management autonomy are collectively referred to as managerial autonomy, in contrast with policy autonomy. We focus here on perceived de facto autonomy.

Table 11.2 presents an overview of the relationships between agency characteristics and the various types of agency autonomy.

11.2.1   Human resource management autonomy

As shown in Chapter 8, of the three aspects of HRM, agencies achieve most autonomy on evaluation of personnel: more than seven out of ten agencies report that, to a large or some extent, they can make decisions on the general criteria for evaluating personnel independently of the parent department (that is, have strategic autonomy). In comparison, around six out of ten agencies report that they have strategic autonomy on promotion of personnel, and around four out of ten on the level of salaries.

In Table 11.2 we see that while some structural, cultural and task features have a clear impact on HRM autonomy, others do not appear to be particularly important. We will discuss here whether and to what extent these observations are in line with what was expected.

While agency type does not make any significant impact on HRM autonomy, the existence of a governing board is highly important for several dimensions. Thus, the positive sign and statistically significant value of gamma for autonomy on promotion and evaluation indicate that agencies with a board have more strategic autonomy on these aspects than agencies without a board. The positive sign and statistically significant value of the estimate indicates that the effect of this structural feature is sustained when controlling for the other agency characteristics. This implies that HA2 gets quite strong support.

In general, agency size seems to be quite important for the perception of human resource management autonomy. For all aspects of HRM autonomy, large agencies regard themselves as being more autonomous than small agencies. For example, with regard to personnel salaries, 58 per cent of large agencies and 30 per cent of small agencies report having strategic autonomy. Likewise, while 23 per cent of small agencies claim no operational or strategic autonomy on the evaluation of personnel, this is not the case for any of the large agencies, and while 41 per cent of small agencies have no

Table 11.2 Agency characteristics and autonomy. Total sample. Gamma (first value) and estimates in logistic regression (second value)

Agency characteristics	HRM autonomy			Financial management autonomy			Policy autonomy
	Salaries	Promotion	Evaluation	Taking loans	Setting tariffs	Shifting budget	
Agency type	0.10	0.22	0.01	0.09	0.02	0.28	−0.10
	−0.49	0.09	−0.21	1.20*	−0.17	0.24	−0.09
Governing board	−0.11	0.37**	0.40**	0.81**	0.56**	0.16	0.19
	−0.29	1.15**	0.91**	2.42**	1.30**	0.17	0.34
Agency size	0.34**	0.39**	0.30**	−0.13	0.13	0.46**	−0.05
	1.30*	1.04	1.25*	−1.40	0.10	2.12**	0.31
Agency age	0.40**	0.18	0.17	−0.10	0.09	0.37**	0.25*
	0.65*	−0.07	0.11	−0.62	−0.16	0.49	0.81**
Service delivery	0.07	0.03	0.17	−0.06	0.45**	0.09	−0.10
	−0.04	−0.13	0.11	−0.66	0.91**	−0.10	0.09
Regulation	0.06	0.20	0.05	0.09	−0.17	0.04	0.38*
	0.27	0.97*	0.58	−0.27	0.06	0.14	0.79
Welfare and social policy	0.05	0.03	−0.25	−0.15	0.01	−0.15	−0.36**
	0.12	0.77	0.07	−0.26	0.20	−0.56	−1.16**
Economic policy	−0.31*	−0.19	−0.38**	0.13	0.23	−0.24	−0.15
	−1.06*	−1.27**	−1.08*	0.43	0.41	−0.70	0.66
Budget size	0.27**	0.33**	0.23	−0.02	0.01	0.20	−0.14
	0.21	0.43	0.14	0.64	−0.54	−1.05	−0.36
Source of income	0.11	0.27*	0.18	0.37**	0.48**	0.32**	−0.05
	0.04	0.60	0.25	1.65**	1.49**	0.93	−0.72
N = 100 % (regression)	201	200	202	205	204	196	196

**(bivariate) sign. < 0.01, *(bivariate) sign. < 0.05.
**p-value < 0.01, *p-value < 0.05.

operational or strategic autonomy on promotion of personnel, this share is only 5 per cent for large agencies. This pattern is in line with what we expected regarding size as an indicator of structure (HA3), but contrasts with what we expected regarding size as an indicator of (a distinct) culture (HA5).

Taking the other agency characteristics into account in a multivariate analysis we find that the effect of agency size on HRM autonomy is to a large extent sustained. This positive relationship may reflect the fact that large organizations have greater capacity for handling these issues themselves and perhaps have been more successful in pressing for autonomy in these matters. It could also be that superior bodies may find it advantageous if such matters are maintained within large organizations themselves, for example by reducing the amount of time and resources spent on these matters by the superior bodies.

Looking at agency age, we find that there is a higher degree of autonomy on salaries of personnel among old agencies than among young agencies. This effect is sustained when controlling for the other agency characteristics. Thus, HA4 gets partial support for HRM autonomy.

With regard to primary task, we observe quite small variations on HRM autonomy. Thus, overall, the results on relationships between primary task and HRM autonomy are not in line with what was expected from HA6 and HA7.

For policy area, there is some variation on HRM autonomy when comparing agencies in the economic policy area with agencies in other policy areas. However, the findings that agencies in the economic policy area perceive themselves as being significantly less autonomous than other agencies, even when controlling for the other agency characteristics, is in contrast with what we expected, based on ideas of credible commitment for these agencies (HA9). Moreover, being in the welfare and social policy area does not have any impact on the perception of HRM autonomy, implying that HA8 also gets no support.

For size of the budget, we find that agencies with a large budget have more HRM autonomy than agencies with a small budget, in contrast to what was expected, based on ideas of political salience for these agencies (HA10). Here the significant effects disappear when controlling for the other agency characteristics, but they are still opposite to what was expected.

Finally, for source of income, the only statistically significant bivariate correlation (with autonomy on promotion of personnel) is not upheld in the multivariate analysis, implying that HA11 does not get any support for HRM autonomy.

Summing up, we see that structural features such as the existence of a governing board and agency size are quite important for the perception of HRM autonomy, and these relationships are also as expected. For cultural and task features the effects are smaller, and also in some instances contrary to what was expected.

11.2.2   Financial management autonomy

For our three aspects of financial management, agencies perceive least autonomy on taking out loans: almost eight out of ten agencies report that they can make decisions on this independent of the parent ministry to a small or no extent (low autonomy), and only 2 per cent can do this to a large extent without limits set by the parent department (high autonomy). Compared to this, four out of ten agencies can set tariffs independent of the parent department to a small or no extent, an equal share report that they can do this to some extent within limits set by their parent department (medium autonomy), while two out of ten can do this to a large extent With regard to shifting budgets between years, the proportion of agencies reporting that they can do this to some or a large extent is about the same as the proportion allowed this to a small or no extent.

As shown in Table 11.2, as with HRM autonomy we find some differences with regard to whether and how structural, cultural and task features have an impact on financial management autonomy. Here, too, agency type has only a minor impact on autonomy, except for taking loans. On the other hand, the existence of a governing board has a major effect on taking loans and setting tariffs. Thus, while only 5 per cent of agencies without a board report high or medium autonomy on taking loans, this applies to 36 per cent of agencies with a board. Likewise, 43 per cent of agencies without a board and 73 per cent of agencies with a board perceive themselves as having high or medium autonomy on setting tariffs. These strong and positive relationships are upheld in the multivariate analyses. This implies that HA2 gets quite strong support for these two aspects of financial management autonomy.

Agency size also seems to be of importance with regard to some aspects of financial management autonomy. Thus, 53 per cent of small agencies and 77 per cent of large agencies report high or medium autonomy on setting tariffs, while 36 per cent of small agencies and 72 per cent of large agencies report high or medium autonomy on shifting budgets. The strong and positive relationship between agency size and shifting budgets is upheld in the multivariate analysis. This pattern is in line with what was expected based using size as an indicator of structure (HA3), but in contrast to what was expected using size as an indicator of culture (HA5).

With regard to agency age there is a greater extent of autonomy on setting tariffs among old agencies than among young agencies. However, this effect disappears when controlling for the other agency characteristics, implying that HA4 does not get any support.

For primary task, the only major difference is in the perception of autonomy for setting tariffs. Here, we find that 30 per cent of service delivery agencies, 5 per cent of regulatory agencies and 18 per cent of other agencies report having high autonomy. The effect of having service delivery as a primary task for autonomy on setting tariffs is upheld in the multivariate analysis. This positive relationship may also reflect that autonomy on setting tariffs is particularly important for service delivery agencies. Overall, while HA6 (on service delivery) gets partial support, HA7 (on regulation) does not get any support for financial management autonomy.

While the variations according to policy area and size of the budget are quite small, source of income makes a clear difference when it comes to taking out loans and setting tariffs, as well as when variables at different levels are included in multivariate analyses, in line with what was expected (HA11). The positive relationship between source of income and autonomy on setting tariffs may reflect that this is particularly important for agencies that depend on generating a large portion of their income independently. However, in general, for most indicators of task, the relationships with aspects of financial management autonomy are weak or even opposite to what we expected.

Summing up, as in the case of HRM autonomy, structural features like the existence of a board and agency size are important for the perception of financial management autonomy, and make a difference, in line with what was expected. On the other hand, our two indicators of culture have no impact, or a negative impact, on these forms of autonomy, in contrast to what we expected. Task features, like having service delivery as a primary task and having a large amount of own income, primarily make a difference for autonomy on setting tariffs, but in the case of source of income also do so in relation to taking out loans.

11.2.3   Policy autonomy

The question here is to what extent can the agency choose policy instruments like use of resources and input factors? Overall, 8 per cent report that the parent department makes most of the decisions, independently of the agency, or that the parent department makes most of the decisions after having consulted the agency, 52 per cent that the agency makes most of decisions itself in accordance with conditions set by the parent department, or following consultation with the ministry, while 40 per cent of the agencies make most of the decisions themselves, where the parent department is only partially involved in the decision-making processes and sets few restrictions.

Table 11.2 shows that, in contrast to managerial autonomy, none of the structural features (agency type, governing board and agency size) make a difference for policy autonomy. On the other hand, agency age makes a difference, also when controlling for other agency characteristics. That old agencies perceive more policy autonomy than young agencies is in line with what we expected from seeing age as an indicator of (a distinct) culture (HA4). This positive relationship may reflect that autonomy on choosing policy instruments to some extent relates to the creation and existence of a specific culture and experience in doing things a certain way. It could also be that older agencies, to a large extent, successfully manage to build up a relationship of trust with superior bodies, based on previous positive experiences of task fulfilment, which grants them more leeway in choosing policy instruments.

With regard to primary task we find that regulatory agencies have a higher degree of policy autonomy, in line with what we expected (HA7). This relationship is, however, weakened when controlling for other agency characteristics. For policy area, agencies within the welfare and social policy area perceive less autonomy than agencies in other areas, in line with what we expected based on ideas concerning the political salience of these agencies (HA8). This relationship is upheld when controlling for other agency characteristics. As for other aspects of autonomy, budget size seems to be of no importance. Source of income and being in the economic policy area also have no effect on policy autonomy. Thus, for task features of agencies, being in the welfare and social policy area only seems to make a difference for the perception of policy autonomy. Together with agency age, this is the main agency characteristic of importance for the perception of policy autonomy.

11.3 Agency control

Here, too, for agency control we differentiate between accountability of the CEO, control through rewards and sanctions and result control. An overview of the relationships between agency characteristics and the various types of agency control is presented in Table 11.3. We focus here on perceived control.

11.3.1 CEO accountability

As noted, the accountability of the CEO to the parent department and other superior bodies may take one of two forms: whether the top manager is accountable for the results of the agency, and whether the top manager is accountable on legality. In general, for both forms of accountability the extent of control is quite high: 82 per cent of the agencies report accountability on results and 84 per cent on legality. Combining the two forms as an overall measure of control through CEO accountability, 77 per cent report accountability on both (high control), 13 per cent on either results or legality (medium control) and 11 per cent on none of them (low control).

In Table 11.3 we see that, in general, structural, cultural and task features make less impact on CEO accountability than on autonomy. Nevertheless, there are some differences across groups of agencies.

As with autonomy, agency type does not make a difference for accountability. This indicates that superior bodies control agencies in a similar fashion, regardless of whether the agency has subordinate units or not. For governing board we find that agencies with a board report a greater extent of accountability on legality and results (81 per cent on overall accountability)

Table 11.3 Agency characteristics and control. Total sample. Gamma (first value) and estimates in logistic regression (second value)

Agency characteristics	Upwards CEO accountability			Rewards and sanctions				Result control
	Results	Legality	Overall	Wages	Resources	Discretion	Overall	
Agency type	0.16	0.38	0.28	0.43	−0.09	0.44*	0.25	0.25
	−0.06	0.91	0.57	0.35	−1.05*	0.78	−0.31	−0.20
Governing board	0.26	0.33	0.26	0.06	0.34*	−0.14	0.20	0.16
	1.10*	1.27**	1.18**	0.24	0.42	−0.51	0.19	0.47
Agency size	0.37*	0.23	0.24	0.48**	0.41**	0.39**	0.53**	0.47**
	0.54	0.46	0.30	1.30	1.81*	0.41	1.60**	1.29*
Agency age	0.10	0.24	0.09	−0.12	0.17	−0.05	0.07	0.05
	−0.26	0.07	−0.19	−0.71	0.21	−0.34	−0.08	−0.09
Service delivery	−0.13	−0.02	−0.12	0.03	0.48**	0.12	0.36**	0.12
	−0.29	−0.54	−0.50	−0.53	0.78	−0.34	0.37	0.10
Regulation	0.17	0.12	0.20	−0.01	−0.51*	−0.23	−0.23	−0.05
	0.79	0.37	0.58	0.39	−0.08	−1.04	−0.00	0.24
Welfare and social policy	0.34*	0.31	0.31*	0.11	−0.20	0.15	−0.05	0.17
	1.86*	1.14	1.41*	−0.74	−0.91	−0.04	−0.72	0.16
Economic policy	0.03	0.11	0.09	0.31	−0.02	0.20	0.12	0.17
	−1.28	−0.59	−0.87	0.99	0.81	−0.07	0.59	0.20
Budget size	0.37*	0.12	0.22	0.55**	0.39**	0.32*	0.49**	0.40**
	0.82	−0.32	0.25	1.94*	0.77	0.58	1.10	0.81
Source of income	0.08	0.26	0.10	0.13	0.16	0.27	0.25*	0.19
	−0.02	0.26	−0.01	−0.93	−1.30	0.95	−0.28	−0.04
N = 100% (regression)	196	198	194	199	199	199	199	196

**(bivariate) sign < 0.01, *(bivariate) sign < 0.05.
***p*-value < 0.01, * *p*-value < 0.0.

than agencies without a board (70 per cent on overall accountability). When the other agency characteristics are included in multivariate analyses, the existence of a board still makes a significant difference However, these positive relationships are the opposite of what we expected (HA2).

With regard to agency size we find that a larger proportion of medium-sized and large agencies, than of small agencies report control through CEO accountability, and particularly on the results of the agency (89 per cent versus 74 per cent). However, the effect of agency size to a large extent disappears when other agency characteristics are included in a multivariate analysis. Agency age also does not make any difference, implying that cultural features are not important.

Looking at primary task, we find only small differences on both forms of accountability between regulatory agencies, service delivery agencies and other agencies. For policy area, the most interesting observation is that agencies in the welfare and social policy area report a higher degree of accountability than agencies in other policy areas, particularly in relation to results. The differences are, to a large extent, upheld when controlling for other agencies. The effect of being in the welfare and social policy area on control through CEO accountability are in line with what we expected, based on ideas of the political salience of these tasks (HA8). As with primary task, the effects of being in the economic policy area, the size of the budget and the source of income on accountability are quite small. This indicates that organizations having more tangible primary tasks, like service delivery, are controlled in much the same manner as organizations with regulation or other kinds of primary tasks with regard to results and legality. It also indicates that organizations having small or more moderate budgets are controlled in similar ways as organizations with large budgets. This pattern reveals that the superior bodies, in general, do not differentiate between different types of agencies with regard to accountability on results and legality.

11.3.2 Rewards and sanctions

Rewards and sanctions may be used for different aspects of an agency. Here, we include rewards through wage increases or bonuses for personnel (and, similarly, sanctions through wage decreases or bonus reduction), rewards through increased resource allocation (and sanctions through reduced resource allocation), and rewards through more discretionary freedom (and sanctions through reduced discretionary freedom).

Overall, we find that 59 per cent of the agencies report no rewards or sanctions of any kind, 24 per cent say that there are either rewards or sanctions of at least one kind, while 16 per cent have both rewards and sanctions of at least one kind. Rewards and sanctions related to wages and bonuses are least common: 89 per cent of the agencies report that there are no rewards and sanctions to any extent on this aspect, 8 per cent have either rewards or sanctions, while 4 per cent have both rewards and sanctions, to some extent. For resource allocation, the corresponding figures are, respectively, 80 per cent, 11 per cent and 8 per cent, while for discretionary freedom they are 79 per cent, 16 per cent and 5 per cent.

As shown in Table 11.3, like CEO accountability, structural, cultural and task features make less impact on these forms of control than on autonomy, but there are some effects that may be of interest.

Agency type has some impact on control through rewards and sanctions, but in different ways. While the finding that agencies having a territorial component are subject to less control through rewards and sanctions on resources than agencies without a territorial component is in line with what we expected; the contrasting finding with regard to control through rewards and sanctions on discretion is not (HA1). For governing board there are only minor differences, particularly when controlling for other agency characteristics. This indicates that the existence of a board is of less relevance for control through rewards and sanctions than for control through CEO accountability.

The effect of agency size on control through rewards and sanctions is larger than the effects on control through CEO accountability. Overall, 76 per cent of small agencies report a low degree of rewards and sanctions, compared to 65 per cent of medium-sized agencies and only 30 per cent of large agencies. There is a positive relationship between agency size and all aspects of rewards and sanctions, but only some of these relationships (on overall control and on control of resources) are sustained when other agency characteristics are included in a multivariate analysis. This pattern is in contrast to what we expected regarding size as an indicator of structure (HA3), but in line with what we expected based on size as an indicator of culture (HA5). However, agency age does not make any difference for control through rewards and sanctions.

With regard to primary task, there are some differences between service delivery agencies and regulatory agencies on overall control, and control through rewards and sanctions on resources. However, the effects of primary task disappear when other agency characteristics are included in a multivariate analysis.

For policy area and source of income there are only minor differences across groups of agencies. But for budget size there are positive relationships on all aspects of rewards and sanctions. The relationships are somewhat weakened when other agency characteristics are included in a multivariate analysis, but there are still statistically significant effects of budget size on overall control and on control through rewards and sanctions on wages. This pattern is in line with what we expected, based on ideas on political saliency (HA10).

The general conclusion on rewards and sanctions is that, with the exception of agency size and budget size, we find no clear indications to suggest that superior bodies produce or use control systems in different ways, in order to suit different types of agencies.

11.3.3 Result control

As noted, result control is measured by the extent to which the CEO is accountable on results and whether or not this result accountability goes hand in hand with the threat of potential performance-based rewards and sanctions. Overall, 37 per cent of the agencies report accountability on results as well as some kinds of rewards and sanctions, 46 per cent accountability on results, but no rewards and sanctions, and only 17 per cent no accountability on results.

Table 11.3 shows that the pattern for result control to a large extent resembles the one we found for control through rewards and sanctions. Thus, there is a statistically significant effect of agency size, in line with what we expected based on size as an indicator of culture (HA5), but in contrast to what we expected regarding size as an indicator of structure (HA3). For budget size, the statistically significant bivariate correlation disappears when other agency characteristics are included in the multivariate analysis. The other agency characteristics do not seem to make any difference for the extent of result control. With regard to control of service delivery agencies, we were particularly interested in result control, expecting a positive relationship for this type of primary task (H6). However, this does not turn out to be the case.

11.4 Conclusion

Overall, we find a quite complex picture with regard to the extent to which agency characteristics influence the level and pattern of autonomy and control. Some characteristics make a difference, but not in a uniform way across all dimensions of autonomy and control. The findings on the extent to which the formulated hypotheses get support are summarized in Table 11.4.

The existence of a governing board is particularly important for some aspects of HRM autonomy, financial management autonomy and CEO accountability, but does not make any difference for policy autonomy and control through rewards and sanctions and result control. Agency size is also important for HRM autonomy, but makes a greater difference on control through rewards and sanctions and result control than on control through CEO accountability. While the effects of agency size on autonomy are in line with what we expected when viewing this as an indicator of structure (HA3), the effects on control are in line with what we expected when viewing this as an indicator of culture (HA5). Of the other structural and cultural features, agency type and agency age seem to be of less relevance for autonomy and control, but here too there are some statistically significant relationships.

Table 11.4 Summary of findings on autonomy and control. Extent of support of hypotheses

Agency characteristics	HRM autonomy	FM autonomy	Policy autonomy	CEO Accountability	Rewards sanctions	Result control
HA1 Type of agency	no	partial	no	no	weak (contradictory)	no
HA2 Governing board	strong	strong	no	no (opposite)	no	no
HA3 Agency size	strong	partial	no	no	no (opposite)	no (opposite)
HA4 Agency age	partial	no	strong	no	no	no
HA5 Agency size	no (opposite)	no	no	no	strong	strong
HA6 Primary task: service delivery	no	partial	–	–	–	no
HA7 Primary task: regulation	no	no	weak	no	no	no
HA8 Policy area: welfare	no	no	strong	strong	no	no
HA9 Policy area: economy	no (opposite)	no	no	no	no	no
HA10 Size of budget	no	no	no	no	strong	weak
HA11 Source of income	no	strong	no	no	no	no

Legend: No = no significant values in bivariate or in multivariate analyses
Weak = only significant values in bivariate analyses, but not in multivariate analyses
Partial = significant values in multivariate analyses for one aspect
Strong = significant values in multivariate analyses for several aspects.

With regard to task features, overall, primary task appears to be slightly less important than policy area. While being in the economic policy area, in particular, makes a difference for HRM autonomy, the effects of being in the welfare and social policy area is greatest for policy autonomy and control through CEO accountability. For welfare and social policy agencies the direction of the relationship was in line with what was expected for policy autonomy, but opposite to that expected for accountability. Having service delivery as a primary task and having a large proportion of own income is primarily important for the perception of some aspects of financial management autonomy, while having a large budget is primarily important for the perception of control through rewards and sanctions. These relationships are in line with what was expected.

Chapter 13 contains a more comprehensive discussion on the impact of agency characteristics, where state-level characteristics also are included in the analysis. This discussion also draws on the results concerning the use of management techniques, as shown in Chapter 12.

12
Comparing Internal Management of Agencies

12.1 Introduction

In Chapter 8 we discussed the extent to which agencies use management techniques, and whether differences or similarities exist in their use between agencies in different states. We emphasized comparisons across states, and whether the similarities and dissimilarities were upheld for agencies with certain features. In this chapter we analyse the extent to which agency characteristics, and the autonomy and control of agencies, make a difference for their use of various management techniques. Thus, we aim to answer the fifth research question:

RQ 5:   What agency-level factors influence the internal management of agencies? To what extent does the level of autonomy and control affect the internal management?

As shown in Chapter 9, there is a wide variation in the degree to which agencies use management techniques – our dependent variables. Taking all agencies in the three states together, we see that half of them use techniques such as allocation of resources internally on the basis of performance and cost-calculation systems. Techniques related to quality management systems are used by approximately 35 per cent of the agencies. Techniques like multi-year planning (85 per cent), public reporting (93 per cent) and customer surveys (68 per cent) are applied by a (large) majority of the agencies in Norway, Ireland and Flanders. In the remainder of this chapter, we summarize the theoretical background and the hypotheses to test, which were developed extensively in Chapter 10. We then present the results of the statistical analysis and look at the extent to which variables belonging to the theoretical perspectives developed above make an impact on the use of management techniques by agencies. Finally, we draw some conclusions about the determinants of the use of management techniques.

12.2   Overview of hypotheses

The theoretical background for this chapter is extensively described in Chapters 3 and 10. In Chapter 10, a set of hypotheses, related to different theoretical perspectives, was developed to explain the extent to which agencies use management techniques, or not.

The theoretical perspectives explain the use of management techniques in relation to certain types of agency characteristics: (1) structural features, (2) cultural features, (3) task features and (4) the extent of managerial autonomy and result control. The hypotheses we developed and the main arguments for why agency characteristics may influence the use of management techniques, are summarized in Table 12.1. We have developed 13 hypotheses, based on different ideas concerning the way certain factors may affect the willingness or potential for agencies to use modern management techniques. We now examine the effect of the variables on the six management techniques in three separate empirical sections. In the first two sections we present the results of the bivariate correlation analyses (gamma) and the binary logistic regression analysis (estimates) of the variables involved. The first section discusses the effects of the variables that belong to the structural, the cultural and the task-specific perspective. The second section discusses the effects of autonomy and control. The third section puts the variables that have a statistically significant effect in the two previous analyses together in an overall model.

12.3   Effects of structure, culture and task of the agencies

Table 12.2 presents an overview of the relationships between agency characteristics (structure, culture and task) and the use of management techniques by these agencies. As with similar tables in Chapter 11, the cells in the table show the bivariate gamma correlation coefficient (top) and the estimate from the binary logistic regression (bottom) when all characteristics are included in a multivariate analysis. Also, indications are given as to whether and to what extent the gamma coefficients and the estimates are statistically significant. As the table shows, differences in the use of management techniques can be related to some specific features of the agency.

The extent to which agencies use multi-year planning is principally related to their primary task. Agencies with service delivery as their primary task report a more extensive use of multi-year planning, when compared with other agencies. This relationship remains valid after controlling for other agency characteristics (positive and statistically significant estimate of logistic regression). The age of the agency, the size of the budget and the size of the agency in terms of staff numbers are related positively to the use of multi-year planning, but these relationships disappear after controlling for other variables.

Table 12.1 Overview of hypotheses on comparing the use of management techniques by state agencies. Main arguments and expectations

Agency characteristics	Effect on the use of management techniques
HA1T Type of agency	Agencies organized according to geography in combination with another principle will use management techniques to a greater extent, owing to the ability of agencies that are embedded in regional or local networks to choose on their own to use management techniques as instruments towards goal and mission attainment.
HA2T Governing board	Agencies with a governing board will use management techniques to a greater extent, owing to the ability of these agencies to choose on their own, without interference from above, to use management techniques as instruments towards goal and mission attainment.
HA3T Agency size	Large agencies will use management techniques to a greater extent than small agencies, owing to their larger structural capacity to use management techniques as instruments for goal or mission attainment.
HA4T Agency age	Old agencies will use management techniques (that are relatively new in the public sector) to a lesser extent than young agencies, because such techniques are regarded as incompatible with established norms and values.
HA5T Agency size	Small agencies will use management techniques (that are relatively new in the public sector) to a lesser extent than young agencies, because such techniques are regarded as incompatible with established norms and values in small organizations (that can be assumed to have a stronger culture and identity, hence are more able to resist using practices that are incompatible with organizational norms and values).
HA6T Primary task: service delivery	Agencies with service delivery as a primary task will use management techniques to a greater extent, because optimizing production and service delivery processes (by using management techniques) may be advantageous for organizational efficiency, and for building trust and legitimacy.

HA7T	Agencies with regulation as a primary task will use management techniques to a larger extent. This is
Primary task: regulation	due to the interest of regulatory agencies to 'prove' their independence and objectivity (assuming that the use of management techniques contributes to objectivity).
HA8T	Agencies in the social and welfare policy area will use management techniques to a greater extent,
Policy area: Welfare	owing to the political salience and increasing competition in that field, and the need for the agency to be efficient, and hence legitimate.
HA9T	Agencies in the economic policy area will use management techniques to a greater extent, in order to
Policy area: economic	prove credible commitment and legitimacy, especially in areas where liberalization and competition are becoming more important.
HA10T	Agencies with a large budget will use management techniques to a greater extent than agencies with a
Size of budget	small budget, owing to their political salience (stemming from the budget size), and their capacity, which urges and enables them to prove efficient and effective.
HA11T	Agencies with a large proportion of own incomes will use management techniques to a greater extent,
Source of income	as they need to 'prove' efficient, effective and display innovative behaviour to the users from whom they receive their income (legitimacy building via the use of management techniques).
HA12T	Agencies with high levels of managerial autonomy will use management techniques to a greater
Managerial autonomy	extent, because their managerial decision-making competences create opportunities to use these techniques ('letting the managers manage').
HA13T	Agencies with high levels of result control will use management techniques to a greater extent,
Result control	because their oversight regime makes it beneficial for the agency to use these techniques (to 'prove' good performance, 'making the managers manage').

Table 12.2 Agency characteristics and the use of management techniques. Total sample. Gamma (first value) and estimates in logistic regression (second value)

Agency characteristics	Multi-year plan	Internal result-based allocation	Cost-calculation	Public reporting	Quality management	Customer surveys
Agency type	0.36	0.30*	0.43**	0.64*	0.59**	0.34*
	−0.42	−0.25	0.23	1.79	0.72	−0.66
Governing board	0.19	−0.04	0.07	0.16	−0.04	0.22
	0.16	−0.48	−0.09	0.98	0.06	0.51
Agency size	0.54**	0.51**	0.56**	0.10	0.62**	0.68**
	1.35	1.1*	1.25*	0.18	2.19**	3.34**
Agency age	0.43*	0.18	0.18	−0.12	−0.01	0.13
	0.50	0.21	−0.11	−0.56	−0.56	−0.30
Service delivery	0.53**	0.47**	0.38**	−0.21	0.15	0.21
	1.2*	1.0**	0.22	−0.81	−0.24	−0.26
Regulation	−0.17	−0.31	−0.32	0.12	−0.12	−0.25
	0.63	0.20	−0.37	0.79	0.10	−0.25
Welfare policy	0.07	0.08	0.05	−0.10	0.20	−0.03
	0.28	−0.18	−0.45	−0.26	−0.00	−0.95
Economic policy	−0.11	0.01	0.01	−0.21	0.19	0.07
	−0.57	0.01	−0.35	−0.58	−0.04	0.37
Budget size	0.49**	0.46**	0.54**	0.38	0.44**	0.57**
	0.80	0.95	1.06*	0.86	−0.15	0.54
Source of income	0.32	0.15	0.45**	−0.14	0.22	0.30*
	0.37	−0.17	1.14*	−0.49	0.27	0.20
N = 100 per cent (regression)	200	197	199	197	195	198

**(bivariate) sign < 0.01, *(bivariate) sign < 0.05.
**p-value < 0.01, *p-value < 0.05.

The extent to which agencies allocate their resources internally on the basis of performance is positively related to the size of the agency and its primary task (having a service delivery task). These relationships remain significant after controlling for other agency characteristics. On the other hand, the positive effects of budget size and agency type on the use of techniques related to internal allocation of resources, as observed in the bivariate correlation analysis, disappear after controlling for other agency characteristics in the multivariate analysis.

Agencies that do not rely on the government for their (financial) resources, and have a large budget and a large number of personnel, tend to make more use of cost-calculation systems. These relationships remain significant after controlling for other agency characteristics. The use of public reporting by agencies, about their results, is not related to any agency characteristics, suggesting that characteristics related to their structure, culture or task do not influence the extent to which agencies report publicly.

The use of quality management systems such as CAF is related positively to the size (in staff numbers) of the agency, suggesting that larger agencies use quality management systems more frequently. This effect remains, having also controlled for other agency characteristics. Finally, we observe that larger agencies tend to survey their customers more frequently than other agencies.

In general, the most important agency characteristic in explaining the use of management techniques appears to be the size of the agency in staff numbers, which is positively related (after controlling for other variables) to four out of six management techniques. This is in line with what we expected based on using size as an indicator of structure (HA3T). Thus, large agencies seem to make more use of management techniques because their larger structural capacity enables them to use these techniques as instruments for goal or mission-attainment (giving them greater legitimacy in the eyes of stakeholders, such as users or government). Also in line with our expectations (HA6T) is the observation that service delivery agencies seem to use more management techniques than other agencies, which is the case for two out of six techniques studied. Some hypotheses achieve only partial support in our findings. Thus, agencies with a large budget and agencies with a lot of self-generated revenues tend to use cost-calculation systems more than others. This observation is in line with HA10T and HA11T. According to these hypotheses, management techniques will be used more frequently by agencies with a large budget and with much of their own revenue, because their political salience (large budget) and independence (own income) provides both the impetus and the opportunity to use management techniques (to prove their efficiency and effectiveness, from which legitimacy may stem). However, this relationship was not observed for any of the other five management techniques.

Other agency characteristics do not seem to have a statistically significant effect on the use of management techniques. Task features like the policy area in which the agency is active, or having a regulative task, as well as structural features such as having a territorial component or a governing board, have no effect.

12.4   Effects of autonomy and control

The second multivariate analysis examines the effects of agency autonomy and control on the use of management techniques. Six aspects of managerial autonomy (human resource management and financial management autonomy) and result control are included in the analysis. The results of the bivariate correlation and binary logistic regression analysis are summarized in Table 12.3.

As the table shows, the extent to which agencies use multi-year planning is determined mainly by the degree to which agencies have the freedom to shift budgets between years (an indicator of financial management autonomy). This positive relationship remains after controlling for the other autonomy and control variables. The level of result control and the extent to which agencies can shift budgets between years, has a positive and statistically significant effect on the extent to which agencies allocate their resources internally to lower units on the basis of performance. The extent to which agencies use cost-calculation systems is positively affected by their financial management autonomy (budgets), by their HRM autonomy (salaries) and by the level of result control they face. Also, there seems to be a negative effect of this form of human resource management autonomy with regard to evaluating personnel on the use of cost-calculating systems; however, this finding is hard to interpret.

No statistically significant effect of autonomy and control variables is found on the extent to which agencies report publicly on their performance. Finally, agencies that face a lot of result control and have a lot of HRM autonomy in the promotion of their personnel, tend to use quality management systems and customer surveys more frequently.

In general, financial management autonomy (in terms of shifting budgets between years) and result control tend to be the strongest explanatory variables for the use of management techniques. The more financial management autonomy and the more result control, the more frequent the use of modern management techniques. This observation confirms our hypotheses HA12T and HA13T, based on ideas that 'making and letting the managers manage' would lead to a greater use of management techniques. Notwithstanding this conclusion, two observations call for care in confirming hypothesis HA12T. First, with the exception of HRM autonomy for promotion, the other indicators of managerial autonomy have far less explanatory power than does the indicator of shifting budgets between

Table 12.3 Agency autonomy and control, and the use of management techniques. Total sample. Gamma (first value) and estimates in logistic regression (second value)

Autonomy and control	Multi-year plan	Internal result-based allocation	Cost-calculation	Public reporting	Quality management	Customer surveys
HRM autonomy	0.51**	0.13	0.52**	0.60**	0.01	0.20
(salaries)	0.38	−0.35	1.2*	1.40	−0.72	−0.28
HRM autonomy	0.46**	0.14	0.13	0.56*	0.18	0.33*
(evaluation)	−0.43	−0.41	−2.2*	0.93	−0.94	−0.61
HRM autonomy	0.60**	0.22	0.39**	0.62**	0.35**	0.47**
(promotion)	1.37	0.61	1.03	0.72	1.59*	1.88**
FM autonomy on	−0.18	−0.07	0.02	−0.14	0.24	0.20
taking loans	−0.42	−0.61	0.47	1.35	0.74	1.48
FM autonomy (setting	0.13	−0.03	0.20	0.06	−0.03	0.20
tariffs)	−0.36	−0.60	0.40	−1.11	−0.63	0.03
FM autonomy	0.77**	0.30*	0.46**	0.27	0.16	0.29
(shifting budgets)	2.07**	0.78*	0.96*	0.06	0.53	0.38
Result control	0.27	0.55**	0.46**	−0.22	0.47**	0.45**
	0.73	2.17**	2.1**	−0.77	2.02**	1.42**
N = 100 per cent (regression)	178	177	177	177	175	177

**(bivariate) sign < 0.01, *(bivariate) sign. < 0.05.
**p-value < 0.01, *p-value < 0.05.

Table 12.4 Overall model of significant variables affecting the use of management techniques. Total sample. Estimates in logistic regression

Retained variables	Multi-year plan	Internal result-based allocation	Cost-calculation	Public reporting	Quality management	Customer surveys
Agency size	NR	1.00*	0.49	NR	1.91**	2.04**
Service delivery	1.24**	0.82*	NR	NR	NR	NR
Budget size	NR	NR	1.14	NR	NR	NR
Source of income	NR	NR	1.10*	NR	NR	NR
HRM autonomy (salaries)	NR	NR	1.42**	NR	NR	NR
HRM autonomy (evaluation)	NR	NR	–1.67*	NR	NR	NR
HRM autonomy (promotion)	NR	NR	NR	NR	0.36	0.91*
FM autonomy (shifting budgets)	2.06**	0.41	0.81*	NR	NR	NR
Result control	NR	1.60**	1.55**	NR	1.15*	0.90
N = 100 per cent (regression)	*199*	*187*	*178*	*–*	*191*	*193*

**p-value < 0.01, *p-value < 0.05.
NR: not retained for this management technique.

years, which is contrary to what we expected. Second, and also contrary to expectation, a negative effect of autonomy in evaluating personnel is found in relation to the extent to which agencies use cost-calculation systems.

12.5   Overall model

In this final overall model, for each management technique we only retain independent variables that turned out to have statistically significant estimates in the two previous multivariate models. The results of this analysis are summarized in Table 12.4.

As the table shows, the most powerful explanatory variables are agency size and the extent to which agencies are subject to result control. Both variables have a positive and statistically significant effect on the extent to which agencies use management techniques (this applies to three out of six management techniques for both variables). Other strong predictors for the use of management techniques are the extent to which agencies enjoy financial management autonomy in shifting budgets over years, and having service delivery as the primary task. Both variables explain the use of management techniques in two out of six techniques. Other variables account for the use of only one management technique, for example, the effect of source of income on the use of cost-calculation systems.

12.6   Conclusion and discussion

Even if the observed effects of agency characteristics on the use of management techniques depend to some extent on whether or not managerial autonomy and result control are included in the multivariate models, some conclusions can be drawn on the extent to which the formulated hypotheses get support. This is summarized in Table 12.5.

Of the agency characteristics related to the structural perspective, only agency size makes an impact (HA3T). However, the observed effects of agency size is contrarary to what we expected, based on regarding this as an indicator of culture (HA5T). Since our other indicator of culture (agency age) also did not make any difference, the cultural perspective does not seem to be of relevance for the use of management techniques. For the task-specific perspective, only some aspects (having service delivery as a primary task and having some sources of own income) seem to be important. The effects of managerial autonomy and result control on the use of managagement techniques is quite strong, in line with what we expected (HA12T and HA13T).

Our analyses point to some interesting findings that may inspire further research into the determinants of agencies in using management techniques or behaving innovatively. If we feed back the results of the analysis to the

Table 12.5 Hypotheses on comparing the use of management techniques based on agency characteristics. Extent of support

Agency characteristics	Multi-year plan	Internal result-based allocation	Cost-calculation	Public reporting	Quality management	Customer surveys	Overall
HA1T Type of agency	no	no	no	no	no	no	no
HA2 T Governing board	no	no	no	no	no	no	no
HA3T Agency size	no	strong	weak	no	strong	strong	strong
HA4T Agency age	weak	no	no	no	no	no	no
HA5T Agency size	no	no (opposite)	no	no	no (opposite)	no (opposite)	no (opposite)
HA6T Primary task: service delivery	strong	strong	no	no	no	no	partial
HA7T Primary task: regulation	no	no	no	no	no	no	no
HA8T Policy area: welfare	no	no	no	no	no	no	no
HA9T Policy area: economy	no	no	no	no	no	no	no
HA10T Size of budget	no	no	weak	no	no	no	no
HA11T Source of income	no	no	strong	no	no	no	partial
HA12T Managerial autonomy	partial	no	strong (contra-dictory)	no	no	partial	partial
HA13T Result Control	no	strong	strong	no	strong	weak	strong

Legend: No = no significant values in multivariate analysis in model without autonomy and control – not included in overall model
Weak = significant values in multivariate analysis in either model without autonomy and control or in model with autonomy and control – included in overall model, but no significant values there
Strong = significant values in multivariate analysis in either model without autonomy and control or in model with autonomy and control – included in overall model, resulting in significant values.

theoretical perspectives we developed above, then we can conclude that all of them only partially explain the variance in the extent to which agencies use management techniques. Also, the overall model cannot fully explain the use of management tools by state agencies. This suggests that variables other than the ones we selected should be taken into account if we wish to fully comprehend why agencies use management techniques.

Nevertheless, some interesting observations can be made. Some variables such as agency size, primary task, managerial autonomy and result control appear to be significantly and positively related to the extent to which agencies use management techniques. The positive influence of these variables may be indicative for agencies using management techniques as a rational and wilful choice. Agencies that have sufficient capacity and ability to use management techniques (size), that have the operational decision-making discretion to manage their organization themselves (autonomy), and that are under pressure for results and good performance (result control by superior bodies, service delivery agencies), may have good reasons and opportunities to use modern management tools (to prove, for example, their will to perform). Using management techniques may thus be the result of wilful choice for the shopping basket on the part of the agencies. On the other hand, an agency's use of management techniques may also result from superior body's wish to control and steer the organization.

In this scenario, management techniques used by agencies are considered as an expression of regulation inside government. This can, for example, be inferred from the observed positive relationship between agency size and the use of management tools. Large agencies can be assumed to be politically salient, hence control on these salient agencies is important for the superior bodies. According to this line of reasoning, it is not the *capacity* of large agencies that induces them to use management techniques (wilful choice), but their *political salience* that prompts government to impose management techniques as a means of (indirect) control.

Apart from general conclusions that we can draw for all or most management techniques under scrutiny, some explanations may vary across management techniques. For example, source of income is linked to the management tool of cost-calculation alone. Agencies that are largely independent of government for their resources use cost-calculation systems more frequently. With regard to the use of management techniques as a wilful choice, it is not surprising that cost-calculation systems are more often used by agencies that rely heavily on resources other than those received from the government. These agencies sell products to users in the markets, and need to calculate costs. As a second example, we found that agencies which are strongly controlled according to results, use management techniques that have an inherent performance element more often than other agencies. This is particularly the case when compared with variations on the use of other management techniques.

For example, in respect of the relationship between result control and the use of customer surveys, this may be explained by the assumption that customer surveys are a good instrument to demonstrate accountability to the public the agency serves, as well as the performance of the agency. Also, result control is related to internal result-based allocation of resources to lower organizational units, which perhaps have more contact points with the organization's users. This management technique can thus be understood as a mechanism to show accountability, by making organizational units that have direct contact with the users responsible for their results. In other words, when discussing the use of management tools by agencies, we must also take into account explanations that are specific for one (type of) tool, as well as generic explanations.

A more comprehensive discussion on the impact of agency characteristics on the use of management techniques follows in Chapter 13, where state-level characteristics are also included in the analysis.

13
Explaining Agency Autonomy, Control and Internal Management: The Importance of Agency- and State-Level Characteristics

13.1 Introduction

In this chapter we bring the analysis to its final stage. Having already analysed the influence of state-level and agency-level characteristics separately, we now focus on the effects of interaction between the two. More specifically, we study those agency-level characteristics that affect the autonomy, control and internal management of agencies in a direct way, independently from the influence of state-level characteristics. Integrating the findings on state-level characteristics outlined in Chapter 9, we now know which characteristics, both at state and agency level, make an impact directly and independently from one another. We discuss whether, and to what extent, the structural-instrumental perspective, the cultural-institutional perspective and the task-specific perspective, as well as the environmental perspective outlined in Chapter 3, may be of relevance in explaining the autonomy, control and internal management of agencies. Chapter 13 thus deals with the final research questions:

RQ 6: How do agency-level characteristics interact with state-level characteristics in explaining agency autonomy, control and internal management?

RQ 7: Which of the four theoretical perspectives has the strongest explanatory power with respect to the level and pattern of autonomy, control and internal management in the three states? Or do all four theoretical perspectives add explanations to the empirical data?

In Chapter 10 we formulated a set of hypotheses on the importance of agency-level characteristics, as derived from three perspectives. Then, in

Chapters 11 and 12 we examined whether the various hypotheses achieved some support or not, based on bivariate correlations for each of the agency-level characteristics separately, as well as on multivariate analyses where the effects of other agency-level characteristics were controlled for. However, as noted in Chapter 3, we are also interested in the combined effects of agency- and state-level characteristics. Thus, we now also control for state-level characteristics by including two dummy variables on states (that is, Norway versus the two other states, and Ireland versus the two other states) in the multivariate analyses.

The results of the multivariate analyses including states are presented in the following section. We then discuss the relevance of the three perspectives (and their underlying theoretical ideas) that emphasize agency-level characteristics in separate sections. This discussion is based partly on summaries of whether, and to what extent, there are statistically significant effects of agency-level characteristics in question. It is also partly based on comparisons of the observed patterns in the multivariate analysis with only agency-level characteristics and those where the two dummy variables on states are included. Here, discrepancies between the two patterns indicate that there is an interaction between agency- and state-level characteristics. In a separate section, we also examine the explanatory power of the theoretical perspectives, and finally (in the last section) draw on some of the findings and interpretations in Part III on comparing states to provide an overall assessment of the theoretical framework as presented in Chapter 3.

13.2   Controlling for state-level characteristics

The results of the multivariate analyses with only agency-level characteristics, and the analyses where the two dummy variables on states are included, are presented in Appendix B. Overall, the importance of agency-level characteristics is about the same whether or not state-level characteristics are taken into account: we find 35 statistically significant correlations when state variables are excluded, compared to 31 statistically significant correlations when they are included. However, only for 21 relationships are there statistically significant correlations in both types of analyses. This means that, in many instances, there is an interaction between agency- and state-level characteristics. This is the case for some effects on autonomy as well as control, and on the use of management techniques.

To what extent, then, does controlling for state variables make an impact on the findings presented in Chapters 11 and 12? This is summarized in Figures 13.1, 13.2 and 13.3, showing the effects of agency characteristics on the autonomy, control and internal management of agencies, respectively, first without controlling for state variables and second when controlling for state variables.

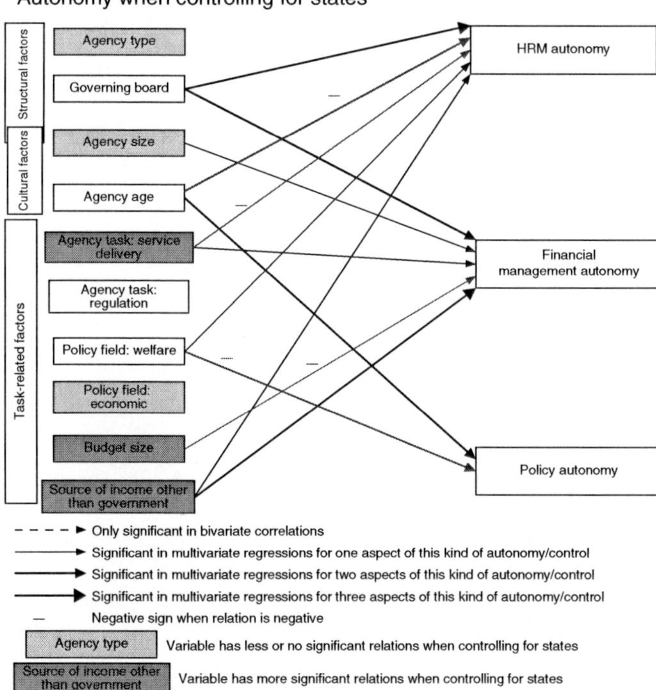

Figure 13.1 Overview of effects of agency-level factors on agencies' autonomy. Significant effects without and with controlling for state-level factors

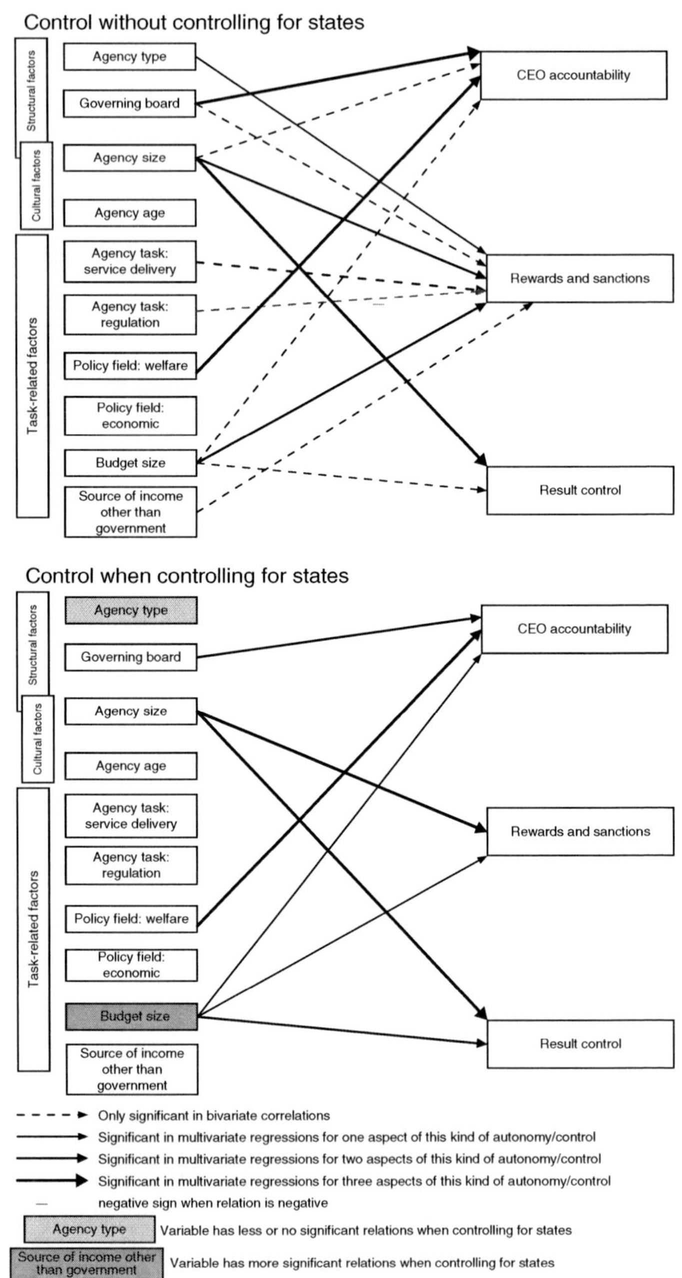

Figure 13.2 Overview of effects of agency-level factors on agencies' control. Significant effects without and with controlling for state-level factors

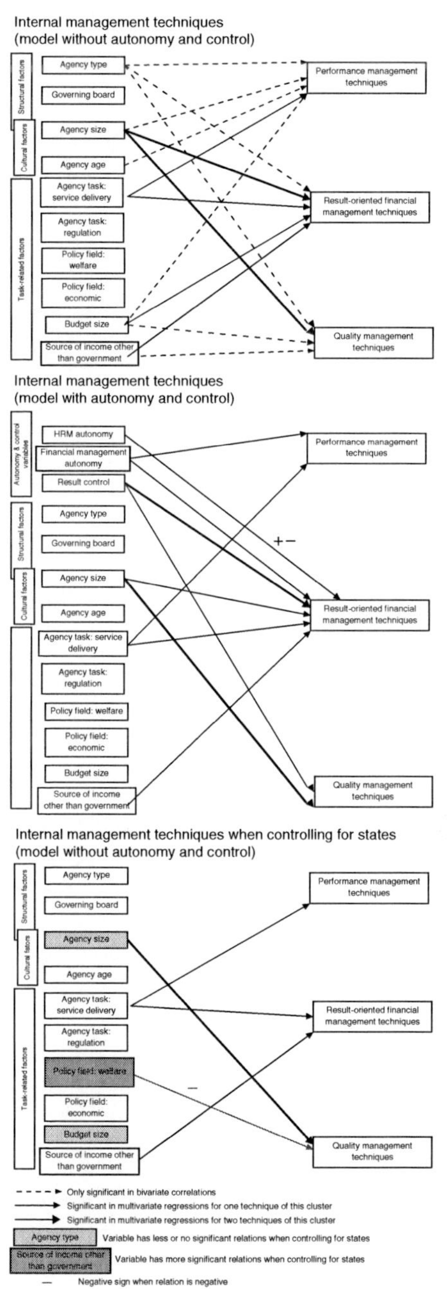

Figure 13.3 Overview of effects of agency-level factors on agencies' internal management. Significant effects without and with controlling for state-level factors

In these three figures, the agency-level characteristics are linked to the three theoretical perspectives. In the following sections we discuss what the findings tell us about the relevance of the perspectives and the theoretical ideas on which the characteristics and perspectives are based.

13.3 The structural-instrumental perspective

In the structural-instrumental perspective, the importance of the formal organizational structure of agencies for their autonomy, control and internal management is emphasized. Aspects of the formal structure of agencies affect whether, and how, superior bodies are willing and able to exercise control over the agencies, and whether, and how, agencies are interested in and able to act on their own, based on a logic of consequentiality. We have examined three structural characteristics of agencies: type of agency, (existence of a) governing board and agency size. All of them turned out to be important for some types of autonomy, control and internal management, but not always in line with what was expected from the structural-instrumental perspective.

For *type of agency*, we differentiated between agencies organized according to geography in combination with another principle, and agencies without a territorial component. We expected that the first group would be more autonomous, subject to less control, and would use management techniques to a greater extent than the second group. When controlling for other agency-level characteristics we found significant correlations for one aspect of autonomy and one aspect of control. However, these correlations were not significant when we controlled for state. With regard to internal management we found some significant bivariate correlations, but they disappeared when the other agency-level characteristics were controlled for. Overall, then, being embedded in regional or local networks does not seem to be of importance for the autonomy, control and internal management of agencies.

With regard to the existence of a *governing board*, our point of departure was with theoretical ideas which imply that agencies with a board will have more autonomy, less control and use management techniques to a greater extent than agencies without a board. For many types of human resource management autonomy and financial management autonomy we also found significant effects for having a board, even after controlling for state. This is in line with previous studies which have demonstrated how a governing board blurs political signals and adds a layer of decision-making (Egeberg 1994; Christensen 2001). However, the lack of significant correlation for the choice of policy instruments may indicate that this additional layer is only important for managerial autonomy and not for policy autonomy.

Looking at different types of control, the existence of a board increases the chances of having CEO accountability for results and legality, but does not affect the use of rewards and sanctions and the extent of result control.

The findings on accountability are in contrast to what we expected, based on ideas of how the existence of a board may enable agencies to avoid control from above. An interpretation more in line with the observations is that superior bodies (like the minister and parent department) particularly want to hold those agencies that are structurally less close accountable, because they are afraid that they may drift away. In sum, agencies which have a governing board simultaneously experience higher levels of managerial autonomy, as well as increased levels of accountability, but without higher levels of result control and control through rewards and sanctions. Finally, with regard to the use of management techniques, we found no significant effects relating to the existence of a governing board. This may indicate that boards do not play a major role in assessments as to whether these techniques are relevant or not.

As argued in Chapter 10, *agency size* may be regarded as an indicator of structure as well as of culture. Taking size as a measure of structural capacity, we expected that large agencies would be more autonomous, subject to less control and use management techniques to a greater extent than small agencies. In Chapter 11 we found quite strong positive correlations between agency size and several aspects of managerial autonomy, even when controlling for the other agency-level characteristics. However, when controlling for state, the effect of size on HRM autonomy disappeared, while the effect on shifting budgets between years remained. Thus, the ability of large agencies to forge autonomy from superior bodies (cf. Carpenter 2001) only seems to be related to some forms of financial managerial autonomy, and not for policy autonomy.

With regard to the control of agencies, most correlations with size were significant, positive and often relatively strong, and this applied also when state dummies were included in the multivariate analysis. Thus, while large agencies perceived themselves as being more autonomous (in terms of financial management) than small agencies, they also perceived themselves as being subjected to more control, particularly through rewards and sanctions and result control. This is the opposite of what we expected, taking size as an indicator of structural capacity. On the other hand, it indicates that large agencies are close to the NPM ideal-type agency model, where high levels of managerial autonomy are combined with high levels of result control and control through rewards and sanction. In other words, for large agencies we find a pattern of compensation between managerial autonomy and control (cf. Roness et al. 2008). Superior bodies give these agencies leeway to act, but also control them through results.

Finally, looking at the use of management techniques, in Chapter 12 we found quite strong positive bivariate correlations between agency size and the use of most management techniques. For some techniques, particularly for those concerned with quality management, this significant effect remained after controlling for other agency-level as well as state-level characteristics. This is in line with what we expected, when viewing this as a wilful choice by agencies, based on their structural capacity. This finding suggests that large agencies have greater internal capacity and expertise to develop and work with innovative quality management techniques, whereas small agencies often seem to lack such capacity. Alternatively, the CEO of a large agency could emphasize management techniques comparatively more often in order to control the lower levels of the agency. Internal principal agent problems, such as information asymmetry and goal incongruence between the CEO and lower hierarchical levels, may be expected to worsen when an agency enlarges, and the span and depth of control increases (Verschuere et al. 2009).

For the structural characteristics of agencies, there are also some differences across types of autonomy. While there were many positive correlations between structural characteristics and the way agencies perceive human resource management and financial management autonomy, these characteristics do not influence the way they perceive policy autonomy. This indicates that structural characteristics are more important for whether, and how, agencies are interested in and able to have managerial rather than policy autonomy. Another interpretation is that the differences are related to whether, and how, superior bodies are willing and able to grant agencies various types of autonomy.

Summing up, the structural-instrumental perspective turns out to be of relevance for the autonomy, control and internal management of agencies. Nevertheless, there are some variations with regard to the effects across structural characteristics, as well as across types of autonomy, control and management techniques. Thus, while many correlations were in line with what we expected and the hypotheses being formulated, some others went in the opposite direction. This combination was particularly evident in relation to the effects of agency size, with larger agencies having higher levels of managerial autonomy and greater use of management techniques, but simultaneously being subjected to higher levels of control in terms of sanctions and rewards, and result control.

13.4   The cultural-institutional perspective

In the cultural-institutional perspective, the importance of the organizational culture of agencies for their autonomy, control and internal management is emphasized. This is seen from below, where aspects of their culture affect whether, and how, agencies regard autonomy, control and the use of management techniques as appropriate and compatible with established norms and values. We have examined the effects of two agency-level characteristics that may be related to organizational culture: age and size.

For *agency age* we differentiated between those agencies established before 1990 (defined as old agencies) and agencies established in 1990 or later (defined as young agencies). We expected that old agencies would be more autonomous, subject to less control and use management techniques to a lesser extent than young agencies. With regard to managerial autonomy, in Chapter 11 we found that age had a statistically significant positive effect on only one aspect of human resource management autonomy (salary), but not on financial management autonomy. However, when controlling for state, the significant effect on HRM autonomy regarding salary disappeared, while there were significant negative effects on the other two aspects of HRM autonomy (promotions and evaluation). On the other hand, there was a strong positive correlation between age and policy autonomy, even when controlling for state. This is in line with what was expected when using age as an indicator of culture. Thus, according to the cultural-institutional perspective, the autonomy of old agencies to decide on policy instruments may be strengthened by the existence of a strongly institutionalized organizational culture and experience in doing things in an organization-specific way (cf. Carpenter 2001). Moreover, such an institutionalized organizational culture and experience seems to be an important resource in securing discretion in policy matters from superior bodies or in shielding such discretion from intervention from above. The mostly negative (and sometimes statistically significant) correlations between age and the types of managerial autonomy, when controlling for states, indicate that the development of a distinct culture does not help agencies to resist interventions from superior bodies on managerial autonomy. An alternative interpretation of the observed importance of age – but not related to the cultural-institutional perspective - is that agencies created from 1990 onwards may have profited from NPM reforms, increasing their managerial autonomy to a greater extent than older agencies.

With regard to control of agencies, we did not find any significant effects for agency age. Thus, assuming that an old agency implies a strong and distinct culture, this aspect of organizational culture does not seem to be of any importance for the way agencies perceive control. Likewise, the institutionalization of a distinct culture, which we assumed to be more prevalent in older agencies, does not seem to affect the use of management techniques in any way.

Taking *agency size* as an indicator of organizational culture was based on ideas that small agencies will have a more homogeneous culture and a more distinct identity than large agencies. Because they are better able to modify signals and resist pressure from superior bodies, we expected that small agencies would be more autonomous than large agencies. However, as noted above, we found positive correlations between agency size and financial management autonomy. On the other hand, we also found that small agencies perceive themselves as being subject to control through rewards and sanctions and through result control to a lesser extent than large agencies, even after including other agency-level and state-level characteristics in multivariate analyses. This is in line with what we expected, assuming that small size implies a strong and distinct culture. Of course, an alternative reason could be that small agencies do not matter as much as agencies of a large size to political and administrative principals, who therefore invest less time and fewer resources in controlling such agencies.

As noted above, we found that small agencies used management techniques to a lesser extent than large agencies. This is also in line with what we expected, based on ideas of what agencies see as being appropriate. The positive effect of size was particularly strong for the use of quality management techniques, implying that these are regarded as being compatible with the established norms and values in small agencies to a lesser extent.

Summing up, we find quite a mixed picture with regard to the relevance of the cultural-institutional perspective for autonomy, control and internal management of agencies. When controlling for the other agency-level characteristics and state-level characteristics, with the exception of policy autonomy, there were no positive effects of agency age on autonomy, and agency age did not make an impact on control and the use of management techniques. The effects of agency size were stronger, but not always in the direction expected, when size is seen as an indicator of culture. However, having a homogeneous culture and more distinct identity, as a result of small size, seems to affect the chances of resisting pressure from above through result control and the use of rewards and sanctions. Moreover, it also affects the chances of being resistant to the use of techniques that are seen as incompatible with established norms and values.

13.5   The task-specific perspective

In the task-specific perspective, the importance of organizational tasks for their autonomy, control and internal management is emphasized. Task characteristics affect whether, and how, superior bodies are willing and able to control agencies, and whether and how agencies are interested in and able to act on their own, based on a logic of consequentiality. We have examined four indicators of task: primary tasks, policy area, source of income and budget size. Here also, all of them turned out to be important for some types of autonomy, control and internal management, but not always in the direction expected from this perspective.

With regard to *service delivery* as a primary task, we expected that service delivery agencies would have more managerial autonomy, be subjected to less result control and use management techniques to a greater extent than agencies with other tasks. For managerial autonomy, we found that having service delivery as a primary task only had a statistically significant positive effect on autonomy in setting tariffs, and in Chapter 11 we argued that this reflected the fact that setting tariffs is particularly important for agencies that deliver services to public and private users. Somewhat unexpectedly, when controlling for states, having service delivery as a primary task affects HRM autonomy (particularly salary), but in a negative way. We also found that having service delivery as a primary task did not have any effect on result control. Thus, overall, although service delivery agencies were assumed to produce outputs which are relatively more measurable and tangible, this does not seem to affect managerial autonomy and result control across agencies.

This is rather surprising, considering the NPM doctrine as well as the results from previous studies emphasizing the importance of measurability and tangibility for the autonomy and control of agencies (OECD 1997; Kickert 1998). Looking at the use of management techniques, we found statistically significant positive effects of having service delivery as a primary task for one performance management technique and one financial management technique, even after controlling for state. This may indicate that service delivery agencies mainly use multi-year planning and internal performance-based allocation of resources in order to optimize production and service delivery processes for organizational effectiveness and to build trust and legitimacy with the main stakeholders.

With regard to *regulation* as a primary task, we expected that this group of agencies would have more autonomy (particularly on policy autonomy), be subjected to less control and use management techniques to a greater extent than other agencies. We found that regulatory agencies perceived having a higher degree of policy autonomy, but that this relationship became statistically insignificant when controlling for other agency-level and state-level characteristics. For the other types of autonomy, as well as for all types of control, there were no statistically significant correlations. There were also no significant effects of regulation as a primary task on the use of management techniques.

For policy area we constructed two dummy variables, focusing on the welfare and social policy area as well as on economic policy. Again, based on the logic of credible commitment, we expected that agencies within the *economic policy area* would have more autonomy, be subject to less control, and would use management techniques to a greater extent than agencies within other policy areas. Contrary to what we expected, in the bivariate and multivariate analyses in Chapter 11, we found a strong negative effect on all aspects of HRM autonomy. However, when controlling for state, we did not find any significant effects of being in the economic policy area. An important conclusion here is that the theoretical ideas of credible commitment do not retain any explanatory power for autonomy, control or internal management with regard to agencies with a regulatory task or agencies in the economic area, when we control for states. Decisions and perceptions on autonomy and control of regulatory agencies, as well as of economic policy agencies, do not seem to be determined strongly by problems of time inconsistency (cf. Thatcher and Stone Sweet 2002; Gilardi 2006).

We now turn to some task features linked to the political salience of that task. We assumed that agencies within the *welfare and social policy area* would be more political salient, and hence expected that they would have less autonomy, be subject to more control, and would use management techniques to a greater extent than agencies within other policy areas. In Chapter 11, we found that being in the welfare and social policy area did not have any effect on the perceptions of managerial autonomy. However, when controlling for states, we found a positive effect on autonomy with regard to promotion. Moreover, there is a statistically significant negative effect on the perceptions of policy autonomy, even after controlling for other agency-level characteristics and for states, in line with what we expected. We also found a statistically significant positive effect of being in the welfare and social policy area on CEO accountability, but no significant effects on control through rewards and sanctions, and results control. Looking at the use of management techniques we only found one statistically significant effect of being in the welfare and social policy area after controlling for state. However, this correlation (on the use of customer surveys) was the opposite of what we expected. In sum, the political salience of welfare and social policy agencies seems to be more reflected in their relatively lower level of policy autonomy than in their level of managerial autonomy. Likewise, CEO accountability seems to be positively affected by their political salience, but it does not seem to affect other forms of control or the use of management techniques.

Budget size was the second indicator for political salience. For *size of the budget*, we expected that agencies with a large budget would have less autonomy, be subject to more control, and would use management techniques to a greater extent than agencies with a small budget. In Chapter 11, we found a very mixed picture with regard to agency autonomy with several positive, as well as negative, correlations. When controlling for state, the only statistically significant effect of the size of the budget on autonomy was on shifting budgets between years, which, as expected, was negative. On the other hand, with regard to control of agencies, almost all correlations were positive, in line with what we expected. Many correlations were also statistically significant even when controlling for state. This may indicate that, for governments, it is more important to control politically salient agencies with large budgets, compared to agencies with small budgets, through accountability on results, rewards and sanctions, and result control. Furthermore, governments tend to restrict their financial managerial autonomy on some aspects. In the bivariate analyses in Chapter 12, we found that having a large budget increases the chances of all types of management techniques being used, in line with what we expected when viewing this as a wilful choice by agencies. Nevertheless, the effects of the size of the budget on the use of management techniques weakened when we controlled for other agency-level characteristics, and it disappeared completely when controlling for state-level characteristics. This is probably due to an intervening effect of characteristics such as agency size and state.

Finally, with regard to *source of income*, we expected that agencies with a large amount of their own income would have more autonomy, be subject to less control, and would use management techniques to a greater extent than agencies with a small proportion of own incomes. When controlling for states, we found that source of income did, indeed, have a statistically significant positive effect on promotion of personnel and on all aspects of financial management autonomy. This indicates that having incomes of their own makes agencies more interested in and able to have managerial autonomy, but not policy autonomy. However, there were no statistically significant correlations on control. Thus, agencies which are partially or fully self-financing have more managerial autonomy, but without being subjected to more control, than agencies without incomes of their own.

In Chapter 12 we found some statistically significant positive correlations between the source of income and the use of management techniques, like cost-calculation systems and customer surveys. However, in the multivariate analyses, the significant effect was only upheld for cost-calculation systems. This seems logical since agencies which predominantly generate their own income from selling services need such cost-calculation systems in order to set their prices and compensations at an appropriate level.

Summing up, for the task-specific perspective we also find a rather mixed picture with regard to understanding the autonomy, control and internal management of agencies. As noted in Chapter 10, the importance of task features was based on different types of ideas. In general, ideas taking political saliency as the point of departure seem to be quite relevant for explaining our findings. Also, several relationships can be explained by simple down-to-earth ideas of pragmatic functionality, referring to the relevance of a particular kind of autonomy for an agency with a specific task feature. However, credible commitment and time consistency logics do not seem to have much explanatory power. Moreover, viewing autonomy, control and the use of management techniques from below as the wilful choice of agencies seems to be somewhat more relevant than seeing this from above as the result of actions taken by superior bodies (see also Lægreid et al. 2007).

13.6 The relative importance of the theoretical perspectives

Returning to RQ7, what, then, do the findings presented above tell us about the explanatory power of the three theoretical perspectives emphasizing agency-level characteristics, in other words, the structural-instrumental, cultural-institutional and task-specific perspectives? When we consider all possible relationships between the respective independent variables from the three different perspectives on the one hand, and the 21 dependent variables on the other hand, all three perspectives seem to have a quasi-equal explanatory power. For the structural-instrumental perspective we found eight statistically significant correlations out of 63 correlations in the direction expected, that is, 13 per cent of all relationships. The expectations based on the cultural-instrumental perspective proved to be significant in five out of 42 relations, and those based on the task-specific perspective in 15 out of 126 relations. Hence, 12 per cent of all relations studied for both the cultural-instrumental and the task-specific perspective proved to be supported by our data.

What does it mean that the three theoretical perspectives have about the same explanatory power? First, even if the overall number of statistically significant correlations is relatively modest, this suggests that the theoretical perspectives are supplementary in their explanatory power, rather than competing, mutually exclusive theoretical frameworks (cf. Roness 2009). This is in line with ideas in a transformative perspective (cf. Christensen and Lægreid 2001b, 2007a), which state that a fuller understanding of organizational features can be understood by combining different theoretical perspectives. It may also suggest that in their decisions about agencies actors combine logics of consequentiality and logics of appropriateness, rather than restricting themselves to one or other logic (March and Olsen 1998; Pollitt et al. 2004: 248–51). We return to this later in the chapter.

Second, there are some interesting variations across perspectives and aspects of autonomy, control and internal management of agencies. The explanatory power of the theoretical perspectives seems to vary quite considerably according to whether we look at the autonomy, control or internal management of agencies. Formulated somewhat simply, the structural-instrumental perspective, followed by the task-specific perspective, is most important for explaining agency autonomy. Agency control is best explained by the cultural-institutional perspective, combined with factors of political salience in the task-specific perspective. The levels of managerial autonomy and result control are most important in explaining the use of management techniques, with the structural-instrumental and task-specific perspectives providing some additional explanatory power.

Third, we could question the extent to which the hypotheses based on our theoretical perspectives are refined enough, since different agency-level characteristics seem to affect both agency autonomy and control in a similar way. For instance, agency size affects agency autonomy positively, which suggests support for the structural-instrumental perspective. Large agencies have more capacity and more resources to resist control from above. However, large agencies do experience more result control. The cultural-institutional perspective suggests that because the organizational culture of agencies is less homogeneous, control signals are less filtered in large agencies. These two logics are hard to reconcile, calling for more refined hypotheses or more refined explanatory variables. We turn to that issue in the next section.

13.7   What about the autonomy-control balance?

Most of our hypotheses in Chapter 11 were formulated in such a way that autonomy and control were treated as opposites. We assumed that when a specific structural, cultural or task-related characteristic lead to more autonomy for agencies, it would also bring about less control. However, these hypotheses did not really take into account the multi-dimensionality of both autonomy and control, as outlined in Chapter 2. Moreover, they hardly took into account that some combinations of high autonomy and high control are plausible, like the combination of managerial autonomy and result control (Roness et al. 2008). As repeatedly stated throughout this book, the NPM doctrine even advocates this combination of managerial autonomy and result control.

This suggests three important conclusions. First, the developed hypotheses at the level of agency autonomy linking high autonomy with low control are too simple. High autonomy and high control can come in pairs, particularly in the case of managerial autonomy and result control. This necessitates building more refined hypotheses based on the aforementioned empirical relations.

Second, these findings also suggest that across the three states the NPM ideal-type agency with a specific combination of high managerial autonomy and result control is to be found relatively more in the groups of agencies with a governing board and a large size, as well as in agencies in the welfare and social policy area. The latter three factors may refer to a higher political salience, or to the existence of intensive relations with users.

Third, these findings add elements to the theoretical discussion on the balance of autonomy and control that agencies experience in practice (Gains 1999) and on the autonomization paradox (Kickert 1998; Van Thiel 2004; Christensen and Lægreid 2006), which point at autonomous agencies who perceive being more controlled than before. Our survey data and analysis demonstrates that perceptions of high autonomy can coexist with perceptions of being strongly controlled, particularly with regard to specific kinds of agencies and in specific states.

13.8   Interaction between agency-level and state-level characteristics

When comparing the outcomes of the multivariate analyses without controlling for state dummies, and the analyses in which we control for state dummies (see Figures 13.1, 13.2 and 13.3), it becomes clear that there are indeed considerable interaction effects between agency-level characteristics and state-level characteristics. For example, when controlling for state-level characteristics, structural aspects such as agency size and type lose some or all of their direct influence on autonomy, control and internal management. On the other hand, some task-related factors like being in the welfare and social policy area, having service delivery as a primary task, and budget size, gain explanatory power when controlling for state-level characteristics. The direct influence of agency age on HRM autonomy even shifts from a positive to a negative influence, when comparing analyses, and controlling for state-level characteristics with analyses, where no such controls are included. Interestingly, differences between the two kinds of analyses are the greatest with respect to characteristics explaining autonomy, and least when it comes to control and management techniques. What can we learn from this?

First, this suggests that the state-specific ways of creating and reforming agencies have substantial explanatory power with regard to (in descending order) autonomy, control and management techniques. When controlling for state, the influence of state-level characteristics is filtered out of our empirical results. We can explain the decreasing explanatory power of several agency-level characteristics quite easily by referring to these state-specific methods of agency creation and reform (see Chapter 6). Agency size becomes less important in explaining autonomy when controlling for state-level characteristics, because Ireland has created many comparatively small agencies, which are very reliant upon their parent department for support in relation to HRM issues. Norway has many old agencies, created before 1990, as well as high levels of HRM autonomy. When filtering out the dominance of older Norwegian agencies with large HRM autonomy, the effect of age on HRM autonomy becomes negative. This means that, taken across the board, young agencies tend to have more HRM autonomy than old agencies. Similarly, the positive effect of agency type on financial management autonomy disappears when we control for the relative dominance of single-integrated agencies in Ireland. Flanders has comparatively much more agencies in the economic policy area, as well as a policy of low levels of HRM autonomy. Hence the negative effect of being in the economic policy area on HRM autonomy disappears when we control for this state difference. Service delivery agencies are more prominent in Norway and Flanders than in Ireland, which may explain the changing influence of service delivery when controlling for states.

Second, these findings strongly support the conclusions in Chapter 9 about the importance of state-level characteristics in explaining state differences in agency autonomy, control and management techniques. As we learned from the analyses in Chapter 9, the three states handled agency creation and reform in different ways. This was because of environmental pressures (for example, a legacy of financial-budgetary crises), cultural aspects (for example, the prominence of an administrative law tradition), elements of polity, as well as the importance of a strong agencification tradition and blueprint when faced with distrusting actor constellations (for example, between central departments, line departments and agencies) and inconsistent deliberate actions. Hence, the fourth theoretical perspective elaborated in Chapter 3, the environmental perspective, also achieves strong support from our multivariate analyses. Thus, institutional environments matters.

13.9 The integrated model revisited

In Chapter 3, we developed an integrated model, combining our four theoretical perspectives. We now revisit this model. Figure 13.4 shows the revised model, as it emerges from the empirical analyses.

Essentially, our analyses show that the integrated model holds very well when confronted with the empirical material. The normative pressure for conformity that comes from international NPM doctrines on optimal

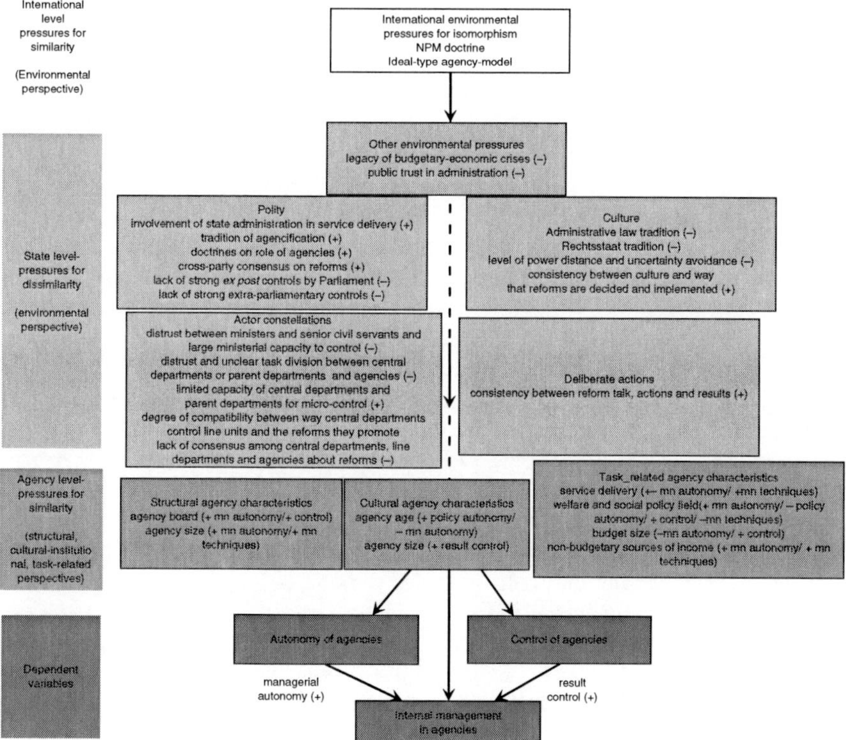

Figure 13.4   The model for comparing and explaining agency autonomy, control and internal management in different states revisited

structure of public administration and the related ideal-type agency image was reported in all three states (see Chapter 6). However, these doctrines were transformed when they met state-specific environmental factors, polity, administrative culture and actor constellations, which led to different responses and deliberate actions in the shape of reform programmes (see Chapter 9). Thus, our evidence strongly supports the transformative perspective of Christensen and Lægreid (2001b, 2007a). We identified several state-level characteristics that pressurize for divergence and dissimilarity between the three states, and create the specific 'implementation habitats' (Pollitt and Bouckaert 2004; Pollitt et al. 2007) that were either conducive or more hostile to these organizational concepts. Our evidence of agency reforms in these three small European states demonstrate that path-dependency indeed matters a great deal, as reflected in the relevance of administrative law tradition, cultural traits, the tradition regarding agencification and common norms on agency roles and positions, or even the legacy of past budgetary and financial crises. Trust, consistent behaviour, clear role divisions and consensus between politico-administrative actors with respect to reforms, the introduction of managerial autonomy and result control also seem to matter also in a positive way.

Most studies on 'implementation habitats' compare states which are NPM forerunners with NPM laggards. Interestingly, this study adds to the literature on 'implementation habitats' as it focuses on how differences of politico-administrative regime may influence the way NPM reforms are adopted in three small European states, which are generally perceived as NPM laggards. The considerable extent to which we have found differences in the adoption of NPM reforms and the extent to which politico-administrative regimes help to explain this adoption strongly suggest that the NPM laggards should not be treated as one equal group and that they deserve more attention in comparative studies.

However, characteristics at the level of agencies also matter. When introducing changes to the autonomy, control and internal management of agencies, politico-administrative actors take agency characteristics into account, either in a logic of consequentiality or in a logic of appropriateness. Across the three states, agencies with a governing board, of a large size, or with a large budget tend to have more managerial autonomy as well as greater (result) control. Agencies which are less dependent on state funding tend to have more managerial autonomy (cf. Gains 1999, 2004). Agencies which were created in the heyday of NPM (after 1990), tend to have more HRM autonomy, but they have less policy autonomy than older agencies (cf. Carpenter 2001). Agencies in the welfare and social policy area report somewhat more managerial autonomy and more accountability, but simultaneously they have less policy autonomy. These characteristics provide agency-level pressures for conformity and similarities of agencies across states.

13.10 Theoretical discussion and conclusions

What do we learn from this, in relation to other recent research and theories with regard to agencification and public administration in general? First, this study supports the basic ideas of the task-specific path-dependency theory, which was formulated by Pollitt et al. (2004) on the basis of a multiple-case study in four states. The autonomy of agencies, as well as the way that they are controlled by ministers or parent departments, is indeed strongly influenced by extensive national path-dependency and politico-administrative regimes (Pollitt et al 2004: 255). Moreover, we have found strong support that the degree of political salience of tasks seems to matter. Like Pollitt et al. (2004) and other researchers (for example, Hogwood et al. 2000), we found that agencies with large budgets tend to be controlled more and have less (financial) management autonomy. Moreover, agencies that have a high degree of face-to-face interaction with large groups of users, like agencies in the welfare and social policy area, tend to be controlled in a stricter way. Also, agencies in the welfare and social policy area may be assumed to perform relatively simple tasks, like the disbursement of social benefits, which are easily understood by their political and administrative principals, in contrast with highly scientific and complex tasks like research agencies (Wilson 1989; Bouckaert and Halachmi 1995; Pollitt et al. 2004). However, contrary to the study by Pollitt et al. (2004), we did not find a straightforward link between the task of the agency and its autonomy or control. Probably, our task variable itself may be operationalized in too rough a way to differentiate between agencies with simple, tangible and measurable tasks and agencies with highly complex, ideal and non-measurable tasks. Moreover, although we did not account for it in our empirical analyses, many agencies reported having multiple tasks, combining, for example, service delivery with policy formulation (see Chapter 6). This mixing of tasks within one agency blurs to some extent the influence of tasks on autonomy, control and internal management. But overall, there are strong indications that the task-specific path-dependency theory seems to pass the test with our survey data from 226 agencies in three states.

We now turn to a short review of the implications of this study for the theories underlying this study. As stated in Chapter 3, our research is primarily based on ideas from organization theory and three different institutional schools (cf. Hall and Taylor 1996; Scott 2001; Peters 2005): rational choice institutionalism with the emphasis on rational behaviour by politicians and administrators, sociological institutionalism with the central concepts of isomorphism, myths and decoupling (Meyer and Rowan 1977; DiMaggio and Powell 1983), and historical institutionalism with path-dependency and punctuated equilibrium (Krasner 1988; Pierson 2004; Thelen 2004). Theories were based on a logic of consequentiality, versus a logic of appropriateness. What do the findings of this study imply for the explanatory power of such grand theories and logics for autonomy, control and internal management techniques?

The logic of consequentiality was developed in several perspectives in this book, and the extent to which these theoretical perspectives help to explain agency autonomy, control and internal management varies considerably. The principal-agent delegation approach which we developed in Chapter 7, in order to explain the effect of state-level characteristics, referred to the structural choice theory of Moe (1990) and others. This theory proved to have quite a strong explanatory power, as described in Chapter 9. However, interestingly enough, the explanatory power was much less for hypotheses that were strongly based on the notions of policy conflict and policy uncertainty, which are at the core of recent developed variants of structural choice theories (cf. Horn 1995; Huber and Shipan 2002; Yesilkagit and Christensen forthcoming). The other hypotheses within that framework, which were more strongly supported, were based more on simple principal-agent elements. Likewise, when we turn to the perspectives developed at the agency level, the ideas of credible commitment, which led us to expect that regulatory agencies and agencies in the economic policy area would have relatively high levels of autonomy and low levels of control, lost their explanatory power when controlling for other agency-level and state-level characteristics. This suggests that actors do not focus primarily on problems of time-inconsistency and credible commitment when designing regulatory agencies or agencies in the economic policy area. At least, this is not common in all three states. These findings raise some doubts about the explanatory power of credible commitment theory which is, however, highly popular in the regulation literature (cf. Thatcher and Stone Sweet 2002; Elgie 2006; Gilardi 2006).

At agency level, other rational choice theories may have some explanatory power. Public choice and principal agent theories, which make up some of the theoretical pillars of NPM doctrines (besides managerialism), find some support in this study. The most clear example of this is that the use of management techniques seems to be enhanced by the extent to which agencies experience result control from their political and administrative principals (besides having high (financial) managerial autonomy, service delivery tasks, a large size and own sources of income). This seems to support the basic idea of NPM and of principal agent theories that actors will perform well if they are forced to do so, by having strong controls placed on their performance ('make the managers manage'), and if they have enough autonomy to do so. Of course, one could also see how agencies whose performance is strongly controlled might introduce these management techniques to achieve legitimacy with their principals, in the hope that control may diminish over time. This was definitively the case in the highly distrusting setting of Flemish agencies, as shown in other research (Verhoest et al. 2007).

This latter explanation would be closer to sociological institutionalism with its concepts of structural decoupling, legitimacy and isomorphism. Other theoretical perspectives based on the logic of appropriateness do have something to add when it comes to explaining agency autonomy and control. Cultural-institutional theories about the importance of organizational culture and history did have some relevance, in that older agencies tend to have more policy autonomy, and larger agencies tend to be controlled more strictly. Path-dependency in particular, and historical institutionalism generally, was central, however, to understanding why the three states have created and changed agencies and their autonomy and control arrangements in different ways. The findings in Chapter 9 stressed the importance of administrative culture and long-standing agencification traditions with explicit normative visions about agency roles.

So theories based on both logics of consequentiality and appropriateness appear to be relevant. This emphasizes the need for a better understanding of how, to what extent, and under which conditions actors behave according to these logics or when they alternate between them (March and Olsen 1998: 952–3; Pollitt et al. 2004: 250). Future multiple case-study based research could provide for refined testing of hypotheses developed in this study, but with a stronger potential to grasp the underlying mechanisms and logics in the minds of the key actors involved. Such future research could also circumvent some of the limitations of operationalization that we faced with this study. For example, our typology of tasks proves to be too general, and mixing of tasks within one agency was not considered in our analyses. Moreover, taking agency age as a proxy for the institutionalization of organizational culture is a second-best choice, at most. Multiple case studies, which take full measures of organizational culture, could foster our understanding of the cultural-institutional factors determining autonomy and control. Future research should also test the relevant findings in other politico-administrative cultures, in order to see if the patterns found do have a general bearing across cultures and administrative traditions, which is wider than our three states. Recently, major cross-country studies are being conducted jointly in different networks (The COBRA 'Comparative Public Organization Data Base for Research and Analysis – network', and the COST Action IS0601 'Comparative Research into Current Trends in Public Sector Organization – CRIPO'), based on both survey and multiple case study methodologies. It is our hope that this study may inspire researchers involved in these and other networks to bring their research forward.

Appendix A
Distribution of Dependent Variables

Table A.1   Distribution of dependent variables

HRM autonomy re: salary – *Can the organization without interference from above (without ministerial or departmental influence) take decisions*

- *on the general policy for the organization re: salary levels (that is 'strategic autonomy')?*
- *to increase the salary of an individual member of staff (that is 'operational autonomy')?*

		Frequency	Per cent
0	No operational and no strategic autonomy	107	49
0.5	Operational, but not strategic autonomy	21	10
1	Operational and strategic autonomy	90	41
	Total	218	100
Missing		8	

HRM autonomy re: promotion – *Can the organization without interference from above (without ministerial or departmental influence) take decisions*

- *on the general policy for the organization re: promotion conditions (that is 'strategic autonomy')?*
- *to promote an individual member of staff (that is 'operational autonomy')?*

		Frequency	Per cent
0	No operational and no strategic autonomy	51	24
0.5	Operational, but not strategic autonomy	31	14
1	Operational and strategic autonomy	135	62
	Total	217	100
Missing		9	

HRM autonomy re: evaluation – *Can the organization without interference from above (without ministerial or departmental influence) take decisions*

- *on the general policy for the organization re: evaluation methods and criteria (that is 'strategic autonomy')?*
- *to evaluate an individual member of staff (that is 'operational autonomy')?*

		Frequency	Per cent
0	No operational and no strategic autonomy	25	11
0.5	Operational, but not strategic autonomy	38	17
1	Operational and strategic autonomy	155	71
	Total	218	100
Missing		8	

Financial management autonomy re: taking loans – *Can your organization itself take loans for investments?*

		Frequency	Per cent
0	No	173	78
0.5	Yes, within limits and conditions set by oversight authority	45	20
1	Yes, fully and without limits and conditions set by oversight authority	5	2
	Total	223	100
Missing		3	

Financial management autonomy re: setting tariffs – *Can your organization itself set tariffs for services or products?*

		Frequency	Per cent
0	No	86	39
0.5	Yes, within limits and conditions set by oversight authority	87	40
1	Yes, fully and without limits and conditions set by oversight authority	47	21
	Total	220	100,0
Missing		6	

Financial management autonomy re: shifting budgets between years – *Can your organization itself shift budgets between different years?*

		Frequency	Per cent
0	No	107	51
1	Yes	101	49
	Total	208	100
Missing		18	

Table A.1   (Continued)

Policy autonomy re: choice of policy instruments – *Which of following statements is most valid, with respect to the choice/selection of the policy instruments (such as subsidies, . . .) of the policy that your organization executes?*

		Frequency	Per cent
0	None – minister/department takes most of the decisions independently of the organization	3	1
.33	Low – minister/department takes most of the decisions after having consulted the organization	15	7
.66	High – when organization takes most of the decisions itself after having consulted minister/department or under explicit restrictions/conditions set by minister	110	52
1.00	Very high – when organization takes most of the decisions itself, minister/department is not, or only, slightly involved and sets no or only minor restrictions	85	40
	Total	213	
Missing		13	

Upwards CEO accountability for results – *Is the CEO of the organization accountable to the oversight authority (cabinet, minister or parent department) on results and goal achievement?*

		Frequency	Per cent
0	No	37	18
1	Yes	173	82
	Total	210	100
Missing		16	

Upwards CEO accountability for legality – *Is the CEO of the organization accountable to the oversight authority (cabinet, minister or parent department) on legality of the agencies' actions and compliance to rules, regulations or precepts?*

		Frequency	Per cent
0	No	33	16
1	Yes	178	84
	Total	211	100
Missing		15	

Overall upwards CEO accountability – *Is the CEO of the organization accountable to the oversight authority (cabinet, minister or parent department) . . . ?*

		Frequency	Valid Percent
0	Not accountable for either results or for legality (none of both)	22	11
0.5	Accountable for either results OR legality (not both)	26	13
1	Accountable for both results and legality	159	77
	Total	207	100
Missing		19	

Rewards and sanctions re: wages of individuals

- *Are there rewards in case of good results or the achievement of the goals or targets for the organization with respect to wage increase or bonus for manager or other staff members?*
- *Are there sanctions in case of bad results or the failure to achieve the goals or targets with respect to wage decrease or bonus reduction for manager or other staff members?*

		Frequency	Per cent
0	No rewards and sanctions re: wages	190	89
0.5	Either rewards or sanctions re: wages	16	7
1	Both rewards and sanctions re: wages	8	4
	Total	214	100
Missing		12	

Rewards and sanctions re: resources

- *Are there rewards in case of good results or the achievement of the goals or targets for the organization with respect to increased financial resources for the organization?*
- *Are there sanctions in case of bad results or the failure to achieve the goals or targets with respect to decreased financial resources for the organization?*

		Frequency	Per cent
0	No rewards and sanctions re: resources	173	81
0.5	Either rewards or sanctions re: resources	24	11
1	Both rewards and sanctions re: resources	17	8
	Total	214	100
Missing		12	

Rewards and sanctions re: discretion

- *Are there rewards in case of good results or the achievement of the goals or targets for the organization with respect to more autonomy for the organization in relation to the oversight authority (cabinet, minister or parent department)?*
- *Are there sanctions in case of bad results or the failure to achieve the goals or targets with respect to less autonomy for the organization in relation to the oversight authority (cabinet, minister or parent department)?*

Table A.1   (Continued)

		Frequency	Per cent
0	No rewards and sanctions re: discretion	169	79
0.5	Either rewards or sanctions re: discretion	34	16
1	Both rewards and sanctions re: discretion	11	5
	Total	214	100
Missing		12	

Overall rewards and sanctions

- *Are there rewards in case of good results or the achievement of the goals or targets for the organization of at least one kind?*
- *Are there sanctions in case of bad results or the failure to achieve the goals or targets of at least one kind?*

		Frequency	Per cent
0	No rewards or sanctions of any kind	127	59
0.5	Either rewards or sanctions of at least one kind	54	25
1	Both rewards and sanctions of at least one kind	33	15
	Total	214	100
Missing		12	

Result control: *Presence of CEO accountability for results, combined with rewards or sanctions of at least one kind*

		Frequency	Per cent
0	No result control (no CEO accountability for results)	37	18
0.5	CEO accountability for results	96	46
1	CEO accountability for results + rewards or/and sanctions of at least one kind	77	37
	Total	210	100
Missing		16	

Management techniques: multiyear planning (recoded dichotomous variable) – *Are the following management techniques used in your organization: planning over years in the form of a multi-year plan or business plan?*

		Frequency	Valid Percent
0	No	32	15
1	Yes	182	85
	Total	214	100
Missing		12	

Management techniques: internal allocation of resources to organisational units on the basis of results (recoded dichotomous variable) – *Are the following management techniques used in your organization: internal allocation of resources to organizational units on the basis of results?*

		Frequency	Valid Percent
0	No	95	45
1	Yes	116	55
	Total	211	100
Missing		15	

Management techniques: development of cost-calculation systems (recoded dichotomous variable) – *Are the following management techniques used in your organization: development of cost-calculation systems?*

		Frequency	Valid Percent
0	No	116	55
1	Yes	96	45
	Total	212	100
Missing		14	

Management techniques: public reporting on performance – *Are the following management techniques used in your organization: public reporting on the performance of the organisation (in annual reports or budget reports)?*

		Frequency	Valid Percent
0	No	14	7
1	yes	195	93
	Total	209	100
Missing		17	

Table A.1   (Continued)

Management techniques: quality management systems – *Are the following management techniques used in your organization: quality management systems, such as ISO, CAF, EFQM, Balanced Score-card?*

		Frequency	Valid Percent
0	No	133	64
1	yes	74	36
	Total	207	100
Missing		19	

Management techniques: Use of customer surveys in the organisation – *Are the following management techniques used in your organization: customer surveys?*

		Frequency	Valid Percent
0	No	67	32
1	yes	143	68
	Total	210	100
Missing		16	

Appendix B
Comparing Agency Autonomy, Control and Internal Management: The Importance of Agency Characteristics Without and with Controlling for State-Level Factors

Table B.1   Agency characteristics and agency autonomy. Total sample. Estimates in logistic regression, without controlling for state-level factors (first value) and with controlling for state-level factors (second value)

	HRM autonomy			Financial management autonomy			Policy autonomy
	Salaries	Promotion	Evaluation	Taking loans	Setting tariffs	Shifting budget	
Agency type	−0.49	0.09	−0.21	1.20*	−0.17	0.24	−0.09
	−0.32	0.10	−0.44	1.33	−0.10	0.36	−0.12
Governing board	−0.29	1.15**	0.91**	2.42**	1.30**	0.17	0.34
	1.42**	2.71**	1.88**	2.40**	1.42**	0.74	0.24
Agency size	1.30*	1.04	1.25*	−1.40	0.10	2.12**	0.31
	0.64	0.92	1.46	−0.17	−0.10	1.98**	0.39
Agency age	0.65*	−0.07	0.11	−0.62	−0.16	0.49	0.81**
	0.02	−1.09*	−0.88*	−0.10	−0.32	0.23	0.82*
Service delivery	−0.04	−0.13	0.11	−0.66	0.91**	−0.10	0.09
	−1.02*	−0.46	0.28	−0.41	0.98**	−0.30	0.16
Regulation	0.27	0.97	0.58	−0.27	0.06	0.14	0.79
	0.04	0.62	0.18	−0.53	0.00	−0.10	0.78
Economic policy	−1.06*	−1.27**	−1.08*	0.43	0.41	−0.70	0.66
	−1.04	−0.86	−0.54	−0.20	0.59	−0.39	0.65

Welfare policy	0.12	0.77	0.07	−0.26	0.20	−0.56	−1.16**
	0.65	1.19	−0.19	−0.20	0.26	−0.53	−1.20**
Budget size	0.21	0.43	0.14	0.64	−0.54	−1.05	−0.36
	0.39	0.56	0.60	0.41	−0.51	−1.34*	−0.29
Source of income	0.04	0.60	0.25	1.65**	1.49**	0.93	−0.72
	0.73	1.53*	0.93	2.08**	1.59**	1.14*	−0.74
Norway	–	–	–	–	–	–	–
	4.31**	5.09**	5.08**	23.36*	.98*	1.76**	0.09
Ireland	–	–	–	–	–	–	–
	−0.82	1.15*	2.26**	−0.53	0.49	−0.29	0.42
N = 100 %	201	200	202	205	204	196	196

**p-value < 0.01, *p-value < 0.05.

Table B.2 Agency characteristics and agency control. Total sample. Estimates in logistic regression, without controlling for state-level factors (first value) and with controlling for state-level factors (second value)

	Upwards CEO accountability			Rewards and sanctions				Result control
	Results	Legality	Overall	Wages	Resources	Discretion	Overall	
Agency type	−0.06	0.91	0.57	0.35	−1.05*	0.78	−0.31	−0.20
	−0.14	0.89	0.54	−0.05	−0.82	0.84	−0.32	−0.27
Governing board	1.10*	1.27**	1.18**	0.24	0.42	−0.51	0.19	0.47
	0.78	1.02*	1.04*	−0.52	0.78	−0.59	0.17	0.33
Agency size	0.54	0.46	0.30	1.30	1.81*	0.41	1.60**	1.29*
	0.63	0.43	0.29	2.96*	1.54*	0.35	1.63**	1.39**
Agency age	−0.26	0.07	−0.19	−0.71	0.21	−0.34	−0.08	−0.09
	−0.55	−0.14	−0.38	−0.43	0.05	−0.50	−0.07	−0.16
Service delivery	−0.29	−0.54	−0.50	−0.53	0.78	−0.34	0.37	0.10
	0.04	−0.33	−0.14	−1.23	0.78	−0.25	0.38	0.25
Regulation	0.79	0.37	0.58	0.39	−0.08	−1.04	−0.00	0.24
	0.69	0.25	0.53	0.51	−0.15	−1.16	0.01	0.26
Economic policy	−1.28	−0.59	−0.87	0.99	0.81	−0.07	0.59	0.20
	−0.75	−0.16	−0.56	0.44	1.12	0.17	0.58	0.38

Welfare policy	1.86*	1.14	1.41*	−0.74	−0.91	−0.04	−0.72	0.16
	1.88	1.14	1.58**	−0.64	−0.87	−0.18	−0.73	0.09
Budget size	0.82	−0.32	0.25	1.94*	0.77	0.58	1.10*	0.81
	1.60*	0.25	0.91	1.39	1.07	0.81	1.11*	1.11*
Source of income	−0.02	0.26	−0.01	−0.93	−1.30	0.95	−0.28	−0.04
	0.30	0.61	0.49	−1.60	−1.32	1.05	−0.28	−0.11
Norway	−	−	−	−	−	−	−	−
	1.82**	1.30*	1.70**	−3.65**	1.87**	1.18*	−0.06	0.76*
Ireland	−	−	−	−	−	−	−	−
	3.94**	3.15**	3.58**	−2.00**	0.96	1.35*	0.04	1.29**
N = 100%	196	198	194	199	199	199	199	196

**p-value < 0.01, *p-value < 0.05.

Table B.3 Agency characteristics and the use of management techniques. Total sample. Estimates in logistic regression, without controlling for state-level factors (first value) and with controlling for state-level factors (second value)

	Multi-year plan	internal result-based allocation	Cost-calculation	Public reporting	Quality management systems	Customer survey
Agency type	−0.42	−0.25	0.23	1.79	0.72	−0.66
	−0.49	−0.21	0.44	2.34	0.66	−0.78
Governing board	0.16	−0.48	−0.09	0.98	0.06	0.51
	0.56	−0.31	0.51	1.48	−0.30	0.14
Agency size	1.35	1.1*	1.25*	0.18	2.19**	3.34**
	0.99	0.99	0.95	−0.21	2.66**	3.54**
Agency age	0.50	0.21	−0.11	−0.56	−0.56	−0.30
	0.24	0.23	−0.29	−0.74	−0.54	−0.34
Service delivery	1.2*	1.0**	0.22	−0.81	−0.24	−0.26
	1.1*	0.88*	−0.50	−1.23	−0.13	0.04
Regulation	0.63	0.20	−0.37	0.79	0.10	−0.25
	0.39	0.19	−0.41	0.72	0.17	−0.29

Economic policy	−0.57	0.01	−0.35	−0.58	−0.04	0.37
	−0.26	−0.03	−0.31	−0.57	−0.13	0.48
Welfare policy	0.28	−0.18	−0.45	−0.26	−0.00	−0.95
	0.30	−0.13	−0.27	−0.04	−0.12	−1.10*
Budget size	0.80	0.95	1.06*	0.86	−0.15	0.54
	0.69	0.79	0.89	0.39	−0.01	1.00
Source of income	0.37	−0.17	1.14*	−0.49	0.27	0.20
	0.42	−0.18	1.34*	−0.47	0.23	0.20
Norway	−	−	−	−	−	−
	1.87**	−0.25	0.27	1.86	−0.43	0.65
Ireland	−	−	−	−	−	−
	0.00	−0.90	−1.72**	−1.13	0.87	1.77**
$N = 100\%$	200	197	199	197	195	198

**p-value < 0.01, *p-value < 0.05.

Appendix C
List of State Agencies

Norway

Statistics Norway
The Norwegian Competition Authority
The Tax Administration – the Directorate of Taxes
Statsbygg – The Directorate of Public Construction and Property
Norwegian Customs and Exercise
The Financial Supervision Authority of Norway
Norwegian School of Economics and Business Administration
The Governor of Svalbard
The Geological Survey of Norway
The Norwegian Water Resources and Energy Directorate (NVE)
The Norwegian Patent Office
Norwegian Petroleum Directorate
Bergvesenet
The Norwegian Peace Corps – fredskorpset
The Norwegian Guarantee Institute for Export Credits
The Norwegian Agency for Development Cooperation (Norad)
Forsvarsbygg (FB)
NSM
Institute of Marine Research
The National Institute of Nutrition and Seafood Research
Norwegian Board of Health
The Norwegian Medicines Agency (NoMA)
Norwegian Institute for Alcohol and Drug Research, SIRUS
The Norwegian Institute of Public Health
The directorate for health and social affairs
The Norwegian Governmental Appeal Board regarding medical treatment abroad
Aetat – The Directorate of Labour
Norwegian Labour Inspection Authority
The Norwegian Pension Insurance for Seamen
The National Insurance Court
The Norwegian Biotechnology Advisory Board
The Norwegian Radiation Protection Authority (NRPA)
The Norwegian Consumer Council

The Norwegian Directorate for Children, Youth and Family Affairs (Bufdir)
The Norwegian Accident Investigation Board
Norwegian Public Roads Administration
The Norwegian Post and Telecommunications Authority
The Norwegian Railway Inspectorate
The Norwegian National Rail Administration
Civil Aviation Authority- Norway
The Norwegian State Housing Bank
The National Institute of Occupational Health
The Norwegian Immigration Appeals Board (UNE)
The Rent Disputes Tribunal
The Product Register
The National Office of Building Technology and Administration
The Office of the Attorney General
The Norwegian Media/Film Authority
Brønnøysund Register Centre
KITT
The Office of the Director of Public Prosecutions
The National Police Directorate
The Correctional Service of Norway Staff Academy
National Mediation Service
The National Institute for Consumer Research
The Centre for Gender Equality
The Consumer Ombudsman
The Gender Equality Ombud
The Government Administration Services
The National Veterinary Institute
The Norwegian School of Veterinary Science
The Norwegian Institute of Land Inventory
'Raindeer Administration'
The Directorate for Nature Management
The Agricultural College University of Norway
The Norwegian Crop Research Institute
The Norwegian Agricultural Authority
The Norwegian Pollution Control Authority
The Norwegian Mapping Authority
Arts Council Norway
The Directorate for Cultural Heritage in Norway
Practical Theological Seminary
The Restoration Workshop of Nidaros Cathedral
University of Oslo
The National Archival Services of Norway
University of Bergen
The Norwegian State Educational Loan Fund
The Norwegian Touring Theatre
The Oslo School of Architecture and Design
The Church Council
University of Tromsø
The Norwegian Touring Orchestra
The Norwegian Institute of Local History

Norwegian Film Institute
Norwegian School of Sports Sciences
School of Longyearbyen
Utsmykkingsfondet for nye statsbygg
The Norwegian Library of Talking Books and Braille
The Research Council of Norway
Norwegian Social Research
The Norwegian Association of Higher Education Institutions
Opplysningsvesenetes fond
VOX
The National Library of Norway
Norwegian Film Fund
The Norwegian Gaming and Foundation Authority
Norwegian Media Authority
Norwegian archive, library and museum authority
Norwegian Agency for Quality Assurance in Education
Npe
Museum of Archaeology, Stavanger
National Insurance Scheme Fund
Statped

Ireland

Agriculture Appeals Office
Bord Altranais
Bord Bia – Irish Food Board
Bord Iascaigh Mhara
Bord Pleanala
Broadcasting Complaints Commission
Building Regulations Advisory Body (BRAB)
Central Statistics Office
Chomhairle Fiacloireachta (Dental Council)
Chomhairle um Oideachas Gaeltachta agus Gaelscolaíochta
Combat Poverty Agency
Commission for Communications Regulation
Commission for Energy Regulation
Commission on School Accommodation
Competition Authority
Courts Service
Crisis Pregnancy Agency
Digital Hub Development Agency
Director of Corporate Enforcement
Dublin Institute for Advanced Studies
Employment Appeals Tribunal
Environmental Protection Agency
Equality Authority
Equality Tribunal
Family Support Agency
Fas
Food Safety Authority

Forensic Science Laboratory
Forfas
Further Education and Training Awards
Garda Complaints Board
Health Research Board
Health and Safety Authority
Health Boards Executive
Higher Education and Training Awards Council
Human Rights Commission
IDA Ireland
Inspectorate of Prisons and Places of Detention
Irish Film Censor's Office
Irish Health Services Accreditation Board
Irish Medicines Board
Irish Museum of Modern Art
Irish Research Council for the Humanities and Social Sciences (IRCHSS)
Irish Sports Council
Irish Water Safety Association
Land Registry/Registry of Deeds
Local Government Management Services Board
Marine Institute
Met Éireann
National Breast Screening Board
National Cancer Registry
National Council for Curriculum and Assessment (NCCA)
National Council for Professional Development of Nursing and Midwifery
National Qualifications Authority of Ireland
National Roads Authority
National Treatment Purchase Fund
NDP Gender Equality Unit
NDP/CSF Evaluation Unit
NDP/CSF Information Office
Office for Health Management
Office of Public Works
Office of the Director of Public Prosecutions
Office of the Information Commissioner
Office of Tobacco Control
Patents Office
Pensions Board
Pensions Ombudsman
Pre-Hospital Emergency Care Council
Probation and Welfare Service
Radiological Protection Institute of Ireland
Rent Tribunal
State Examinations Commission
Sustainable Energy Ireland
Teagasc
Valuation Tribunal
Veterinary Council
Women's Health Council

Flanders

Centre for Agricultural Research
Agency for Pilotage Services
Agency for Cleaning Services
Flanders Foreign Investment Office
Agency for Shipping Services and Canal Infrastructure
Agency for Infrastructure of the Subsidized Schools
Fund for Agriculture and Fishery
Fund for Special Youth Care
Fund for Economic Policy
Institute De Zande
Institute for Special Youth care De Kempen
Public Schools Agency
Agency for Regional Promotion Flemish-Brabant
Fund for Shingle Exploitation
Reallocation Fund
Institute for Forest and Wildlife Research
Agency for Investments in Flemish Institutions for Higher Education
Institute for the Promotion of Innovation by Science and Technology in Flanders
Child Care and Adoption Agency
Royal Academy for Dutch Language and Literature
Landcommandery Alden Biesen
Airport Antwerp Agency
Airport Ostend Agency
Agency for Sea Canal Brussels
Psychiatric Institute Rekem
Agency for Waste Management
Social Economic Council of Flanders
University Hospital Ghent
Public Employment Agency
Agency for Technological Research
Flemish Architectural Service
Flemish Regulator for Media
Flemish Agency for Reintegration of Persons with Disabilities
Flemish Agency for Literature
Flemish Fund for Investments in Agriculture
Flemish Fund for Care
Flemish Social Housing Agency
Flemish Agency for Land Management
Flemish Agency for Water Distribution
Flemish Council for Education
Flemish Agency for Tourism
Flemish Public Bus Transport Agency
Fund for Housing Policy in Flemish Brabant
Agency for Cultural Activities in Voeren
Centre for Information, Communication and Training for the Social Sector
Flemish Institute for Entrepeneurs

Bibliography

Aberbach, J. D., Putnam, R. D. and Rockman, B. A. (1981) *Bureaucrats and Politicians in Western Democracies* (Cambridge, MA, Harvard University Press).

Armstrong, M. (1988) *A Handbook of Human Resource Management* (London, Kogan Page).

Aucoin, P. (1990) 'Administrative Reform in Public Management: Paradigms, Principles, Paradoxes and Pendulums', *Governance*, 3 (2), 115–37.

Bergman, T., Müller, W. C., Strøm, K. and Blomgren, M. (2003) 'Democratic Delegation and Accountability: Cross-national Patterns', in K. Strøm, W. C. Müller and T. Bergman (eds), *Delegation and Accountability in Parliamentary Democracies* (Oxford, Oxford University Press).

Berman, M. and West, J. P. (1995) 'TQM in American Cities: Hypotheses Regarding Commitment and Impact', *Journal of Public Administration Research and Theory*, 5 (2), 213–30.

Beuselinck, E., Verhoest, K. and Bouckaert, G. (2007) 'Reforms of Central Government Coordination in OECD-Countries: Culture as Counterforce for Cross-National Unifying Processes?', in K. Schedler and I. Proeller (eds), *Cultural Aspects of Public Management Reforms* (Amsterdam, Elsevier).

Boston, J., Martin, J., Pallot, J. and Walsh, P. (1996) *Public Management. The New Zealand Model* (Auckland, Oxford University Press).

Bouckaert, G. and Auwers, T. (1999) *De modernisering van de Vlaamse Overheid* (Brugge, die Keure).

Bouckaert, G. and Halachmi, A. (1995) 'The Range of Performance Indicators in the Public Sector: Theory Vs. Practice', in A. Halachmi and D. Grant (eds), *Reengineering and Performance Measurement in Criminal Justice and Social Programmes* (Perth, International Institute of Administrative Sciences).

Bouckaert, G. and Peters, B. G. (2004) 'What is Available and What Is Missing in the Study of Quangos?', in C. Pollitt and C. Talbot (eds), *Unbundled Government. A Critical Analysis of the Global Trend to Agencies, Quangos and Contractualisation* (London, Routledge).

Bouckaert, G., Peters, B. G. and Verhoest, K. (forthcoming) *The Coordination of Public Sector Organizations: Shifting Patterns of Public Management* (Basingstoke, Palgrave Macmillan).

Bouckaert G. and Verhoest, K. (1999) 'A Comparative Perspective on Decentralisation as a Context for Contracting in the Public Sector: Practice and Theory', in Y. Fortin (ed.), *La Contractualisation dans le Secteur Public des Pays Industrialisés depuis 1980* (Paris, L'Harmattan).

Boyle, R. (2004) *The Role of the Centre in Promoting Civil Service Modernisation* (Dublin, Institute of Public Administration, CPMR Discussion Paper No. 27).

Boyle, R. and Humphreys, P. (2001) *A New Change Agenda for the Irish Public Service* (Dublin, Institute of Public Administration, CPMR Discussion Paper No. 17).

Boyne, G. A. (2004) 'Explaining Public Service Performance: Does Management Matter?', *Public Policy and Administration*, 19 (4), 110–7.

Braun, D. and Gilardi, F. (2006) 'Introduction', in D. Braun and F. Gilardi (eds), *Delegation in Contemporary Democracies* (London, Routledge).

Brunsson, N. (1989) *The Organization of Hyprocricy. Talk, Decisions and Actions in Organizations* (Chichester, Wiley).

Callanan, M. (2003) 'Where Stands Local Government?', in M Callanan and J. F. Keogan (eds), *Local Government in Ireland: Inside Out* (Dublin: Institute of Public Administration).

Carpenter, D. P. (2001) *The Forging of Bureaucratic Autonomy: Reputations, Networks, and Policy Innovation in Executive Agencies, 1862–1928* (Princeton, NJ, Princeton University Press).

Christensen, J. G. (2001) 'Bureaucratic Autonomy as a Political Asset', in B. G. Peters and J. Pierre (eds), *Politicians, Bureaucrats and Administrative Reform* (London, Routledge).

Christensen, J. G. and Yesilkagit, K. (2006) 'Delegation and Specialization in Regulatory Administration: A Comparative Analysis of Denmark, Sweden and the Netherlands', in T. Christensen and P. Lægreid (eds), *Autonomy and Regulation. Coping with Agencies in the Modern State* (Cheltenham, Edward Elgar).

Christensen, T. (2007) 'The Norwegian State Transformed?', in Ø. Østerud (ed.), *Norway in Transition. Transforming a Stable Democracy* (London, Routledge).

Christensen, T. and Lægreid, P. (eds) (2001a) *New Public Management – The transformation of Ideas and Practice* (Aldershot, Ashgate).

Christensen, T. and Lægreid, P. (2001b) 'A Transformative Perspective on Administrative Reforms', in T. Christensen and P. Lægreid (eds), *New Public Management – The Transformation of Ideas and Practice* (Aldershot, Ashgate).

Christensen, T. and Lægreid, P. (2001c) 'New Public Management: The effects of contractualism and devolution on political control', *Public Management Review*, 3 (1), 73–94.

Christensen, T., Lægreid, P. and Roness. P. G. (2002) 'Increasing Parliamentary Control of the Executive? New Instruments and Emerging Effects', *Journal of Legislative Studies*, 8 (1), 37–62.

Christensen, T. and Lægreid, P. (2003) 'Administrative Reform Policy: The Challenges of Turning Symbols into Practice', *Public Organization Review*, 3 (1), 3–27.

Christensen, T. and Lægreid, P. (2005) 'Autonomization and Policy Capacity: The Dilemmas and Challenges Facing Political Executives', in M. Painter and J. Pierre (eds), *Challenges to State Policy Capacity: Global Trends and Comparative Perspectives* (Basingstoke, Palgrave Macmillan).

Christensen, T. and Lægreid, P. (2006) 'Agencification and Regulatory Reform', in T. Christensen and P. Lægreid (eds), *Autonomy and Regulation: Coping with Agencies in the Modern State* (Cheltenham, Edward Elgar).

Christensen, T. and Lægreid, P. (2007a) 'Introduction – Theoretical Approach and Research Question', in T. Christensen and P. Lægreid (eds), *Transcending New Public Management: The Transformation of Public Sector Reforms* (Aldershot, Ashgate).

Christensen, T. and Lægreid, P. (2007b) 'Regulatory Agencies – The Challenges of Balancing Agency Autonomy and Political Control', *Governance*, 20 (3), 497–519.

Christensen, T., Lægreid, P., Roness, P. G. and Røvik, K. A. (2007) *Organization Theory and the Public Sector: Instrument, Culture, Myth* (London, Routledge).

Clancy, P. and Murphy, G. (2006) *Outsourcing Government: Public Bodies and Accountability* (Dublin, Tasc New Island).

Coe, C. K. (1989) *Public Financial Management* (Englewood Cliffs, NJ : Prentice-Hall).

Collins, N., Cradden, T. and Butler, P. (2007) *Modernising Irish Government: The Politics of Administrative Reform* (Dublin, Gill & Macmillan).

Dahl, R. A. and Lindblom, C. E. (1953) *Politics, Economics, and Welfare* (New York, Harper & Row).

De Bruijn, H. (2002) *Managing Performance in the Public Sector* (London, Routledge).

De Jong, M., Lalenis, K. and Mamadouh, V. (2002) 'Families of Nations and Institutional Transplantation', in M. De Jong, K. Lalenis and V. Mamadouh (eds), *The Theory and Practice of Institutional Transplantation: Experiences with the Transfer of Policy Institutions* (Dordrecht, Kluwer Academic Publishers).

De Jong, M., Lalenis, K. and Mamadouh, V. (eds) (2002) *The Theory and Practice of Institutional Transplantation. Experiences with the Transfer of Policy Institutions* (Dordrecht, Kluwer Academic Publishers).

DeLeon, L. (2003) 'On Acting Responsibly in a Disorderly World: Individual Ethics and Administrative Responsibility', in B. G. Peters and J. Pierre (eds), *Handbook of Public Administration* (London, Sage).

Department of Finance (2001) *Code of Practice for the Governance of State Bodies* (Dublin, Department of Finance).

De Winter, L. and Dumont, P. (2003) 'Belgium: Delegation and Accountability under Partitocratic Rule', in K. Strøm, W. C. Müller and T. Bergman (eds), *Delegation and Accountability in Parliamentary Democracies* (Oxford, Oxford University Press).

Dill, W. R. (1958) 'Environment as an Influence on Managerial Autonomy', *Administrative Science Quarterly*, 2 (4), 409–43.

DiMaggio, P. J. and Powell, W. W. (1983) 'The Iron Cage Revisited: Institutional Isomorphism and Collective Rationality in Organizational Fields', *American Sociological Review*, 48 (2), 147–60.

Dimitrakopoulos, D. G. and Passas, A. G. (2003) 'International Organizations and Domestic Administrative Reform', in B. G. Peters and J. Pierre (eds), *Handbook of Public Administration* (London, Sage).

Dunleavy, P. (1991) *Democracy, Bureaucracy and Public Choice: Economic Explanations in Political Science* (London, Harvester Wheatsheaf).

Dunsire, A. (1978) *Control in a Bureaucracy.* Oxford: Martin Robertson.

Dunsire, A., Hartley, K. and Parker, D. (1991) 'Organizational Status and Performance: Summary of the Findings', *Public Administration*, 69 (1), 21–40.

Egeberg, M. (1994) 'Bridging the Gap Between Theory and Practice: The Case of Administrative Policy', *Governance*, 7 (1), 83–98.

Egeberg, M. (2003) 'How Bureaucratic Structure Matters: An Organizational Perspective', in B. G. Peters and J. Pierre (eds), *Handbook of Public Administration* (London, Sage).

Elgie, R. (2006) 'Why Do Governments Delegate Authority to Quasi-Autonomous Agencies, the Case of Independent Administrative Authorities in France', *Governance*, 19 (2), 207–27.

Elgie, R. and McMenamin, I. (2005) 'Credible Commitment, Political Uncertainty or Policy Complexity? Explaining Variations in the Independence of Non-majoritarian Institutions in France', *British Journal of Political Science*, 35 (3), 531–48.

Embleton, E. (1999), 'Ireland: modernising the public service' (paper prepared for OECD *Symposium on Government of the Future: Getting from Here to There*, Paris, 14–15 September).

Esping-Andersen, G. (1999) *Social Foundations of Postindustrial Economies* (Oxford, Oxford University Press).

Esping-Andersen, G. and Myles, J. (n.d.) The Welfare State and Redistribution. Downloaded from http://dcpis.upf.edu/~gosta-esping-andersen/materials/welfare_state.pdf on 18 March 2009.

Fedele, P., Galli, D. and Ongaro, E. (2007) 'Disaggregation, Autonomy and Re-Regulation, Contractualism: Public Agencies in Italy (1992–2005)', *Public Management Review*, 9 (4), 557–85.

Flinders, M. (2001) *The Politics of Accountability in the Modern State* (Aldershot, Ashgate).

Flinders, M. and Smith, M. J. (eds) (1999) *Quangos, Accountability and Reform: the Politics of Quasi-Government* (Basingstoke, Macmillan).

Flynn, N. (2002) *Public Sector Management*. Fourth edition (London, Pearson).

Gains, F. (1999) *Understanding Department – Next Steps Agency Relationships* (Sheffield, University of Sheffield, Department of Politics, PhD Thesis).

Gains, F. (2004) 'Adapting the Agency Concept: Variations within "Next Steps"', in C. Pollitt and C. Talbot (eds), *Unbundled Government: A Critical Analysis of the Global Trend to Agencies, Quangos and Contractualisation* (London, Routledge).

Gilardi, F. (2006) 'Delegation to Independent Regulatory Agencies in Western Europe. Credibility, Political Uncertainty, and Diffusion', in D. Braun and F. Gilardi (eds), *Delegation in Contemporary Democracies* (London, Routledge).

Goetz, K. (2000) 'European Integration and National Executives: A Cause in Search of an Effect?' *West European Politics*, 23 (4), 211–31.

Greer, P. (1994) *Transforming Central Government: The Next Steps Initiative* (Buckingham, Open University Press).

Gulick, L. (1937) 'Notes on the Theory of Organization', in L. Gulick and L. F. Urwick (eds), *Papers on the Science of Administration* (New York, Institute of Public Administration).

Hall, P. A. and Soskice, D. (eds) (2001) *Varieties of Capitalism. The Institutional Foundations of Comparative Advantage* (Oxford, Oxford University Press).

Hall, P. A. and Taylor, R. C. R. (1996) 'Political Science and the Three New Institutionalisms', *Political Studies*, 44 (4), 936–57.

Hardiman, N. and MacCarthaigh, M. (2008) *Administrative Reform in a Liberal Market Economy: NPM and Quality of Government in Ireland.* (Dublin, UCD Geary Institute Discussion Series 25/2008).

Hardiman, N. and MacCarthaigh, M. (2009) *Breaking with or Building on the Past? Reform of Irish Public Administration 1958–2008* (Dublin, UCD Institute for British Irish Studies Working Paper Series 2009).

Hardiman, N. and Scott, C. (forthcoming) 'Governance as Polity: An Institutional Approach to the Evolution of State Functions', *Public Administration*.

Hesse, J. J. (ed.) (1991), *Local Government and Urban Affairs in International Perspective: Analyses of Twenty Western Industrialised Countries* (Baden-Baden: Nomos Verlaggeselschaft).

Heyman, D. B. (1988) *Input Controls in the Public Sector: What Does Economic Theory Offer?* (Washington, D.C., IMF Working Paper WP/88/59).

Hofstede, G. (2001) *Culture's Consequences: Comparing Values, Behaviors, Institutions and Organizations Across Nations* (Thousand Oaks, CA, Sage).

Hofstede, G. and Hofstede, G. J. (2005) *Cultures and Organizations: Software of the Mind* (New York, McGraw-Hill).

Hogwood, B., Judge, W. D. and McVicar, M. (2000) 'Agencies and Accountability', in R. A. W. Rhodes (ed.), *Transforming British Government*, Volume 1 (Basingstoke, Macmillan).

Hood, C. (1991) 'A Public Management for all Seasons?', *Public Administration*, 69 (1), 3–19.

Hood, C. (1998) *The Art of the State: Culture, Rhetoric, and Public Management* (Oxford, Oxford University Press).

Hood, C. and Dunsire, A. (1981) *Bureaumetrics* (Farnborough, Gower).

Hood, C. and Jackson, M. (1991) *Administrative Argument* (Aldershot, Dartmouth).

Horn, M. J. (1995) *The Political Economy of Public Administration: Institutional Choice in the Public Sector* (Cambridge, Cambridge University Press).

Huber, J. and Shipan, C. (2002) *Deliberate Discretion? The Institutional Foundation of Bureaucratic Autonomy* (Cambridge, Cambridge University Press).

Ingraham, P. W., Joyce, P. J. and Donahue, A. K. (2003) *Government Performance: Why Management Matters* (Baltimore, MD, Jouns Hopkins University Press).

Ingraham, P. W. and Moynihan, D. P. (2001) 'Beyond Measurement: Managing for Results in State Government', in F. Dall (ed.), *Quicker, Better, Cheaper? Managing Performance in American Government* (Albany, NY, Rockefeller Institute Press).

Institute of Public Administration (1970) *The Devlin Report: A Summary* (Dublin, Institute of Public Administration).

Institute of Public Administration (2005) *Administration Yearbook & Diary 2005* (Dublin, Institute of Public Administration).

Jacobsson, B., Lægreid, P. and Pedersen, O. K. (2004) *Europeanization and Transnational States. Comparing Nordic Central Governments* (London, Routledge).

James, O. (2003) *The Executive Agency Revolution in Whitehall: Public Interest Versus Bureau-Shaping Perspectives* (Basingstoke, Palgrave Macmillan).

Jann, W. and Döhler, M. (eds) (2005) *Agencies in Westeuropa* (Wiesbaden, VS Verlag für Sozialwissenschaften).

Jensen, M. C. and Meckling, W. H. (1976) 'Theory of the Firm: Managerial Behaviour, Agency Costs and Ownership Structure', *Journal of Financial Economics*, 3 (4), 305–60.

Kaufmann, F.-X., Majone, G. and Ostrom, V. (eds) (1986) *Guidance, Control, and Evaluation in the Public Sector* (Berlin, de Gruyter).

Kettl, D. F. (2000) *The Global Public Management Revolution. A Report on the Transformation of Governance* (Washington, D.C., Brookings Institution).

Kickert, W. J. M. (1998) *Aansturing van Verzelfstandigde Overheidsdiensten. Over Publiek Management van Hybride Organisaties* (Alphen aan den Rijn, Samsom).

Kickert, W. J. M. and Hakvoort, J. L. M. (2000) 'Public Governance in Europe: A Historical – Institutional Tour d'horizont', in O. Van Heffen, W. J. M. Kickert and J. J. A. Thomassen (eds), *Governance in Modern Society: Effects, Change and Formation of Government Institutions* (Dordrecht, Kluwer Academic Publishers).

Kickert, W. J. M., Klijn, E.-H. and Koppenjan, J. F. M. (eds) (1997) *Managing Complex Networks: Strategies for the Public Sector* (London, Sage).

Knill, C. (2001) *The Europeanisation of National Administrations: Patterns of Institutional Change and Persistence* (Cambridge, Cambridge University Press).

Krasner, S. (1988) 'Sovereignty: An Institutional Perspective', *Comparative Political Studies*, 21 (1), 66–94.

Krause, G. A. (2003) 'Agency Risk Propensities Involving the Demand for Bureaucratic Discretion', in G. A. Krause and K. J. Meier (eds), *Politics, Policy and Organizations: Frontiers in the Scientific Study of Bureaucracy* (Ann Arbor, MI, University of Michigan Press).

Kravchuk, R. S. and Leighton, R. (1993) 'Implementing Total Quality Management in the United States', *Public Productivity & Management Review*, 17 (1): 71–82.

Laking, R. (2002) 'Distributed Public Governance: Principles for Control and Accountability of Delegated and Devolved Bodies', in OECD, *Distributed Public Governance: Agencies, Authorities and other Autonomous Bodies* (Paris, OECD).

Lane, J.-E. and Ersson, S. O. (1998) *Politics and Society in Western Europe* (London, Sage).

Lawton, A. and Rose, A. D. (1994) *Organisation and Management in the Public Sector.* 2nd ed. (London, Pitman).

Lijphart, A. (1999) *Patterns of Democracy: Government Forms and Performance in Thirty-Six Countries* (New Haven, CT, Yale University Press).

Lindblom, C. E. (1977) *Politics and Markets* (New York, Basic Books).

Listhaug, O. (2007) 'Oil Wealth Dissatisfaction and Political Trust in Norway: A Resource Curse?', in Ø. Østerud (ed.), *Norway in Transition: Transforming a Stable Democracy* (London, Routledge).

Lonti, Z. (2005) 'How Much Decentralization? Managerial Autonomy in the Canadian Puclic Service', *American Review of Public Administration*, 35 (2), 122–36.

Lonti, Z and Woods, X. (2008) *Towards Government At a Glance: Identification of Core Data and Issues Related to Public Sector Efficiency* (Paris, OECD Working Papers on Public Governance 7/2008).

Loughlin, J. and Peters, B. G. (1997) 'State traditions, administrative reform and reorganization', in M. Keating and J. Loughlin (eds), *The Political Economy of Regionalism* (London, Frank Cass).

Lægreid, P. (2001) 'Transforming Top Civil Servant Systems', in T. Christensen and P. Lægreid (eds), *New Public Management – The Transformation of Ideas and Practice* (Aldershot, Ashgate).

Lægreid, P., Rolland, V. W., Roness, P. G. and Ågotnes, J.-E. (2003) *The Structural Anatomy of the Norwegian State 1947–2003* (Bergen, Rokkan Centre, Working Paper 21- 2003).

Lægreid, P., Rolland, V. W., Roness, P. G. and Ågotnes, J.-E. (forthcoming) 'The Structural Anatomy of the Norwegian State 1947–2007', in P. Lægreid and K. Verhoest (eds), *Governance of Public Sector Organizations* (Basingstoke, Palgrave Macmillan).

Lægreid, P. and Roness, P. G. (1999) 'Administrative Reform as Organized Attention', in M. Egeberg and P. Lægreid (eds), *Organizing Political Institutions: Essays for Johan P. Olsen* (Oslo, Scandinavian University Press).

Lægreid, P. and Roness, P. G. (2003) 'Administrative Reform Programmes and Institutional Response in Norwegian Central Government', in J. J. Hesse, C. Hood and B. G. Peters (eds), *Paradoxes in Public Sector Reform: An International Comparison* (Berlin, Duncker & Humblot).

Lægreid, P., Roness, P. G. and Rubecksen, K. (2006a) 'Performance Management in Practice – the Norwegian Way', *Financial Accountability and Management*, 22 (3), 251–70.

Lægreid, P., Roness, P. G. and Rubecksen, K. (2006b) 'Autonomy and Control in the Norwegian Civil Service: Does Agency Form Matter?', in T. Christensen and P. Lægreid (eds), *Autonomy and Regulation: Coping with Agencies in the Modern State* (Cheltenham, Edward Elgar).

Lægreid, P., Roness, P. G. and Rubecksen, K. (2007) 'Modern Management Tools in State Agencies: The Case of Norway', *International Public Management Journal*, 10 (4), 387–413.

Lægreid, P., Roness, P. G. and Rubecksen, K. (2008) 'Performance Information and Performance Steering: Integrated System or Loose Coupling?', in W. Van Dooren and S. Van de Walle (eds), *Performance Information in the Public Sector: How it is Used.* (Basingstoke, Palgrave Macmillan).

MacCarthaigh, M. (2005) *Accountability in Irish Parliamentary Politics* (Dublin, Institute of Public Administration).

MacCarthaigh, M. (2007) *The Corporate Governance of Regional and Local Public Service Bodies in Ireland* (Dublin, Institute of Public Administration, Committee for Public Management Research Report No. 8).

MacCarthaigh, M. (2008) *Government in Modern Ireland* (Dublin, Institute of Public Management).

March, J. G. (1994) *A Primer on Decision-Making* (New York, Free Press).

March, J. G. and Olsen, J. P. (1989) *Rediscovering Institutions: The Organizational Basis of Politics* (New York, Free Press).

March, J. G. and Olsen, J. P. (1998) 'The Institutional Dynamics of International Political Orders', *International Organization*, 52 (4), 943–69.

March, J. G. and Simon, H. A. (1958) *Organizations* (New York, Wiley).

Massey, A. (1995) *After Next Steps – An Examination of the Implications for Policy Making of the Developments in Executive Agencies* (London, Cabinet Office).

Matheson, A., Weber, B., Manning, N. and Arnould, E. (2007) *Study on the Political Involvement in Senior Staffing and on the Delineation of Responsibilities Between Ministers and Senior Civil Servants* (Paris, OECD Working Papers on Public Governance, No. 6).

McGauran, A.-M. and Humphreys, P. (2004) *The Corporate Governance of Agencies in Ireland: Preliminary results of the 2004 Survey of Irish Public Sector Agencies* (Dublin, Institute of Public Administration, CPMR Report 31/04).

McGauran, A.-M., Verhoest, K. and Humphreys, P. (2005) *The Corporate Governance of Agencies in Ireland* (Dublin, Institute of Public Administration, Committee for Public Management Research Report No. 6).

McKinney, J. B. (1995) *Effective Financial Management in Public and Nonprofit Agencies: A Practical and Integrative Approach*. Second edition (Westport, CT, Quorum Books).

Meyer, J. W. and Rowan, B. (1977) 'Institutionalized Organizations: Formal Structure as Myth and Ceremony', *American Journal of Sociology*, 83 (2), 340–63.

Migué, J.-L., Bélangér, G. and Niskanen, W. (1974) 'Toward a General Theory of Managerial Discretion', *Public Choice*, 17 (1), 27–47.

Miller, H. T. and Fox, C. J. (2007) *Postmodern Public Administration*. Revised edition (Armonk, NY, M. E. Sharpe).

Mitchell, P. (2003) 'Ireland: 'O What a Tangled Web…' – Delegation, Accountability, and Executive Power', in K. Strøm, W. C. Müller and T. Bergman (eds), *Delegation and Accountability in Parliamentary Democracies* (Oxford, Oxford University Press).

Mizruchi, M. S. and Fein, L. C. (1999) 'The social construction of organizational knowledge: a study of the uses of coercive, mimetic and normative isomorphism', *Administrative Science Quarterly*, 44 (4), 653–83.

Moe, T. M. (1990) 'The Politics of Structural Choice: Toward a Theory of Public Bureaucracy', in O. Williamson (ed.), *Organization Theory: From Chester Barnard to the Present and Beyond* (Oxford, Oxford University Press).

Moynihan, D. P. and Pandey, S. K. (2006) 'Creating Desirable Organizational Characteristics: How Organizations Create a Focus on Results and Managerial Authority', *Public Management Review*, 8 (1), 119–40.

Mulgan, R. (2003) *Holding Power to Account: Accountability in Modern Democracies* (Basingstoke, Palgrave Macmillan).

Müller, W. C., Bergman, T. and K. Strøm (2003) 'Parliamentary Democracy: Promise and Problems', in K. Strøm, W. C. Müller and T. Bergman (eds), *Delegation and Accountability in Parliamentary Democracies* (Oxford, Oxford University Press).

Murray, J. (2001) 'Looking Forward' (unpublished paper presented to the Committee for Public Management Research Conference, Dublin).

Naschold, F. (1996) *New Frontiers in Public Sector Management* (Berlin, de Gruyter).

National Competitiveness Council (1999) *Report on Social Partnership* (Dublin, National Competitivenes Council).

Niskanen, W. A. (1971), *Bureaucracy and Representative Government* (Chicago, IL, Aldine-Atherton).

Norman, R. (2003) *Obedient Servants? Management Freedoms & Accountabilities in the New Zealand Public Sector* (Wellington: Victoria University Press).

NOU 1984: 23 Produktivitetsfremmende reformer i statens budsjettsystem (Haga Commission).

NOU 1989: 5 En bedre organisert stat (Hermansen Commission).

OECD (1994) *Performance Management in Government: Performance Measurement and Results-Oriented Management* (Paris: Public Management Committee, OECD).

OECD (1997) *In Search of Results: Performance Management Practices in Ten OECD Countries* (Paris, Public Management Committee, OECD).

OECD (1999) *Performance Contracting: Lessons from Performance Contracting Case Studies: A Framework for Public Sector Performance Contracting.* (Paris, OECD-PUMA. unclassified document).

OECD (2002a) *Distributed Public Governance: Agencies, Authorities and Other Autonomous Bodies* (Paris, OECD).

OECD (2002b) *Regulatory Policies on OECD Countries: From Interventionism to Regulatory Governance* (Paris, OECD).

OECD (2007) *OECD Reviews of Human Resource Management in Government Belgium: Brussels-Capital Region, Federal Government, Flemish Government, French Community, Walloon Region* (Paris: OECD).

OECD (2008) *Ireland: Towards an Integrated Public Service* (Paris, OECD).

Olsen, J. P., Roness, P. G. and Sætren, H. (1982) 'Still Peaceful Co-existence and Revolution in Slow Motion?, in J. J. Richardson (ed.), *Policy Styles in Western Europe* (London, Allen & Unwin).

Ongaro, E. (2006) 'The Dynamics of Devolution Processes in Legalistic Countries: Organizational Change in the Italian Public Sector', *Public Administration*, 84 (3), 737–70.

O'Riordan (2004) *Developing a Strategic Approach to HR in the Irish Civil Service* (Dublin, Institute of Public Administration, CPMR Discussion Paper No.26).

Osborne, D. and Gaebler, T. (1992) *Reinventing Government: How the Entrepreneurial Spirit is Transforming the Public Sector* (Reading, MA, Addison-Wesley).

Osborne, S. (ed.) (2002) *Public Management: Critical Perspectives.* Volume 1 (London, Routledge).

O'Toole, L. J., Jr. and Meier, K. J. (2003) '*Plus ca Change*: Public Management, Personnel Stability, and Organizational Performance', *Journal of Public Administration Research and Theory*, 13 (1), 43–64.

Ouchi, W. G. (1979), 'A Conceptual Framework for the Design of Organizational Control Mechanisms', *Management Science*, 25 (9), 833–48.

PA Consulting Group (2002) *Evaluation of the Progress of the Strategic Management Initiative/Delivering Better Government Modernisation Programme* (Dublin, PA Consulting Group).

Painter M. and Pierre, J. (eds) (2005) *Challenges to State Policy Capacity Global Trends and Comparative Perspectives* (Basingstoke, Palgrave Macmillan).

Pelgrims, C. (2008) *Bestuurlijke hervormingen vanuit politiek perspectief. Politici als stakeholders in Beter Bestuurlijke Beleid en de Copernicushervorming* (Brugge, VandenBroele).

Peters, B. G. (1987) 'Politicians and Bureaucrats in the Politics of Policy-Making', in J.-E. Lane (ed.), *Bureaucracy and Public Choice* (London, Sage).

Peters, B. G. (1998) 'Managing Horizontal Government: The Politics of Coordination', *Public Administration*, 76 (2), 295–311.

Peters, B. G. (2001) *The Politics of Bureaucracy.* Fifth edition (London, Routledge).

Peters, B. G. (2005) *Institutional theory in political science. The 'New Institutionalism'.* Second edition (London, Continuum).

Pierre, J. (ed.) (1995) *Bureaucracy in the Modern State* (Aldershot, Edward Elgar).

Pierson, P. (2000) 'The Limits of Design: Explaining Institutional Origins and Change', *Governance*, 13 (4), 475–99.

Pierson, P. (2004) *Politics in Time: History, Institutions, and Social Analysis* (Princeton, NJ, Princeton University Press).

Pollack, M. A. (2002) 'Learning from the Americanists (Again): Theory and Methods in the Study of Delegation', *West European Politics*, 25 (1), 200–19.

Pollitt, C. (1995) 'Management Techniques for the Public Sector: Pulpit and Practice', in B. G. Peters and D. J. Savoie (eds), *Governance in a Changing Environment* (Montreal, McGill-Queen's University Press), 203–38.

Pollitt, C. (2001) 'Convergence: The Useful Myth?', *Public Administration*, 79 (4), 933–47.

Pollitt, C. (2004) 'Theoretical Overview', in C. Pollitt and C. Talbot (eds), *Unbundled Government: A Critical Analysis of the Global Trend to Agencies, Quangos and Contractualisation* (London, Routledge).

Pollitt, C. (2005a) 'Ministries and Agencies: Steering, Meddling, Neglect and Dependency', in M. Painter and J. Pierre (eds), *Challenges to State Policy Capacity: Global Trends and Comparative Perspectives* (Basingstoke, Palgrave Macmillan).

Pollitt, C. (2005b) 'Performance management in practice: a comparative study of executive agencies', *Journal of Public Administration Research and Theory*, 16 (1), 25–44.

Pollitt, C. (2008) *Time, Policy, Management* (Oxford, Oxford University Press).

Pollitt, C., Bathgate, K., Caulfield, J., Smullen, A. and Talbot, C. (2001) 'Agency Fever? Analysis of an International Policy Fashion', *Journal of Comparative Policy Analysis: Research and Practice*, 3 (3), 271–90.

Pollitt, C., Birchall, J. and Putnam, K. (1998) *Decentralising Public Service Management* (Basingstoke, Macmillan).

Pollitt, C. and Bouckaert, G. (2004) *Public Management Reform: A Comparative Analysis.* Second edition (Oxford, Oxford University Press).

Pollitt, C. and Talbot, C. (eds) (2004) *Unbundled Government: A Critical Analysis of the Global Trend to Agencies, Quangos and Contractualisation* (London, Routledge).

Pollitt, C., Talbot, C., Caulfield, J. and Smullen, A. (2004) *Agencies: How governments do Things Through Semi-Autonomous Organizations* (Basingstoke, Palgrave Macmillan).

Pollitt, C., Van Thiel, S. and Homburg, V. (eds) (2007) *New Public Management in Europe* (Basingstoke, Palgrave Macmilan).

Pratt J. W. and Zeckhauser, R. J. (1991), 'Principals and Agents: An Overview', in J. W. Pratt and R. J. Zeckhauser (eds), *Principals and Agents: The Structure of Business* (Boston, MA, Harvard Business School Press).

Premfors, R. (1998) 'Reshaping the Democratic State: Swedish Experiences in a Comparative Perspective', *Public Administration*, 76 (2), 141–59.

Roness, P. G. (1995) *Stortinget som organisator* (Oslo, TANO).

Roness, P. G. (2001a) 'Reforming Central Governments and Parliaments: Structural Recoupling and Institutional Characteristics', *International Review of Administrative Sciences*, 67 (4), 673–90.

Roness, P. G. (2001b) 'Transforming State Employees' Unions', in T. Christensen and P. Lægreid (eds), *New Public Management – The transformation of Ideas and Practice* (Aldershot, Ashgate).

Roness, P. G. (2007) 'Types of State Organizations: Arguments, Doctrines and Changes Beyond New Public Management', in T. Christensen and P. Lægreid (eds), *Transcending New Public Management: The Transformation of Public Sector Reforms* (Aldershot, Ashgate).

Roness, P. G. (2009) 'Handling Theoretical Diversity on Agency Autonomy', in P. G. Roness and H. Sætren (eds), *Change and Continuity in Public Sector Organizations* (Bergen, Fagbokforlaget).

Roness, P. G., Verhoest, K., Rubecksen, K. and MacCarthaigh, M. (2008) 'Autonomy and Regulation of State Agencies: Reinforcement, Indifference or Compensation?' *Public Organization Review*, 8 (2), 155–74.

Scharpf, F. W. (1997) *Games Real Actors Play. Actor-Centered Institutionalism in Policy Research* (Boulder, CO, Westview Press).

Schedler, K. and Proeller, I. (eds) *Cultural Aspects of Public Management reforms* (Amsterdam, Elsevier).

Schick, A. (2002) 'Agencies in Search of Principles', *OECD Journal on Budgeting*, 2 (1), 7–26.

Scott, W. R. (2001) *Institutions and Organizations*. Second edition (London, Sage).

Scott, W. R. (2003) *Organizations: Rational, Natural, and Open Systems*. Fifth edition (Upper Saddle River, NJ, Prentice-Hall).

Selznick, P. (1957) *Leadership in Administration* (New York, Harper & Row).

Smullen, A. (2004) 'Lost in Translation? Shifting Interpretations of the Concept of Agency: The Dutch Case', in C. Pollitt and C. Talbot (eds), *Unbundled Government: A Critical Analysis of the Global Trend to Agencies, Quangos and Contractualisation* (London, Routledge).

Smullen, A., Van Thiel, S. and Pollitt, C. (2001) 'Agentschappen en de verzelfstandigingsparadox', *Beleid & Maatschappij*, 28 (4), 190–201.

Spanhove, J. and Verhoest, K. (2008) *Deugdelijk Bestuur in de Vlaamse Overheid anno 2008: een kwalitatieve analyse van nieuwe Government Governance mechanismen in BBB* (Leuven, Steunpunt Bestuurlijke Organisatie Vlaanderen).

Stinchcombe, A. L. (1965) 'Social Structure and Organizations', in J. G. March (ed.), *Handbook of Organizations* (Chicago, IL, Rand McNally).

Strøm, K. (2003) 'Parliamentary Democracy and Delegation', in K. Strøm, W. C. Müller and T. Bergman (eds), *Delegation and Accountability in Parliamentary Democracies* (Oxford, Oxford University Press).

Strøm, K., Müller, W. C. and Bergman, T. (eds) (2003a) *Delegation and Accountability in Parliamentary Democracies* (Oxford, Oxford University Press).

Strøm, K., Müller, W. C., Bergman, T. and Nyblade, B. (2003b) 'Dimensions of Citizen Control', in K. Strøm, W. C. Müller and T. Bergman (eds), *Delegation and Accountability in Parliamentary Democracies* (Oxford, Oxford University Press).

Strøm, K. and Narud, H. M. (2003) 'Norway: Virtual Parliamentarism', in K. Strøm, W. C. Müller and T. Bergman (eds), *Delegation and Accountability in Parliamentary Democracies* (Oxford, Oxford University Press).

Talbot, C. (2004) 'The Agency Idea: Sometimes Old, Sometimes New, Sometimes Borrowed, Sometimes Untrue', in C. Pollitt and C. Talbot (eds), *Unbundled Government:*

A Critical Analysis of the Global Trend to Agencies, Quangos and Contractualisation (London, Routledge).

Talbot, C. and Caulfield, J. (eds) (2002) *Hard Agencies in Soft States? A Study of Agency Creation Programmes in Jamaica, Latvia and Tanzania* (Pontpridd, University of Glamorgan).

Ter Bogt, H. J. (1998) *Neo-Institutionele Economie, Management Control En Verzelfstandiging Van Overheidsorgansiaties: Overwegingen Voor Verzelfstandiging en Effecten Op Efficiëntie En Financieel-Economische Sturing* (Groningen, University of Groningen).

Thatcher, M. and Stone Sweet, A. (2002) 'Theory and Practice of Delegation to Non-Majoritarian Institutions', *West European Politics*, 25 (1), 1–22.

Thelen, K. (1999) 'Historical Institutionalism in Comparative Politics', *Annual Review of Political Sciences*, 2, 369–404.

Thelen, K. (2004) *How Institutions Evolve* (Cambridge, Cambridge University Press).

Thompson, F. (1993) 'Matching Responsibilities with Tactics: Administrative Controls and Modern Government', *Public Administration Review*, 54 (3), 303–18.

Thompson, G., Frances, J., Levavic, J. and Mitchell, J. (eds) (1991) *Markets, Hierarchies and Networks: The Coordination of Social Life* (London, Sage).

Thompson, J. D. (1967) *Organizations in Action* (New York, McGraw-Hill).

Thompson, J. D. and Tuden, A. (1959) 'Strategies, Structures and Processes of Organizational Design', in J. D. Thompson et al. (ed.), *Comparative Studies in Administration* (Pittsburgh, PA, University of Pittsburgh Press).

Trosa, S. (1994) *Next Steps: Moving on: An Examination of the Progress to Date of the Next Steps Reform Against a Background of Recommendations Made in the Fraser Report* (London: HMSO).

Van de Walle, S., Van Roosbroek, S. and Bouckaert, G. (2008) 'Trust in the Public Sector: Is There Any Evidence for a Long-Term Decline?' *International Review of Administrative Sciences*, 74 (1), 47–74.

Van Leerdam, J. (1999) *Verzelfstandiging en politieke economie* (Delft, Eborun).

Van Thiel, S. (2001) *Quangos: Trends, Causes and Consequences* (Aldershot, Ashgate).

Van Thiel, S. (2004) 'Quangos in Dutch Government', in C. Pollitt and C. Talbot (eds), *Unbundled Government: A Critical Analysis of the Global Trend to Agencies, Quangos and Contractualisation* (London, Routledge).

Verhoest, K. (2002) *Resultaatgericht verzelfstandigen. Een analyse vanuit verruimd principaal agent perspectief (Result-driven agencification. An extended Principal-Agent Perspective analysis)* (Leuven, Katholieke Universiteit Leuven, Faculteit Sociale Wetenshappen, PhD-dissertation).

Verhoest, K. (2005) 'The Impact of Contractualisation on Control and Accountability in Government-Agency Relations: The Case of Flanders (Belgium)', in G. Drewry, C. Greve and T. Tanquerel (eds), *Contracts, Performance and Accountability* (Amsterdam, IOS Press).

Verhoest, K., Peters, B. G., Bouckaert, G. and Verschuere, B. (2004a) 'The Study of Organisational Autonomy: A Conceptual Review', *Public Administration and Development*, 24 (2), 101–18.

Verhoest, K., Verschuere, B. and Bouckaert, G. (2003) *Agentschappen in Vlaanderen: een beschrijvende analyse* (Leuven: Steunpunt bestuurlijke organisatie Vlaanderen).

Verhoest, K., Verschuere, B. and Bouckaert, G. (2007) 'Pressure, Legitimacy and Innovative Behaviour by Public Organisations', *Governance*, 20 (3), 469–97.

Verhoest, K., Verschuere, B., Peters, B. G. and Bouckaert, G. (2004b) 'Controlling Autonomous Public Agencies as an Indicator of New Public Management', *Management International/International Management/Gestion Internacional*, 9 (1), 25–35.

Verschuere, B. and Verhoest, K. (2003). *Agentschappen in Vlaanderen*. Research Report. SBOV: Leuven.

Verschuere, B. (2005) *Determinants of Organizational Autonomy: A Political Approach of Structuring Public Organizations* (Paper 14ème colloque international de la Revue Politiques et Management Public: Le Management Public à l'Epreuve de la Politique, Bordeaux, 17–18 March 2005).

Verschuere, B. (2006) *Autonomy & Control in Arm's Length Public Agencies: Exploring the Determinants of Policy Autonomy* (Leuven, Katholieke Universiteit Leuven, Faculteit Sociale Wetenshappen, PhD-dissertation).

Verschuere, B. (2007) 'The Autonomy-Control Balance in Flemish Arm's Length Public Agencies', *Public Management Review*, 9 (1), 107–33.

Verschuere, B., Demuzere, S., Verhoest, K. and Meyers, F. (2009) 'Why do Public Agencies use Management Techniques?' *International Journal of Public Sector Management*, 22.

Verschuere, B., Verhoest, K., Meyers, F. and Peters, B. G. (2006) 'Accountability and Accountability Arrangements in Public Agencies', in T. Christensen and P. Lægreid (eds), *Autonomy and Regulation: Coping with Agencies in the Modern State* (Cheltenham, Edward Elgar).

Waterman, R. W., Rouse, A. A. and Wright, R. L. (2004) *Bureaucrats, Politics, and the Environment* (Pittsburgh, PA, University of Pittsburgh Press).

Weaver, R. K. and Rockman, B. A. (eds) (1993) *Do Institutions Matter?* (Washington, D.C., Brookings Institution).

Wettenhall, R. (2005) 'Agencies and Non-Departmental Public Bodies: The Hard and Soft Lenses of Agencification Theory', *Public Management Review*, 7 (4), 615–35.

Williamson, O. E. (1981) 'The Economics of Organisations: The Transaction Cost Approach', *American Journal of Sociology*, 87 (3), 548–77.

Williamson, O. E. (1985) *The Economic Institutions of Capitalism: Firms, Markets, Relational Contracting* (New York, Free Press).

Wilson, J. Q. (1989) *Bureaucracy: What Government Agencies Do and Why They Do It* (New York, Free Press).

Wirth, W. (1986) 'Control in Public Administration: Plurality, Selectivity and Redundancy', in F.-X. Kaufmann, G. Majone and V. Ostrom (eds), *Guidance, Control and Evaluation in the Public Sector* (Berlin, de Gruyter).

Wolf, P. (1993) 'A Case Survey of Bureaucratic Effectiveness in U.S. Cabinet Agencies: Preliminary Results', *Journal of Public Administration Research and Theory*, 3 (2), 161–81.

Wollmann, H. (ed.) (2003a) *Evaluation in Public-Sector Reform* (Cheltenham, Edward Elgar).

Wollmann, H. (2003b) 'Evaluation in Public-Sector Reform: Trends, Potentials and Limits in International Perspective', in H. Wollmann (ed.), *Evaluation in Public-Sector Reform* (Cheltenham, Edward Elgar).

Wollmann, H. (2004) 'Policy Change in Public-Sector Reforms in Comparative Perspective: Between Convergence and Divergence', in S. Munshi and B. P. Abraham (eds), *Good Governance, Democratic Societies and Globalisation* (New Delhi, Sage).

Yesilkagit, K. (2004a) 'The Design of Public Agencies: Overcoming Agency Costs and Commitment Problems', *Public Administration and Development*, 24 (2), 119–27.

Yesilkagit, K. (2004b) 'Bureaucratic Autonomy, Organizational Culture and Habituation', *Administration and Society*, 36 (5), 528–52.

Yesilkagit, K. and Christensen, J. G. (forthcoming) 'Institutional Design Within National Contexts: Agency Independence in Denmark, the Netherlands and Sweden', *Journal of Public Administration Research and Theory*, 19.
Zuna, H. R. (2001) 'The Effects of Corporatization on Political Control', in T. Christensen and P. Lægreid (eds), *New Public Management – The transformation of Ideas and Practice* (Aldershot, Ashgate).

Index